RELIGION AND POLITICS
IN AMERICA

RELIGION AND POLITICS IN AMERICA

A Conversation

MICHAEL CROMARTIE

Copublished with EPPC

ROWMAN & LITTLEFIELD PUBLISHERS, INC.
Lanham • Boulder • New York • Toronto • Oxford

ROWMAN & LITTLEFIELD PUBLISHERS, INC.

Published in the United States of America
by Rowman & Littlefield Publishers, Inc.
A wholly owned subsidary of The Rowman & Littlefield Publishing Group, Inc.
4501 Forbes Boulevard, Suite 200, Lanham, Maryland 20706
www.rowmanlittlefield.com

PO Box 317
Oxford
OX2 9RU, UK

British Library Cataloguing in Publication Information Available

Library of Congress Cataloging-in-Publication Data

Cromartie, Michael.
  Religion and politics in America : a conversation / Michael Cromartie.
    p. cm.
  Includes index.
  ISBN 0-7425-4470-2 (hardcover : alk. paper)—ISBN 0-7425-4471-0 (pbk. : alk.
paper)
  1. Religion and politics—United States. 2. Chrisitanity and politics—United States.
  3. United States—Religion. I. Title.
  BL2525.C76 2005
  322'.1'0973—dc22   2004021925

Printed in the United States of America

⊗™ The paper used in this publication meets the minimum requirements of American National
Standard for Information Sciences—Permanence of Paper for Printed Library Materials,
ANSI/NISO Z39.48-1992.

Contents

Introduction
Michael Cromartie

Martin Marty, the dean of American religion historians, remarked several years ago that there is "almost no major news in the world today that does not have a religious dimension or component underlying it." His observations are confirmed by research sponsored by the Ethics and Public Policy Center. In a report commissioned by the Center, Robert Lichter and his colleagues at the Center for Media and Public Affairs conducted a study of "Media Coverage of Religion in America 1969–1998," a random sample of 2,365 stories that appeared from 1969 through 1998 in the *New York Times*, the *Washington Post*, *Time*, *Newsweek*, *U.S. News & World Report*, and the ABC, CBS, and NBC newscasts.

One of the results unearthed in this study was that religious news stories have nearly doubled in the mainstream press from the 1980s to the 1990s. However, the researchers also found that there was very little understanding of theology or religious belief in religious news. Only 1 story in 14 mentioned any religious beliefs or doctrines. This figure dropped to 1 in 20 for stories about Protestants, Catholics, and Jews. Lichter and his colleagues drew the following conclusion from this study:

> In recent years, religious faith and its institutional expression have commanded greater attention in the national media newsrooms that set the tone for their profession. If this intensely personal yet inextricably communal sphere of human experience is to play a great role in the national dialogue, journalists need to be aware of the content and consequences of the narrative they craft. The ephemeral events and deadline pressure that define their profession do not encourage self reflection.

In a column devoted to these same survey results, Gregg Easterbrook, a senior editor at *The New Republic*, reiterated this claim:

> Journalists seemed comfortable discussing the politics and scandals of religion but not what people believe—though what they believe, and why they decide to

believe it, is in many ways the most important issue. Important for individuals, anyway; perhaps still too complicated for the big media.

As religiously grounded moral arguments have become ever more influential factors in the national debate—particularly reinforced by recent presidential elections and the creation of the faith-based initiative office in the White House—journalists' ignorance about theological convictions has often worked to distort the public discourse on important policy issues. Pope John Paul II's pronouncements on stem-cell research, the constitutional controversies regarding faith-based initiatives, the emerging participation of Muslims in American life—issues like these require political journalists in print and broadcast media to cover religious contexts that many admit they are ill-equipped to understand. Put differently, these news events reflect subtle theological nuances and deep faith commitments that shape the activities of religious believers in the public square. Inasmuch as a faith tradition is an active or significant participant in the public arena, journalists will need to better understand the theological sources and religious convictions that motivate this political activity.

The current national discourse has brought faith and its relationship to public policy to the forefront of our daily news. Since 1999, the Ethics and Public Policy Center, through the generosity of the Pew Charitable Trusts, has hosted six conferences for national journalists to help raise the level of their reporting by increasing their understanding of religion, religious communities, and the religious convictions that inform the political activity of devout believers. This book contains the presentations and conversations that grew out of those conferences.

In chapter 1, historians Nathan Hatch and Grant Wacker discuss the roles, both political and cultural, that conservative Protestant evangelicals have played in American history. Nathan Hatch, professor of history and provost at the University of Notre Dame, discusses the origins of evangelicalism in America starting in the colonial era. Grant Wacker, professor of the history of religion at Duke University Divinity School, gives a "cultural profile of evangelicals in modern America," defines their beliefs and identifies what accounts for their success. Rejecting the notion that God no longer acts in special ways toward people, Wacker argues that evangelicals continue to believe in the miraculous power of God to change common people. Hanna Rosin of the *Washington Post* responds to Hatch and Wacker by pointing out that the faith of evangelicals is surprisingly less concerned with broad societal transformation and has become more therapeutic, domesticated, and focused on individual reform.

In chapter 2, papal biographer George Weigel describes the diversity of Catholics in America and how it is at odds with the black-and-white terminology used in reporting them. The categories of "liberal" and "conservative" often oversimplify the larger discussion. Respondent Kenneth Woodward, veteran religion reporter of *Newsweek*, disagrees with Weigel about the state of American Catholicism and is less hopeful about the future of American Catholicism. He points to the decline in those studying for the priesthood and expresses concern over Catholics who do not take their positions into the public arena.

In chapter 3, Jack Wertheimer, provost of the Jewish Theological Seminary of America, discusses the contributions that Judaism has made and is making to American society. He argues that the importance of Jewish citizens to America is twofold: they play an influential role in society in professions, media, academia, entrepreneurial endeavors; and they are a model ethnic and religious minority for others in similar situations. Today, however, he says it is not totally clear what a Jew in America really is, and thus Jews are preoccupied with "fitting in." David Brooks, at the time a senior editor of *The Weekly Standard* and now a columnist for the *New York Times*, observes that as a result of outside intellectual pressures, there has been a return recently to serious Judaism as "self-created religions" have proved insufficient. But this new turn has been characterized by what he calls "flexidoxy," a merger of flexible orthodoxy and this causes him to question its durability.

In chapter 4, Yale law professor Stephen Carter notes that religion and God-talk tend to increase in presidential election years. But he sees it as shallow and superficial if the candidates do not give us an indication of how their faith matters in their policies. The electorate tends to see religion as a proxy for a candidate's morality, but too close a relationship between religion and politics can have negative ramifications for religion, especially if people put too much faith in a candidate whose religious views seem closer to theirs than others. In response, syndicated columnist Charles Krauthammer argues for continued religious talk in politics. He notes that former vice presidential candidate Joseph Lieberman's appeals to civil religion had an appeal that crossed denominational lines. Krauthammer also argues that the use of "God language" has been central to the American political experience. Historian Leo Ribuffo of George Washington University, the second respondent, highlights the religiosity of numerous presidents in American history. Nonetheless, he expresses ambivalence and caution about too much religious talk in politics.

In chapter 5, political scientists John Green and John DiIulio look at how different religious groups voted in the 1992, 1996, and 2000 presidential elections. John Green gives an overview of his survey that measured the influence of religion on voting behavior. He notes that white evangelical Protestants have become the dominant religious group in the Republican party. Both religiously observant blacks and Hispanics, and less observant religious groups tend to vote Democratic. John DiIulio responds by addressing the remaining race variables and importance of party identification, since non-white religious groups vote mostly Democratic. He also doubts the degree of influence of Christian activist groups.

In chapter 6, Jean Bethke Elshtain of the University of Chicago Divinity School and William McGurn, editorial page editor of *The Wall Street Journal*, discuss the use of religious and theological language in public discourse. Elshtain borrows heavily from Alexis de Tocqueville's observations about the religious basis of American culture and politics. Tocqueville observed that there is an unabashed mixing of religion and politics in America even while there is a clear tradition of separation of church and state. Elshtain argues that while every political issue does not have an explicitly Christian response to it, Christians should not resign themselves to operating merely on the world's terms. McGurn emphasizes that all of our political concerns must go back to first principles. For "human rights" to have substantial meaning, they must be rooted in religious authority.

In chapter 7, historian Leo Ribuffo surveys the history of the rise of the new Christian Right in American politics. After World War II, there was a spiritual revival in America. However, the evangelical and fundamentalist culture that grew out of it has been updated from the conservative Protestantism of the 1920s and 1930s: they are less legalistic, they are far less anti-Catholic, and they use modern technology well. In the future, the Christian right will be an important factor in American politics, but journalists should realize that the "pious" should not lumped together in one religious pot. The picture is much more complicated than that. In response, David Shribman observes that religious conservatives are now at the center of our politics and have "changed the American conversation." "Values" have now become the language of politics, and religious conservatives have become an indisputable part of the political process.

In chapter 8, law professors Stephen Carter and Jeffrey Rosen discuss the proper relationship between religion and politics in American society. Carter points out that compromise is good for political organizations but dangerous for religion. He is concerned that religious believers not compromise their deeply held doctrinal convictions in favor of political expediency. Rosen is encouraged that both strict separationists and religious supremacist views have been rejected in the legal community but this has yet to find great resonance in the larger public.

In chapter 9, eminent historian Mark Noll gives a summary of the history and tenets of American evangelicals. In the last twenty-five years he notes that diversity, pluralism, and political activism have become much more important to evangelicals. Evangelicals today tend to worry more about secularism and postmodernism than they do about liberalism. Respondent Jay Tolson of *U.S. News and World Report* argues that there are a variety of doctrinal interpretations within evangelicalism which can potentially lead to confusion for those seeking to understand it. He suggests that greater theological clarity will aid the discussion about evangelicals, especially as it pertains to issues of literalism, women's roles, the sanctity of life, Israel, and problems related to international politics.

I would like to thank several colleagues at the Ethics and Public Policy Center. Senior editor Carol Griffith, with her usual consummate skill, did a masterful job of both editing the papers and retrieving the most important comments buried within the many pages of transcript. Laura Fabrycky provided invaluable assistance in numerous ways. She handled all the details concerning conference arrangements, did heroic work in transcribing tapes, and always provided thoughtful timely assistance on matters great and small. The Ethics and Public Policy Center has always been blessed with talented interns; Anna Kaufmann came along at just the right time to render indispensable service. Ian Corbin and Kirsten Hasler, both students at Gordon College, generously gave of their time to proof read the final manuscript.

"Disagreement is a rare achievement," said the great Jesuit scholar John Courtney Murray, "and most of what is called disagreement is simply confusion." You will find considerable disagreement within these pages but we trust many points of clarification. At all of these conferences it was our express purpose to have diverse viewpoints expressed and argued. We trust the reader will find that this purpose was achieved in the discussions preserved in this book.

Evangelicalism and American Life   I
A Conversation with Nathan Hatch, Grant Wacker, and Hanna Rosin

NATHAN HATCH: Americans have long considered religious liberty to be a crowning achievement of their revolution and at the heart of their national identity. They have also naturally linked liberty of conscience to such legendary heralds as Roger Smith and William Penn, who struggled against heavy odds to achieve religious freedom during the colonial era. After independence a strange coalition of humanists and evangelicals—including Thomas Jefferson, James Madison, and the Baptists Isaac Backus and John Leland—joined forces to ensure that religion would not serve as an engine of civil policy.

To focus on such individuals creates a narrative of religious freedom as a heroic enterprise. Without underestimating the symbolic role of these champions of liberty, however, we may usefully consider whether there truly was such a close connection between intention and outcome. Perhaps, as the historians Sidney Mead and Perry Miller argue, most early Americans were not following the cloud and pillar of high principle but rather walking down the road to religious freedom without knowing it.

In retrospect, the evolution of religious freedom in North America seems so natural and uncomplicated—almost foreordained—that it is easy to overlook how unusual, even extravagant, was the hothouse of religious diversity within those colonies that became the United States. By the middle of the eighteenth century, any traditional European churchmen would have found the religious environment of America disruptive and disorienting. Colonial America surged with religious diversity well before any theory could fully explain or justify it. The weakness of the English state and the strength of commercial capitalism conspired to make North America a haven for a variety of British and European dissenters, many of whom had compelling religious or ethnic reasons to flee the Old World. Religion became massively deregulated in the English colonies, not by design, but because of governmental and ecclesiastical weakness. This functional deregulation of religion is a stark contrast to the centralist tradition that characterized both the Spanish and the French experience in America.

English North America was also distinctive for the remarkable and unprecedented wave of immigration that mixed English, German, Swiss, Scottish, Scotch-Irish, Dutch, and African ethnic groups. Religious persecution accounted for some of them. French Huguenots barred from Quebec helped build Charleston, Philadelphia, and New York, while Jews fleeing the Inquisition in Spain and Brazil also established communities in Charleston and New York.

In the twenty years before the American Revolution, about three hundred thousand people poured into English America—a number equivalent to the entire Spanish migration to America during the colonial period. As many as sixteen thousand flooded into the English colonies each year, more than the total number of French settlers to Quebec in 150 years. "The movement of hundreds of thousands of displaced Europeans and Africans into the half billion acres that lay east of the Mississippi," Bernard Bailyn has written, "produced a culture unlike any other then known."

I would suggest that within this culture religious liberty developed, in a legal sense, by default: the withering of state and ecclesiastical authority allowed rampant religious improvisation. At the time of the Revolution, for instance, South Carolina had what Richard Hofstadter called a "vacant establishment." On paper, the Anglican church was the official establishment, and around Charleston it had some institutional coherence. Yet for commercial reasons South Carolina had always welcomed promising settlers, whatever their religious convictions, and Presbyterians actually outnumbered Anglicans. The backcountry of the colony, moreover, simmered with religious and ethnic dissent. With the exception of New England, the British colonies in North America had given up a monopolistic relationship between religion and the state prior to the adoption of the First Amendment.

The experience of the revolution and of building a democratic polity further undermined the already fragile foundations of church tradition. Episcopalians, Presbyterians, and Congregationalists, closely tied to elite institutions and civil authority, had a difficult time competing in the religious free market of the early republic. While they commanded a certain high ground of culture and power, they were too weak to restrain upstart vernacular religious movements that blurred the distinction between church and popular religion. Lay-driven, voluntary, participatory, and enthusiastic, these movements became endemic. Methodists, a counterculture in England, outstripped all other churches in the United States and helped to define its core culture.

Colonial America bequeathed a unique and untidy diversity to the United States. The early republic, in turn, profoundly altered the relationship of class and religion in America. The upper classes in the United States would never control religion; nor would its diverse and democratized churches allow the state to control or centralize cultural life. No other Western democracy, not even Canada, would develop a system of higher education so decentralized, independent of state control, and open to the entrepreneurial efforts of religious dissenters.

Recognizing the religious diversity within the thirteen states, members of the Constitutional Convention adopted the First Amendment, which prohibited any governmental establishment of religion and guaranteed free exercise of religious choice. Jefferson's drive for religious liberty had arisen from his assumption that religious corruption sprang from the privileged status of established churches. Freedom of religion, Jefferson thought, would release churches from ecclesiastical hierarchy and sectarian enthusiasm and set them on a path of rationality and restraint.

What Jefferson actually witnessed, however, was anything but measured decorum. He and other Founders who lived into the first decades of the nineteenth century were deeply disturbed by the rising revivalist and populist faiths that were transforming the classical republic of their dreams into a "fiery furnace of democracy." The early republic was swept off its feet by what Sean Wilentz deemed "one of the most extraordinary spells of sectarian invention that the nation and world has ever seen." The most powerful social movement of the new nation was the very embodiment of enthusiasm and authoritative religion—the Methodists.

Rise of the Methodists

That the Methodists would achieve such a formidable position in the new United States was curious and unexpected. At the dawn of the American republic, New England Congregationalists, Middle Colony Presbyterians, and Southern Anglicans cast a dominant shadow in society, politics, and religion. While a few followers of John Wesley had made their way to colonial cities, the Methodists were not yet a separate church from the Anglicans and were insignificant in the American religious economy.

The explosive growth of the Methodist Episcopal Church was a surprising development in a republic that shunned state-sponsored religion. The American followers of John Wesley, who could boast no more than four ministers and three hundred lay people in 1771, were threatened with extinction during the revolution. All their leaders except Francis Asbury returned to England, leaving the Methodist faithful to struggle with the stigma of Toryism throughout the war.

Under the tireless direction of Asbury, however, the Methodists advanced from Canada to Georgia by emphasizing three themes that Americans found captivating:

God's free grace, the liberty of people to accept or reject that grace, and the power and validity of popular religious expression—even among servants, women, and slaves. Led by uneducated preachers committed to sacrifice and travel, the Methodists organized local classes—or cells—and preaching circuits at a rate that alarmed more respectable denominations. Between 1776 and 1850, Methodists in America experienced a miraculous growth. Comprising less than 3 percent of all church members in 1776, Methodist ranks swelled to encompass more than 34 percent of all church members by 1850, becoming by far the largest religious body in the nation.

Unlike Methodism in Great Britain, moreover, which remained a dissenting movement despite its strength and never occupied the high ground of culture and power held by the Church of England, Methodism in America came to embody the nation's preeminent religious and cultural ethos. The whole American style, which emphasized sincerity and openness rather than form and privacy, became "Methodist." While the culturally prestigious style remained Anglican in England, enthusiasm of all kinds—religious, cultural, and personal—reigned in America.

The message and structure of Methodism also embodied a liberal conception of reality that broke decisively with the prerevolutionary pursuit of homogeneous community. As a movement of self-conscious outsiders, Methodism embraced pluralism, competition, and the marketing of religion in every sphere of life—far beyond the narrow confines of ecclesiastical space. The Methodist itinerant Peter Cartwright recounted how a Presbyterian minister objected to his starting another church within the "bounds of his congregation." Cartwright responded that his were a free people in a free country and they would do as they pleased.

Disestablishment in the early republic was not attributable solely to law. Rather, the free religious market emerged as the presumptive authority of traditional churches withered. While European churches were shoring up their authority following the convulsion of the French Revolution and Napoleon, America's established churches and their college-educated ministers continued to read sermons and staid liturgies despite a tremendous assault. In *The Churching of America, 1776–1990*, Roger Finke and Rodney Stark point out that, as a percentage of religious adherents, between 1776 and 1850 Congregationalists dropped from 20 to 4 percent, Presbyterians from 19 to 11.6, and Episcopalians from 15.7 to 3.5.

It is difficult to give a coherent account of this period. Churches and religious movements after 1800 operated in a climate of tottering ecclesiastical establishments, the federal government had almost no internal functions, and the rampant migration of people continued to short-circuit old networks of personal authority. Established religious institutions linked to the upper classes remained too weak to make a whole society accept their language and analysis. In America's rapidly expanding society, fluid structures of institutional control allowed new and dynamic religious movements to take root and thrive. There was virtually unlimited social space, without hardened distinctions of social class or religious denomination.

As Americans moved into new areas—from the hill country of New England, to the Ohio River Valley, to central Tennessee and Kentucky—staid churches could not make the transition. On the New England frontier, the slow-growing Congregationalists established only five churches during the 1790s while Baptists started twenty-six new congregations and the Methodists started nine. By 1800, these dissenters outnumbered Congregationalists by three to one. By 1810, only one in eight back-country communities had a Congregational church. Similar conditions prevailed on the frontier in Kentucky and Ohio, where the Methodists easily outstripped the Presbyterians.

In the young United States, religious power, influence, and authority were dispersed and based on popular appeal. Nothing better illustrates this fact than the marked pluralism of religious publishing, which exploded in the early nineteenth century and stood in sharp contrast to the tightly controlled and centralized traditions of publishing in Quebec and in Latin America. The historian Gaylord P. Albaugh has estimated that, of the 605 distinct religious journals founded in America by 1830, only 14 had existed before 1790. Journals appeared as quickly as they vanished, creations of common people for a broad popular audience. Before 1789, all religious journals had issued from either Boston, New York, or Philadelphia. By 1830, religious journals had been published in 195 different cities and towns and in every state but Mississippi. Of the 70 locations with such publications still active in 1830, over half were west of the Alleghenies.

Methodist and Mormon Success

These vernacular religious movements, which arose in the wake of religious liberty, blurred the distinctions between church and popular religion. While outbreaks of enthusiasm were common in European and British Christianity in the era of the democratic revolutions, America was unique because of the absence of a revived state church. In the United States, high culture was too weak to inhibit or restrict enthusiastic popular religiosity, and the cultural periphery remained far more powerful and unobstructed. In this ideal climate for churches growing out of the popular culture, the Methodists and Mormons thrived.

Both Methodism and Mormonism broke decisively with the kind of churches that had dominated the American colonies. They succeeded because they were willing to market religion outside traditional ecclesiastical space and to cater to the interests of specific market segments—a proliferation that Adam Smith had predicted would result with government deregulation of religion. Both movements empowered ordinary people by taking their deepest spiritual impulses at face value, by shattering formal distinctions between lay people and clergy, by providing an arena for the entrepreneurial instincts of religious upstarts, and by communicating the gospel message in the vernacular—in preaching, print, and song. Methodists and the Mormons were also strikingly alike in two other ways: in their focus on the reality of the supernatural in everyday life, and in their recruitment and organization of disciplined bands of young followers who were hungry for achievement, sacrificial in their zeal, and driven by a sense of providential mission.

In the first two decades of the nineteenth century, Methodist experience brimmed with overt enthusiasm, supernatural impressions, and reliance on prophetic dreams and visions, as is evident from Methodist journals and autobiographies. Methodism dignified religious ecstasy, unrestrained emotional release, and preaching by blacks, by women, by anyone who felt the call. Two African-American women who became successful Methodist exhorters, Jarena Lee and Zilpha Elaw, were dramatically converted through direct revelation and found guidance in prophetic dreams. The most celebrated and notorious Methodist itinerant of his day, "Crazy" Lorenzo Dow, was celebrated as a holy man with unusual powers. Even Nathan Bangs, who eventually set his face to rid Methodism of the stigma of enthusiasm, began his itinerant career as a white-hot enthusiast. The historian John Wigger argues that the defining characteristic of American Methodism under Francis Asbury was not a theological abstraction but a quest for the supernatural in everyday life.

In America, the rapid expansion of Methodism created conditions that allowed women and African Americans to assume religious leadership. The Methodists gave women extraordinary freedom to speak, encouraging them to share their religious experiences in public, and also granted African Americans the right to preach the Gospel. They even ordained black ministers, though some attempted to keep black leaders on the fringe of the movement. This gave rise to independent black churches, the first being the African Methodist Episcopal Church founded by Richard Allen in Philadelphia.

By the time Joseph Smith announced his prophetic mission, the Methodist Episcopal Church was pushing enthusiasm to the margins, but the popular yearning for divine intervention in day-to-day experience remained. Joseph Smith issued a clarion call to a militant supernaturalism: a demonstrable revelation from heaven, the reality of miracles and apostolic gifts, and a sure and ongoing channel of prophecy. "I am a God of Miracles," the Lord proclaimed in the Book of Mormon, and the Latter-day Saints insisted on taking that claim literally.

Mormons and Methodists shared a common longing for the miraculous power of the biblical world. They also shared a genius for organizing and consolidating the expansion of their faiths. Methodists and Mormons were, at their core, youth movements with an extraordinary capacity to mobilize people for a cause and to build an organization sustained by obedience and discipline rather than ties of parish, family, and patronage. In both movements a battery of young leaders without elite pedigree constructed fresh religious ideologies around which the movement coalesced.

Mormons and Methodists were also both driven by a consuming passion to convert the unconverted. They saw an urgent missionary purpose as the principal reason for their existence, and their preaching was aimed at warning people of the wrath to come. Their proselytizing took the form of a relentless and systematic deluge. Unlike the young itinerants of the early eighteenth-century Great Awakening, whose efforts were largely uncoordinated and short lived, these movements developed regimented and ongoing schemes for sending out lay preachers to the most remote pockets of American civilization. Both Methodists and Mormons, furthermore, rejected the Puritan tradition of painstaking study. Mormon preachers—who included hatters, cobblers, glaziers, potters, and farmers—were advised against using careful forethought, written notes, or detailed plans. Their overriding goal was to convince the unconvinced by whatever means possible.

The organizational genius of Methodists and Mormons was to embrace and empower common people in a system that was centrally directed in a fixed, even authoritarian way. In their early years, both movements were volatile and unstable, as a variety of fledgling and self-ordained leaders vied for influence, tested the limits of the prescribed authority, and frequently defected to form their own churches. Yet Mormons and Methodists, unlike Disciples and Baptists, swore by institutional coherence. In the face of clamoring dissent—sometimes fueled by democratic impulses, sometimes by visionary ones—Methodists and Mormons were willing to exercise discipline, even ruthlessly, to preserve a movement in the name of God.

In their authoritarian extreme, the Latter-day Saints symbolize the disorienting instability that accompanied a free-market religious economy—its crisis of authority and its failure to integrate meaning or to care for the lonely and forlorn. The primitive Mormons were an apocalyptic sect, intent on expansion and willing to unsheathe the sword in retaliation for the persecution of their own. At its inception, Mormonism throbbed with diversity, multiple revelations, and an array of spiritual gifts, but internal dissent and external threats led Smith to deny freedom of thought and demand the strictest loyalty to his commands. In 1843, Smith announced that all earthly commitments were null and void save the ones sealed by himself. No human obligation—even the solemn vow of marriage—had any meaning unless it was sanctioned by the prophet Joseph. As divine prophet, military general, political boss, and even candidate for the presidency of the

United States, Smith consolidated power into his own hands and equated obedience to his will with compliance to the divine will. In submitting to their prophet and revelator, Mormon followers were willing to dismiss the architecture of classic Christian theology and practice. In Missouri and Illinois, such radicalism led to persecution that, far from disbanding the movement, set in motion the pilgrimage to Utah, where the Mormons flourished.

This religious marketplace—what one Congregational missionary to Illinois called in 1829 "religious anarchy" and "a sea of sectarian rivalries"—could give rise to intolerance and sometimes even persecution. As in the case of Joseph Smith, denials of religious liberty were generally a function not of government but of popular action, of mobs. It was not the oppression of the powerful that dissenters had to fear in America, Alexis de Tocqueville noted, but the tyranny of the majority. During the 1830s and the 1840s, mob action was rampant in America—against Catholics in Boston and Philadelphia, against Mormons in Ohio, Missouri, and Illinois, and against abolitionist preachers in a variety of locations.

Intolerance and persecution, nonetheless, were rarely effective in suppressing religious dissent. Instead, the availability of space in the United States meant that dissent and pluralism generally proceeded apace. America's vast hinterland allowed the oppressed Mormons to trek beyond the writ of law or mob rather than be crushed in Missouri and Illinois. The very experience of that pilgrimage solidified the identity of the Latter-day Saints and helped Brigham Young turn a highly fragmented and fragile apocalyptic sect into a major religious community.

Severe popular prejudice against Roman Catholics, particularly with respect to education, emboldened the immigrant Catholic Church to begin its own system of parochial education and, in time, its own colleges and universities. To a lesser degree, mid-nineteenth-century Methodists felt discriminated against by Calvinists, who controlled most colleges. They responded by founding thirty-five colleges between 1840 and 1860 and another thirty-five plus between the Civil War and 1900.

In the United States, religious liberty proceeded with almost unrestrained fury, generating a popular culture "awash in a sea of faith" and unmediated by traditional religious leaders or government officials. The people of America turned out to be more free to practice religion than their European cousins. This does not mean that Americans possessed greater foresight or tolerance; it simply means that their institutions were too weak and their communities too diverse to restrain the religious whirlwind that descended upon them. At the founding of the republic, no one wanted or envisioned such a state of religious freedom. However, the deregulation of religion, the popular contagion of the American Revolution, the vast expanse of land, and the continual mixing of peoples all conspired to make religion a pervasive, if divisive, reality in American life.

GRANT WACKER: I would like to offer a cultural profile of evangelicals in modern America, that is, in post–World War II America. Some historical references are inevitable, but my primary focus is on the modern scene.

To offer a profile, of course, I must first identify the people I am talking about. Who are these evangelicals? Anecdotal insights can be revealing. Suppose someone comes up to you on a big-city bus and says, "Is this seat saved? Oh, incidentally, are you?" That's a tip-off that you are probably sharing your seat with an evangelical rather than a high-church Episcopalian. An evangelical can also be defined as someone who really, *really* likes Billy Graham, while a fundamentalist is someone who really likes Billy Graham but worries that he's going soft on liberals. Another chestnut, which historian Joel Carpenter borrows from Bob Jones, Sr., is that an evangelical is someone who says to a liberal, "I'll call you a Christian if you'll call me a scholar."

Social science probably gives us less insight than the anecdotal evidence does into what the evangelical animal is. First, the data vary wildly. Under the strictest definition, evangelicals number only a few million, but with some criteria the figure can go as high as fifty million. I think the best estimate, which I draw from Christian Smith, a sociologist at the University of North Carolina, is that roughly 25 to 29 percent of Americans are associated with conservative Protestant churches. Smith bases this figure on massive polling that his research team has done, as well as on general surveys. But whether it's twenty million or forty million, we're dealing with a lot of people.

I call these people "culturally self-conscious evangelicals," which is a much broader category than "Christian Right." Politically active members of the Christian Right probably number no more than a couple hundred thousand, but the number of evangelicals who could be mobilized on a given issue swells rapidly to millions. Though the definitions become very loose when the count goes that high, I would argue that what evangelicals *believe* is central to any reasonable definition.

Evangelical Beliefs

Belief is important, because that is how evangelicals instinctively define themselves. While the Jewish community, for instance, may give preeminence to ritual rather than to doctrinal affirmation, evangelicals give preeminence to belief. There is a great deal of flexibility in how they manifest those beliefs in ordinary life, but no evangelical would ever say, "Oh, well, it really doesn't matter what you think about the birth of Jesus Christ." To them it *does* matter. Belief counts. That is the first crucial tenet of evangelicalism.

Its second crucial tenet—the theologian's "formal principle"—is the authority of the Bible. All Protestants believe in the authority of the Bible, of course, and all

Christians believe in the Bible in one way or another. But evangelicals distinguish themselves on the religious landscape by their insistence that the Bible be interpreted without benefit of the church, the community, or the clergy. In other words, one reads the Bible and makes a judgment as to what it means. A well-known Pentecostal once said, "We believe that God has no grandchildren." That reveals a great deal about the ethos and the deepest assumptions of the movement. There are no grandchildren. All evangelicals are responsible for doing their own reading and making their own decisions—which is not to say that they actually do so, only that they have the desire to do so. Most evangelicals will add to the point about the authority of the Bible their belief that the Bible doesn't make mistakes—the doctrine of inerrancy—and that the best way to understand it is to interpret it as literally as possible. But the bottom line is the authority of the Bible.

Evangelicals' third item of belief, or their "material principle," is the necessary affirmation of Jesus Christ's redeeming act on the cross. Theologians call it "justification by faith"; most evangelicals would simply say, "God has taken care of the past. He has taken care of our brokenness, our sins, whatever defiles us." Sometimes this affirmation can generate a kind of unappealing smugness: "My problem has been taken care of. Now what about yours?" So there are both positive and negative implications to this manifestation of faith.

A fourth, more implicit belief among most evangelicals is that some parts of the Bible are more significant than others. Such variations in emphasis have, in fact, generated the variety of denominations within the evangelical family: Pentecostals, Holiness groups, Adventists, Baptists, African-American Baptists and Methodists, and several others. Almost all these bodies have come into existence because they have stressed one particular part of the Bible, usually a passage in the New Testament. Pentecostals, for example, focus on the practice of speaking in other tongues, which the book of Acts describes as having occurred on the day of Pentecost; this they take to be normative for the devout believer.

A fifth evangelical tenet is that time counts. Evangelicals talk about millennialism of all sorts. The great majority of them are premillennialists, who think that Christ will return to earth before the millennium, a period when peace and righteousness will prevail on earth. Some are postmillennialists, who think he will return *after* the millennium. A few are amillennialists, who believe that the millennium is in the heart rather than being an actual time on earth. But however they see the future, all their eschatological schemes involve a sense that time counts; we fritter it away at our peril. Of course, evangelicals may be as likely to fritter away their time as anyone else, but they feel guilty about it. They feel that they should be doing the Lord's work.

Lastly, evangelicals believe strongly in the autonomy of the individual, and particularly the individual decision. They stress that every individual must, of necessity, make a personal decision to follow Christ. God has no grandchildren; everyone must make his or her own decision. If you had asked evangelicals back in the 1950s to name their favorite radio program, they might well have said, "The Hour of Decision." They probably would have liked it, not only because of Billy Graham, but also because of the title itself. This emphasis on autonomous decision making, moreover, bleeds into a related emphasis on autonomous churches. Even those that are hierarchically structured, like Methodist churches, display considerable freedom at the local level.

Evangelical Behaviors

In addition to these distinctive beliefs, evangelicals display distinctive behavior patterns. The first distinctive behavior is evangelizing. One simply does not have the good news of the Gospel unless one shares it. Though Christian Smith's recent work and extensive polling data show that evangelicals are very reluctant to buttonhole people and share their faith, they feel they *should* do so, and they try to. A very important Southern Baptist periodical is called *Tell*—not *Take It and Hold It*, or *Keep It to Yourself*, but *Tell*. One prominent evangelical preacher insisted that it was important to keep the cookies on the bottom shelf. In other words, make the message accessible.

The second noteworthy behavior is the embrace of social reform. The particular causes change—from temperance in the 1820s and abolition in the 1840s, through prohibition in the 1920s, to abortion and school prayer more recently—but evangelicals' desire to change society is part of their cultural DNA. This effort to reach out creates inevitable friction with the elite secular culture. In many of their reform campaigns, evangelicals deny the validity of the public-private distinction so precious to the Enlightenment culture. If abortion is wrong for me, they reason, it's wrong for everybody. If it is wrong for everybody, it's wrong for me. These are social concerns, corporate concerns.

A third behavioral characteristic—especially glaring in the last twenty years—is the adversarial posture toward the wider culture. In the past this posture has at times receded, and evangelicals have become more accommodating toward the culture. In the last quarter century, however, the adversarial posture has been dominant. Such representative voices as Tim and Beverly LaHaye describe a great secular humanist conspiracy out there. Most evangelicals also see the wider culture as full of defrauders: pseudoscientists who know the scientific evidence for creationism but refuse to let it enter the classroom; dishonest educators who tell local school boards they are teaching value-free social science when in truth what they teach is packed with an agenda; historians of religious history who hijack the American story and suppress the role of Christians; liberal clergy who leave out a vast amount of the historic Christian story when they preach. These people and others like them are duplicitous and cannot be trusted. While evangelicals don't have much of a problem with the openly unsympathetic John Deweys of the world, they fear and resent the wolf in sheep's clothing.

Their disgust at such duplicity has not only animated the Christian Right but also created an unprecedented panevangelical sense of a common threat. In recent years—very recent—Southern Baptists, Pentecostals, and Mormons have begun joining hands, despite their deep theological differences, to oppose defrauders.

In dealing with the outside world, evangelicals favor a variety of tactics. One is what Robert Wuthnow has called "procedural rationalism." By this he means that they file lawsuits, elect people to town councils, follow the rules, do what they can do to set venues. While I don't think that such actions have been terribly effective, procedural rationalism is certainly part of the evangelical tool kit.

A more important tactic is the effort to gain control of the key symbols of society. Think about the title "Moral Majority." Who is going to claim to be part of an immoral minority, except tongue in cheek? Most people want to think of themselves as part of a moral tradition that is widely shared. Think how evangelical groups try to do their work, in one way or another, in Washington, D.C. Most have some kind of an organization there; others, like Promise Keepers, have made symbolic gestures there. Washington itself is key. The desire to gain symbolic control is also behind the issue of school prayer. I doubt that any evangelical thinks prayer in schools has much catechetical value, but most do credit its symbolic significance.

The last behavior pattern I would highlight, and probably the most important of late, is the effort among evangelicals to take control of their own lives. The burgeoning home-schooling movement offers the premier, but not the only, example of this tactic. Evangelicals are trying, in a very pragmatic way, to create parallel institutions where their values can be played out.

This catalogue of evangelical beliefs and behaviors does not address, of course, two crucial questions: What brought evangelicalism into existence in the first place? What gives it its particularly visible, aggressive edge in American life today?

Evangelical Origins

To understand the origins of the evangelical tradition, and its prominence, we need to look at the ideology of modernity. One critical feature of modernity is the Enlightenment emphasis on individual choice, which lies at the heart of the church-state distinction. David Bebbington, a marvelous historian of evangelicals in England, has in fact argued that evangelicalism is properly understood, not as a reaction to the modern world, but as an expression of it. Evangelicalism is the premier expression of modernity, precisely because it emphasizes choice and the conscious embracing of one's life. But the downside of that choice is the denial of tradition.

Here's the rub. Evangelicals embrace part of modernity, the emphasis on individual choice, but they worry about and react against other parts, especially those that would deprive them of God's special acts in the Bible and in history. Beginning in the late nineteenth century, traditional supernaturalism came under attack in many spheres, and especially in biblical criticism. The Bible became a book among other books, opened to tools of investigation. In addition, the study of evolution, the emergence of anthropology, and the growing awareness of world religions all supported the assumption that God does *not* act in special ways. In other words, God is accessible to all, and the divine is simply a part of culture. This notion of the divine is what we often call romanticism, and it can be argued that romanticism is far more important than secularism for understanding evangelicals. Secularists are not the problem; romantics are the problem. Because they see the divine in all of culture, in all of history, they neutralize it. Secularists we can deal with; romantics are dangerous because of their perceived duplicity.

Of greater consequence for evangelicals even than the ideology of modernity, however, are the distinctive social arrangements that have accompanied modernization, such as compartmentalization, centralization, and bureaucratization. Modernization forces a mixing of communities and of world views. The interstate highway system, for example, has had the effect of mixing up society, of forcing people into proximity, in ways that were unimaginable before the 1950s. Effective contraceptives have dramatically increased the possibility of both geographic and occupational mobility. All kinds of late-twentieth-century social arrangements bring about a mixing that would not take place in a less modernized society.

Faced with such mixing, evangelicals have become enormously self-conscious about who they are. And their awareness of this identity is particularly evident in their reactions to the federal government. Perhaps the feature of modernization that has had the profoundest effect on evangelicals is the growth of the federal government. That growth increases the ability of government, and of other mass structures, to intrude upon the enclave, and this is what creates in evangelicals their sense of being besieged. Kevin Phillips has written, "The world of Manhattan, Harvard, and Beverly Hills was being exported to Calhoun County, Alabama, and Calhoun County did not like it."

Now, this sense of being besieged is discussed by many different groups. All talk about how the rest of the world is intruding on them. But not all react the way evangelicals react. Evangelicals react organizationally. They *do* something about it. They have the resources, the money, and a social location that makes it possible for them to mobilize, to organize, to publish, to get on the airwaves, to create schools. They don't create universities—they are singularly inept at that—but they are very good at creating schools and colleges and parachurch organizations.

There is extraordinary strength and density in the evangelical infrastructure. Part of this is historic, part a sense of mission, part has to do with the real or perceived necessity of defending themselves. Evangelicals follow the maxim "the best defense is an offense." Their aim is to restore a traditional world, even if that world is for the most part an illusion—a Norman Rockwell world of small towns and summer nights and stable values. It never existed, but they think it did, and they are mobilizing to restore it.

What then keeps them going? I suggest that there are three sustaining factors that go beyond all the cultural reasons already discussed. The first, which is counterintuitive, is that they provide a place for women. While women may be excluded from the pulpit, they have an extraordinary range of obligations and opportunities within the evangelical world. The second factor that helps evangelicals continue to thrive is the emphasis upon biblical authority, which provides a great sense of security. And lastly, most evangelicals believe in an eschatology that tells them they are part of a larger design. Life isn't just an accident. As Martin Marty has said, "Religion makes sad hearts glad or it does nothing at all." That's true of all Bible-based religious traditions, and it's certainly true of the evangelical tradition at its best. Historians, journalists, and social scientists should keep that in mind.

HANNA ROSIN: My experience in the evangelical world is that of an outsider, and I can speak about it only as an outsider and a journalist. I've tried to discover the wider cultural significance of today's evangelical fervor. Do America's evangelicals represent a certain cultural vanguard about to usher in another Great Awakening and an era of social reform, or do they merely represent pockets of seething nostalgia, some sort of counterculture?

But first I want to talk about my credentials as an outsider. I come from a family that, like many, has become successively less religious over the generations. The easiest way to summarize this heritage is to describe a time when I was in Israel and four generations of my family were living in the same house. On the Sabbath, my great-grandmother would just not move—not because she was 100 years old but because she believed it was a sin even to chew on the Sabbath. We would sit at the table and not move so as not to offend God. My grandmother would move, but only to go to the synagogue. I remember going with her to her Orthodox synagogue, where the women were confined to a dark chamber behind dingy curtains. The rationale for this was that the women would distract the men, which struck me as preposterous at the time because my dear grandmother didn't pose that sort of threat.

Meanwhile, my mother was the first generation formed by a Zionist education, which turned all religion into Israeli national myth. She could tell you everything about the Jewish resistance to the Romans at Masada, for instance, but almost nothing about the importance of Yom Kippur. And then there's me, now out of Israel and wondering what it's all about.

I now find myself, moreover, a religion reporter. I wrote about evangelicals a little bit at the *New Republic*, mostly contemptuously and without much understanding. When I first heard the former California congresswoman Andrea Seastrand, I thought that her descriptions of her apocalyptic visions of California and the Second Coming were absolutely off the wall. But after a year of spending a lot of time in the evangelical world, I've come to think it's the *Washington Post* newsroom that's crazy. I now have the feeling that everyone is an evangelical, that I could get on any plane in America and ask the person sitting next to me, "When did you accept Jesus Christ?" and he or she wouldn't even blink. Back in my newsroom, however, no one will believe me when I tell them that 44 percent of Americans are biblical creationists. They think it's time to transfer me off my beat.

Grant Wacker was right to draw attention to evangelicals' refusal to recognize the validity of the public-private distinction. My own experience entirely confirms this. Some of the people I write about call me at home all the time because, to them, there is no distinction between my public life as a reporter and my private life as a person.

I am also the target of their missionary zeal. When I'm out on the beat, people always ask, "What are you?" I'm not a reporter, I'm an opportunity for evangelizing, so they want to know who and what I am. When I tell them I'm Jewish, they'll say, "So you're a Messianic Jew," as if that were the most natural thing in the world. One time, at a Waffle House, a preacher I was interviewing just kept staring at me. I became uncomfortable and couldn't eat, and he finally said, "You know, you look just like Jesus Christ. You have the blood of Jesus running through you!" Another time, in Kansas, a guy played good cop/bad cop in his efforts to get me to convert. He stared at me intently, without blinking, and said, "Hanna, I love you." And I thought, "God, we just met!" That was the good cop side. Then the bad cop started to talk to me about the Second Coming and the pit of hell. Neither of those tactics worked, but they impressed me. As I've wandered through the world of evangelicals, I've discovered that their religion is not theoretical. It is a living faith for them. As Grant Wacker said, it affects their behavior all the time.

My day-to-day experience, however, doesn't answer the fundamental question: Do these small episodes in Kansas, Alabama, and elsewhere add up to anything? To the Fourth Great Awakening? To a cultural vanguard? Can we put it all together? At the end of his great book *Revivals, Awakening, and Reform*, William McLoughlin speculated about the religious meaning of the 1960s. Was that decade an example of a Great Awakening? Are we in another period of, as Pat Robertson and Jerry Falwell say, a great spiritual revival? When I look around, this period does not seem comparable to the one in which nineteenth-century New England teemed with religious prophets and the quest for the supernatural in everyday life lasted a generation. That period added up to something large—to a definition of what it means to be an American and what America's place is in God's universe. It actually redefined the culture.

Today's ferment seems to have less transformative potential. The structure of churches and the craving for respectability are obstacles. With Methodists now exemplars of the middle class, the churches seen as heralding a great revival are the evangelical Calvary churches and the charismatic Vineyard churches that started out in California. A short time ago the Vineyard churches were quite radical, converting barefoot surfers to go out into the world and work for Jesus. But they've already begun their quest for respectability. Like the Methodists before them, Vineyard churches have already moved on to wanting to populate the country with Vineyard churches and develop an institutional structure. So they've lost a bit of their spontaneity and spark.

The megachurches may also sabotage a more sweeping spiritual revival. They are so media ready and so ready to respond to all their members' needs that they may subsume discontent too quickly. Lastly, new churches that thrive because of a cult of charisma and one personality, such as that of Lon Solomon at the McLean Bible Church in Virginia, are unlikely to survive into the next generation.

In exploring how the legacy of the sixties fosters or undercuts spiritual revival, I've noticed another interesting phenomenon. The therapeutic jargon that evangelicals so love to hate has become, ironically, the idiom of many of evangelicals' own churches. It is common in these churches to hear that the parable of Moses and the burning bush is a story about depression, and that David is a story about leadership. At the close of a rousing sermon at a megachurch in Virginia, the minister declared, "Jesus is your greatest antidepressant." Songs refer to Jesus as your buddy. At the church Kenneth Starr attends, the emphasis is on the members' various self-help groups. While religion is ostensibly about something larger, it often seems to be about something small and narrow, such as whether you are depressed or what happened to you at home that day. As Robert Wuthnow has written, God has become quite domesticated.

At the same time, this therapeutic impulse coexists with a kind of traditionalism. A study of child-rearing practices concluded that while evangelicals use physical forms of discipline more than others, they also hug their kids and cry with their kids more than others. This synthesis seems to encapsulate the traditional and therapeutic sides of evangelicals today.

As evangelicals now embrace the therapeutic, they resist the supernatural. The tale of Cassie Bernall, the young woman who died in the Columbine shooting, is revealing. A sort of teenage revival sprouted around her, but people quickly became uncomfortable with the view of Cassie as a spiritual martyr. Her parents published a book detailing her troubled childhood, saying she had simply found happiness in one way. They tried very hard to bring the story many notches down, from being about something big and supernatural to being about something much smaller, domesticated, and manageable.

Lastly, I think that affluence is hindering a sweeping revival. It's true that increasing modernization and suburbanization have generated many new anxieties and that modern evangelicals react viscerally to the soullessness of the suburbs, of the malls, of public education. They feel that they have too much contact with the world. On the other hand, however, the suburbs provide a competing idea—the idea that there is too much to lose. It's hard to think about the end of the world when you're somewhat affluent. A survivalist family I met in Kansas was worried about the Second Coming. They talked to me about how they wanted to buy a generator in case the power went out, but they wondered where to put it so that it wouldn't ruin their garden. A nice suburban life creates problems for apocalyptic visions.

There is a contradiction. Ken Starr's evangelical congregation is typical of many. It defines itself as a place that heals broken people, but it looks like a sterile suburban church. It doesn't display much bleeding in the hallways. Rather, it is a very orderly place, where people come in to worship for an hour and then leave. Several cycles of people come through on a Sunday morning. It feels very proper and suburban; it's already straining for respectability. The same is true of the Calvary churches and Vineyard churches: they may rail against modernity and over-sexualized teenagers, but they do so in sermons that are full of references to Madonna.

All this makes evangelical social work quite convenient but not radical or transforming. Changing the world comes entirely through individual reform. No larger dimension is required. If you believe you have the power to change yourself, and are working every day to change yourself, you don't need to think about the structural reasons for poverty or about what should be done for the underclass. You see poverty and AIDS and other problems as symptoms of human flaws. If people just found Jesus, then they would overcome their problems. Social reform at a large level is unnecessary.

Discussion

MICHAEL CROMARTIE: I'd like to ask Grant Wacker to tell us a little about the data in Christian Smith's new book *Christian America? What Evangelicals Really Want.*

GRANT WACKER: Smith's data come from a multiyear project that involved a lot of telephone sampling and assiduously focused on what ordinary people in the pew think. Most striking is how paradoxical, how inconsistent the data are. By standards of systematic theology, many of those interviewed made little sense. They readily affirmed virtually contradictory claims at the same time. The other key finding, Smith says, is that evangelicals are a great deal more likable than their leaders. They are very humane people who have the same problems that everybody else does. It's their leaders who often display this kind of jut-jaw mentality.

KATHY LEWIS: I have a basic journalistic question for Hanna. How do you arrange your visits to churches? Do you go invited or unannounced?

HANNA ROSIN: It depends. Another thing I've learned about evangelicals is that they are not phone people. You can call them 800 times and they won't call you back, but they love you when you show up. So if I need to talk to a pastor who's not calling me back, I just go. As soon as evangelicals see your face, they love you. In a way, they are nice people to report about; they are very easy to get along with, just as Grant said. In another way, of course, I'm uncomfortable hearing "I love you" from people I've never met before. It's not part of my tradition, and it's certainly calculated. In effect, Southern Baptists give out guidebooks about how to treat strangers in a church, how to invite them over immediately. Their extreme friendliness is almost a caricature.

Whether they trust me or not is also beside the point, because they have a mission to accomplish. They are sort of fatalistic about my writing. They expect someone at the *Washington Post* not to be on their side, and they are pleasantly surprised when sometimes I am. But all their interactions with me give them a chance to reaffirm their faith, to define themselves in reaction to me and my clinical, evaluating attitude. A reporter has the opposite mentality of an evangelical. That makes my job hard because I'm exactly what evangelicals don't like.

NATHAN HATCH: A wonderful book called *Defenders of God*, by Bruce Lawrence and Frederick Denny, points out that no traditional religious fundamentalists—be they Jewish, Islamic, or Protestant—like to be studied, to be the objects of analytic attention. (Nor do historians, for that matter.)

E. J. DIONNE: My questions relate to politics, and the first is for Professor Hatch. Two prominent Methodists are running for office in 2000—George Bush and Hillary Clinton—and it strikes me that the two represent two different sides of Methodism. She represents a very strong social-reforming tradition, and he represents reform through individual self-improvement. Would you comment on that?

NATHAN HATCH: I think your perception is accurate. In some ways Methodism is like America—a big tent with many different ways to fit in. Radical Pentecostalism and Holiness had Methodist roots, after all. But despite their fiery beginnings, Methodists were building Gothic churches by the 1850s. It's a full, amorphous tradition that certainly has a strong activist element. Hillary Clinton comes out of that, with a 1960s sort of coloring. And among Southern Methodists, Texas Methodists, there is still a strong revivalist tradition, which Bush reflects.

GRANT WACKER: Looking at a cross section of America at its core is a lot like looking at the Methodist church today. In a sense, saying that somebody is a Methodist tells you nothing anymore.

E. J. DIONNE: My other question is whether something is shifting in terms of the political engagement of evangelicals. Not that the Christian Coalition is going to go away, but there is a sense—from people like Paul Weyrich and Cal Thomas, as well as on the ground—that evangelicals are entering a period of radical withdrawal similar to their withdrawals after the Scopes trial and Prohibition. I'm curious about where you think this movement is going.

GRANT WACKER: I'll try to separate my answer into two entities: the culturally self-conscious evangelicals I discussed, and the much smaller, more active subgroup called the Christian Right. It does seem to me that the Christian Right is in a moment of retrenchment. Certainly its leaders—Paul Weyrich, Jerry Falwell, Ralph Reed, Cal Thomas, and Chuck Colson—are in a tempered mood. They are not despairing but reflective, eager to stop and reassess.

But I don't see retrenchment in the larger group. While not exuberant, perhaps, that basic, church-going component of many millions of people is quite stable. These evangelicals are expecting neither huge successes in the near future— although that would please them—nor a great deal of loss. In a wonderful book called *Redeeming America*, Michael Lienesch likens evangelicalism to the cyclical spectacular phenomenon of a comet. When a comet comes back, it looks flashy and aberrational, but it does so with quite a bit of regularity. The press, nevertheless, always seems to be taken unawares by the evangelical phenomenon and looks like the proverbial deer in the headlights.

NATHAN HATCH: I think that Hanna made some good points about the effect on evangelicals of suburbanization, materialism, and therapeutic Christianity. Their universe is not radical; it's very much part of core, middle-class society. Evangelicals face all the dilemmas that other middle-class people face. In a culture that is fragmenting, that is becoming more secular and more religious at the same time, they are just trying to make some sense of it all. I don't see anything that could be called revival.

JAY AMBROSE: It may not be a revival, but I think that a lot of people, not just evangelicals, are responding to the large problem of modernity by asking religious questions. They recognize that modernism has brought us to extreme relativism and left us with little to hold on to. For instance, we hear all the time that all cultures are of equal value, and yet we know that they are very different in some important respects. We are told that there are no final truths that can be objectively ascertained. I once heard Carl Sagan say on TV, "This is science: there is no difference in kind between humans and other animals." What I wonder is whether we aren't seeing many Americans today reaching out for something more than our modern-day culture is delivering. Isn't this why bookstores are now filled with religious books? I know this is a big question.

GRANT WACKER: And it's a terribly important question, but it may have a surprising answer. One interesting finding of Smith's extensive religious survey is how *little* the distinctive questions of modernity trouble ordinary people. What trouble them are the enduring questions that have troubled folks for millennia: Why did my wife die? Why did my children go astray? Why is there so much suffering, disease, and poverty? While the elites may worry about the problem of modernity, most people seem more consumed by the perennial human problems.

DAVID SHRIBMAN: I'd like to shift back to politics. Prior to the elections of 1988, 1992, and 1996, religious conservatives seemed to be a far more prominent and consequential group of voters, particularly in the Republican primaries, than they are now, at a similar point in the political cycle. God does not seem to be taking part in this election. Is that true? If so, why?

GRANT WACKER: It seems true, but I don't know why.

NATHAN HATCH: I sense there's a backlash against the kind of shrill, partisan message that people heard during the impeachment crisis. A lot of evangelicals are good, middle-class, suburban people who want morality but morality without the partisan rancor.

DAVID SHRIBMAN: Do you consider the religious conservative movement that began with Carter and continued through Reagan and Robertson to be one of the main moments in twentieth-century religious history? Is it historically significant?

NATHAN HATCH: Yes. I think the decline of the mainline churches and the rise of evangelicals is indeed a central story of the second half of the twentieth century. The fact that George W. Bush and Elizabeth Dole are both self-proclaimed evangelicals is significant, and I suspect that they are more representative of evangelicals than the Christian Coalition is. They take a certain stance, but it's not shrill.

JODY HASSETT: I'd like to know more about why a large number of evangelicals are now defecting to Orthodoxy and Catholicism. I tend to think that says more about the psychology of evangelicalism than about its theology.

NATHAN HATCH: A lot of thoughtful people within the evangelical world do seek a real religious tradition and are drawn to Orthodoxy and to the Roman Catholic Church. The structures and seeker-friendliness of evangelical Christianity can make it seem more like a market than a church. By always catering to people's feelings and needs, evangelicals undermine their ability to sustain a viable religious tradition that focuses on human obligations to a transcendent being.

HANNA ROSIN: The early Methodists created a more emotional witnessing. Why do their religious responses seem more authentic and transcendent to you than those of their current heirs?

NATHAN HATCH: The early Methodists wanted real conversions from one thing to another. They would tell you to take off your fancy clothes, cut your long hair, and radically change your life. They didn't appeal to people to make them feel better; they made a transformative demand by preaching that the divine was very active in the world.

MICHAEL BARONE: Having described much of the politics of the last dozen years or so as an argument between therapy and discipline, I am fascinated to discover the amount of therapy that exists in the culture of churches I had assumed embraced discipline. Now I discover that they rely on therapy, just as many therapeutic organizations—Alcoholics Anonymous, for example—rely on discipline. Some drug rehabilitation programs even put you back in jail if you slip up. Most institutions now recognize, as parents long have, that a mixture of therapy and discipline is the best way to achieve desired results. The problem is finding the most effective balance.

ELLIOTT ABRAMS: I'd like to know whether the evangelical population is more or less fixed, like the American Catholic population or the American Jewish population, or do different people float in and out of the movement? Stability certainly affects any movement's political impact.

JOHN GREEN: Evangelicals are a very fixed portion of the population who are able to retain their young in the faith better than most traditions. There's been much less change over the last fifty years than we might imagine. It's an identifiable population that persists. There is, however, a lot of flux in American religion, period—particularly among Catholics and mainline Protestants—and even more so in the large secular population. If anybody moves, secular people move.

NATHAN HATCH: We should also note that new religious influences continually sweep across denominational traditions, introducing new kinds of worship and music in both Protestant and Catholic congregations. How does Elizabeth Dole, whose family is deeply Presbyterian, suddenly become an evangelical? She considers herself both Presbyterian and evangelical.

GRANT WACKER: In the last twenty years we have witnessed a growing willingness among evangelicals to identify themselves generically. We see that elsewhere as well. For example, when the occasion demands, Native Americans do not identify themselves tribally but as Native Americans.

BARBARA BRADLEY: According to statistics, about 40 percent of the people who join megachurches leave within a couple of years. That certainly indicates a kind of churning. Is the megachurch simply a demographic phenomenon that appeals to baby boomers who like self-help groups and professional-sounding music? Is it, therefore, likely to fade and be replaced in the evangelical movement by a different model, like the first-century model of home churches? Is the megachurch running out of steam because its theology is shallow? Will it evolve into something else? What might supplant it?

NATHAN HATCH: I don't see it running out of steam. In suburban areas the megachurch is a multifaceted organization that can target a lot of people. It's in tune with the shape of modern society.

GRANT WACKER: A distinguished sociologist named Steve Warner has spoken about the internal structure of megachurches and revealed that the "mega" is an illusion. In fact, these churches break up into a great many cells. Each is an aggregation of cells that mirrors small-town America drawn together in one large parking lot.

HANNA ROSIN: I'll add that the children of baby boomers really like megachurches. Every suburban megachurch has a youth cell and a youth minister, and sponsors all sorts of youth revivals and meetings.

GRANT WACKER: One thing that megachurches don't have, however, is cemeteries, which indicates a lack of long-term commitment to traditions over generations.

DEBORAH HOWELL: I'd like to turn to the supernatural element, which was so strong in America's early history, and ask, Why did supernaturalism go away? Is there evidence that it might return? Many New Age religions certainly manifest supernaturalism.

NATHAN HATCH: Growing respectability stamps it out. The early Methodist leader Nathan Bangs had visions and dreams early in his career and believed in the miraculous. Then he went to New York, became more respectable, and worked to purge that element from the movement. His own tradition bothered him.

GRANT WACKER: I differ with Nat on this. I think supernaturalism is always there. It just moves from one group to another. Today Pentecostals and Mormons still exhibit some supernaturalism, and charismatics, many of whom are Episcopalians and Roman Catholics, are as wide open to it as they were generations ago.

KENNETH WOODWARD: I have been studying contemporary miracles. The miracles of the Bible are signs and wonders that were given meaning by an interpretive community. The miracles people claim today, on the other hand, are very vague. They don't belong to a particular community but have to do only with the self, the transcendent self. They are less religious than spiritual. This spiritual tradition is important to Pentecostals, but the Catholic tradition, my own tradition, is very rational. We believe that God operates in the world through special divine action, so we need miracles and process them through the saints. We prove where God has acted and where he hasn't in an interesting combination of faith and rationalism. I also happen to think that when everything becomes a miracle—when people claim that God found their car keys and the like—then nothing's a miracle anymore.

PETER BEINART: I'm interested in group identity and have been struck by the way evangelicals and members of other religions differ when they speak about themselves. Catholics, like Ken Woodward, and Jews almost always use the pronoun "us," but my sense is that people who have an evangelical background never talk about "us." They talk about "them." Obviously, this is related to the fact that evangelicals see the elite institutions—the media and the universities—as adversarial in a way that most Catholics and Jews don't. But doesn't this pose a problem for journalists and academics? The media and the universities should try to figure out a way in which evangelicals can speak as self-consciously evangelicals. It's important to control the dissemination of knowledge about one's own group, to write one's own history, as Jews do, for instance.

NATHAN HATCH: That's a most interesting observation. Evangelicals continue to be very populist, and when their leaders acquire more education, they tend to develop a certain distance from their own tradition. I would say that I am an evangelical Presbyterian, but I am also a believer who feels like a person without a country. I'm the son of a mainline Presbyterian minister, a graduate of an evangelical college, and a professor at a Roman Catholic institution, and I feel somewhere in between. Like a lot of my evangelical peers who have become scholars, I think of myself as evangelical but with a sense of distance and of appreciation of other Christian traditions.

BARBARA BRADLEY: Are intellectuals embarrassed to be classified as evangelicals because evangelicals are considered anti-intellectual? *Are* they anti-intellectual, across the board?

NATHAN HATCH: Evangelicalism is a popular movement with many of its own institutions that parallel those in mainline culture. It has separate colleges, separate Bible institutes, separate seminaries. People who come out of those institutions do have to adjust when they move into the mainstream. They are not immediately accepted, even though the general understanding of evangelicals is more sophisticated today than it was twenty years ago.

Elias Smith, Joseph Smith, and other interesting figures of the early republic were popular geniuses, but they were untrained in traditional ways. They were substantive, but they didn't read Aristotle. The same holds true today among many Pentecostals, evangelicals, and fundamentalists. Their leaders are talented but populist, and they come across in angular ways. They are not on the same page as those who received their liberal arts education at Yale. People of learning who come out of the evangelical tradition, therefore, are ambivalent about acting as its spokesmen. Over the last generation, on the other hand, there has been an intellectual maturing of the movement as more evangelicals have become more educated.

JAY AMBROSE: Why do evangelicals inspire such extraordinary fear? The Christian Coalition especially inspires fear, and yet what impact is it having? The popular culture is certainly immune. Evangelicals are accused of wanting to impose their values on the whole of society, but so do environmental groups and many other liberal groups.

GRANT WACKER: To some extent, evangelicals bring criticism on themselves by talking about missionizing all the time. It's not surprising that outsiders sometimes take them seriously. Most groups hold normative views about the way society ought to be structured, but evangelicals make such a big deal of it that it gets them into trouble. For a couple of centuries, evangelicals did indeed have a broad power base. Historically, they have been associated with power, with the ability to impose their will upon broader segments of the population. This creates the impression, false though it may be, that they have power now and can use it in malign ways.

The behavior of irresponsible evangelical leaders also casts light on the subject of embarrassment. Many faithful evangelicals may shun the designation because they are embarrassed by a lot about the tradition and find it hard to defend publicly.

JACK WERTHEIMER: I'm interested in hearing about internal religious coercion, rather than about imposing values on others. To what extent do peer pressure, ostracism, or other forms of coercion operate within the institutions themselves?

HANNA ROSIN: Coercion is definitely present. James Dobson and others like him are very absolutist. For example, Dobson doesn't make a distinction between *Penthouse* and *Vogue*; there's no continuum of "bad culture." It's bad or good, and his followers must conform at every level. He's particularly adamant about the evils of homosexuality. The only thing he has relented on is divorce. For whatever reason, divorce has become vaguely acceptable, in certain situations. You cannot be a gay person and be in James Dobson's empire, but you can be a divorced person.

GREGG EASTERBROOK: I'd like to ask how immigration affects the growth of religious movements. Where do the million recent immigrants fit in? Do they become evangelicals or join more established churches?

JOHN GREEN: The data show that about 20 percent of Hispanic and Latino immigrants are Pentecostals, and many of the rest are nominally Catholic but may not be particularly religious. When they come to the United States, they confront our enormous religious kaleidoscope and, like many immigrant groups in the past, they begin to join churches. Evangelical churches have been particularly effective at recruiting both Latinos and Asian immigrants. A large portion of Asians attend evangelical churches, and another substantial group are attracted to mainline Protestant churches. One of the fastest growing components of the United Methodist Church is Korean Methodists. So immigration does have an effect. It both reinforces existing churches and generates new ones. Many churches we now take for granted were considered to be new and strange a hundred years ago. American religion has always been, and continues to be, reinvigorated by immigration.

MICHAEL BARONE: I have examples from my own travels. Many Brazilian immigrants in Framingham, Massachusetts, belong to the Assemblies of God, a Pentecostal denomination that has more members in Brazil than in the United States. In Latin America, as well as among Latinos here, the evangelical and Pentecostal churches are truly competitive with the Catholic Church. Contrary to their image among many American political commentators, Latinos are not ready to vote in the way that the bishop tells them.

KENNETH WOODWARD: I'd like to return to the question of just who evangelicals are. As a working journalist, when should I use the word evangelical? I would lop off most Pentecostals and also Southern Baptists. But if I eliminate those two communities, who's left? The number of evangelicals is then substantially reduced.

GRANT WACKER: In the 1920s, a pastor named J. C. Massey noted that there were fundamentalists and damn fundamentalists. One draws distinctions as the occasion requires, and I think that in some ways Southern Baptists and Pentecostals are indeed different from Wheaton College evangelicals. But historians and journalists gain a great deal by thinking in terms of a small *e*. Evangelicals do share a common culture that has increasingly seen itself as a counterculture, and this has created a sense of fidelity to a panevangelical group.

MICHAEL CROMARTIE: Thanks again to our three speakers, Nathan Hatch, Grant Wacker, and Hanna Rosin, and thanks to each participant in this stimulating conversation about evangelicalism and American life.

New Century, New Story Line: 2
Catholics in America
A Conversation with George Weigel
and Kenneth L. Woodward

GEORGE WEIGEL: The Roman Catholic Church in the United States is the nation's largest and most complex religious organization. Its 61.5 million members live in nearly 20,000 parishes, served by more than 400 bishops and 47,000 priests. "Religious professionals" also include some 85,000 sisters, 6,000 brothers, and 4,500 seminarians; among the "paraprofessionals" are some 12,000 permanent deacons, usually married laymen, who are reviving a ministry that had lain fallow in the Church for many centuries. In 1997, more than a million infants and some 73,000 adults were baptized into the Catholic Church, while another 88,000 men and women already baptized in other Christian communities were received into full communion. The Catholic Church in the United States maintains an extensive health-care system (some 600 hospitals), a large network of social-service agencies, and the world's largest independent educational system (with roughly 240 colleges and universities, 1,300 high schools, and 7,000 elementary schools). These 61 million Catholics speak dozens of languages and espouse the full range of political views on offer in the American republic. They are probably the most varied, multihued religious community in the nation. Yet for almost forty years, the Catholic story has been reported in starkly black and white terms.

The story line was set in the fall of 1962, when the *New Yorker* published a series of "Letters from Vatican City" written by the pseudonymous Xavier Rynne. "Rynne" described his *New Yorker* reports on the Second Vatican Council (later expanded into a series of books) as "essays in theological journalism." Their urbanity, wit, and literary elegance, combined with what seemed to be the author's intimate familiarity with the mysterious Vatican, made Rynne a literary phenomenon during the Council years (1962–1965).

On Rynne's reading, the Council was the Gettysburg of a civil war between "liberals" and "conservatives" that had been under way in Roman Catholicism since the late eighteenth century. For the first 170 years of that conflict, the forces of "reaction" had been largely successful in controlling the Church, which they saw as a fortress protecting the faithful from the onslaught of modernity. Now Vatican II had been summoned by Pope John XXIII to change the terms of the relationship between Catholicism and the modern world. The pope's blunt criticism of those "prophets of gloom" who "in these modern times . . . can see nothing but prevarication and ruin" signified that the forces of progress had been given a new chance.

Rynne (who turned out to be an American Redemptorist priest, Francis X. Murphy) clearly favored the "liberal" forces of light over the "conservative" princes of darkness. He provided a framework in which otherwise arcane issues— for example, whether divine revelation proceeded from Scripture alone or from Scripture and tradition—could be grasped by reporters and made intelligible, even fun, to a mass audience. *This was like politics.* There were good guys and bad guys, and the division ran along familiar liberal/conservative political lines.

Triumph of the Conventional Story Line

By 1965, the "liberal/conservative" framework had become *the* matrix for reporting and analyzing virtually everything Catholic. There were "liberal" and "conservative" positions on worship, doctrine, church management, philosophy, spirituality, and theology. There were liberal and conservative theories of mission, ecumenism, preaching, religious education, interreligious dialogue, priestly formation, vowed religious life, marriage, sexual morality, and social ethics. Popes, bishops, priests, dioceses, theologians, lay organizations, seminaries, newspapers, magazines, and parishes were categorized as either liberal or conservative. When someone didn't quite fit the categories—for example, when political radical Dorothy Day, founder of the Catholic Worker movement, attended Mass wearing a black mantilla and praying from a Latin missal—this was chalked up to personal eccentricity rather than to a possible flaw in the taxonomy.

Now there was *something* to all of this. Vatican II—the Council itself, and the processes of debate it set loose in the Church—was in fact the moment when the long-delayed encounter between the Roman Catholic Church and modern intellectual, cultural, and political life took place. Those who had urged the Church to leave the fortress and sally forth to confront modernity did gain control of the Council's machinery and agenda, and were largely vindicated by the Council's formal product, its sixteen documents. And there were in fact forces of reaction at Vatican II that fiercely resisted the Catholic encounter with modernity, deeming it lethal to the maintenance of orthodoxy and institutional vitality. The problem was that the liberal/conservative framework was thought capable of explaining *everything*, and it could not do so.

Reporting within the standard account focused excessively on the Church as institution. But the Church is, more importantly, a mystical communion of believers, a "sacrament" of God's presence to the world, a herald making a proposal about the truth of the human condition, a servant of suffering humanity, and a community of disciples. The institution exists only to facilitate these other aspects of the Church's life. Thus "the Church" cannot be identified exclusively or even primarily with the ordained hierarchy; to do so is, in a word, clericalism. And although it is usually thought a particular sin of Catholic conservatives, an intensified clericalism in coverage of the Catholic Church has resulted from the dominance of the standard account. The standard account also led to distorted analysis in other ways:

1. Once the liberal consensus in favor of incremental social change shattered (in 1968 or thereabouts) and political liberalism was radicalized, the liberal/conservative taxonomy proved even more incapable of accurately describing new ideas and movements in the Church. A prime example was the world media's coverage of liberation theology. This complex intellectual and pastoral phenomenon was reduced to a view of liberation theologians as the Latin American version of the "good" forces of Catholic progress, doing battle for the future against the reactionary conservatives who controlled the Latin American hierarchy in cahoots with repressive Latin American regimes. There were, again, elements of truth in this analysis. For far too long the Church in Latin America had been allied with local oligarchies and had not been effective in empowering the poor, socially or politically. Vatican II had rejected classic Iberian Catholic altar-and-throne (or, in the Latin American variant, altar-and-junta) arrangements. This conciliar teaching did presage profound changes, religious and political, throughout Latin America, and those changes were indeed being resisted by the usual suspects.

   But the standard account was hopelessly inadequate for grasping the more complex truths of the situation. Among the distortions it induced were: (1) Liberation theology was seen as an indigenous phenomenon, an authentic Latin American "inculturation" of Vatican II. But in reality liberation theology was invented in Louvain, Münster, and other Catholic intellectual centers where the European fascination with Marxism and neo-Marxism was at its height, and then carried to Latin America by Latin American theologians trained in those European centers. (2) Liberation theology was seen as the Latin American expression of the liberal reformism implied in the Vatican II *Pastoral Constitution on the Church in the Modern World*. But in fact by 1969 virtually all liberation theologians had flatly rejected liberal incrementalism and were openly committed to various radical reconstructions of social, political, and economic life, usually Marxist in inspiration. (3) Liberation theology was seen as the intellectual expression of a popular, grassroots movement throughout Latin America. But in fact liberation theology was an elite movement that eventually had an impact on both popular and institutional thinking in Latin American Catholicism.

2. A similar deficiency could be observed in coverage of the emergence of feminism in the Church. Here, of course, the most visible issue was that of women and the priesthood. As usually reported, this reduced quickly to another struggle between the forces of progress and the forces of reaction. The real question, which was not whether the Church *would* ordain women to the priesthood but whether it *could* do so, was rarely considered. That there were profound issues about the Church, the ordained ministry, and indeed the nature of created reality itself engaged in this debate was almost never acknowledged. Further, the growth among Catholic feminist theologians of a far more radical critique that opposed the very notion of a "hierarchy" was not well understood; it didn't fit the conventional framework, any more than unabashedly Marxist liberation theologians did.

3. The standard account has also proven seriously deficient for understanding the pontificate of Pope John Paul II. For nearly two decades, reporters and analysts have struggled to portray a pope who seems to occupy several positions along the conventional spectrum. Much has been written about John Paul the "doctrinal conservative," who relentlessly underscores the most challenging aspects of the Church's sexual ethic and refuses to ordain women to the priesthood; yet little has been reported about the pope who describes marital intimacy as an icon of the interior life of God, who teaches that the Church symbolized by the Virgin Mary is more fundamental to the Christian reality than the Church symbolized by the Apostle Peter, and who insists that, in making its case to the world, "the Church proposes; she imposes nothing." Then there is John Paul the "social progressive," extolled as the great defender of human rights, the reconciler of the Church with democracy, the social democrat greatly concerned about the impact of a triumphant capitalism on the post–Cold War world. But little has been reported about his empirically sensitive approach to economics, his celebration of entrepreneurship, his affirmation of the "business economy," and his sharp critique of the welfare state. The attempt to confine John Paul II within the conventional categories really short-circuits when the great papal defender of democracy blasts the functioning of contemporary

democracies and warns against a "thinly disguised totalitarianism" (*Centesimus Annus*, 46).

In an attempt to resolve these seeming contradictions, analysts have portrayed the Pope as an angry old man incapable of understanding a world he helped create, or as a kind of uniquely Polish schizophrenic, doctrinally "rigid" but socially "progressive" on at least some issues. In both cases, the tendency has been to set this pontificate *against* Vatican II. But in fact the Pope, who played a significant role at the Council and as archbishop of Kraków conducted one of the world's most extensive implementations of Vatican II, sees himself as the particular heir of the Council.

4. According to the standard account, churches and movements that have identified with the inevitable triumph of the "liberal" side should be prospering. But that is not what has happened. In a striking parallel to the experience of world Protestantism, liberal local Catholic churches are dying or struggling in prosperous, free lands (such as Germany, Austria, Switzerland, Canada, Australia, and New Zealand), while self-consciously orthodox Catholic communities are flourishing in Africa, usually under conditions of poverty and sometimes under serious persecution. In the United States, Catholic practice tends to be lower (and in some cases dramatically lower) in self-consciously "progressive" dioceses than in "conservative" ones.

A similar pattern prevails among religious professionals. The only communities of nuns that are growing in the United States are communities that have broken ranks with the liberal consensus among religious women, as embodied by the Leadership Conference of Women Religious. The seminaries that are growing are replete with candidates for the priesthood who identify with John Paul II. Dioceses that are self-consciously "liberal" have a difficult time attracting candidates for the priesthood.

Since Vatican II, world Catholicism has seen a historically unprecedented explosion of lay renewal movements. Although considerable ink has been spilled on reporting such activist organizations as "Call to Action," "We Are Church," and the fraudulent "Catholics for a Free Choice," the numbers involved in these "liberal" enterprises are simply dwarfed by the numbers involved in renewal movements that identify with the Church's center of unity, the Bishop of Rome.

Rerum Novarum, So to Speak

A good "model" suggests how to organize our understanding of a complex reality and what to expect from that reality in the future. When a model cannot account for large portions of the relevant data and cannot trace a plausible outline for the evolution of what it attempts to describe, the time has come to discard it.

I have no substitute model to propose. Rather, what I would like to suggest is something both old fashioned and quite compelling: real *reporting* on the lived experience of American Catholics, concentrating on those aspects that have been underreported or ignored *and* that bid fair to be major factors shaping the Church's life and impact in the next several decades. Ten such "new things" suggest themselves:

1. The new *Catechism* and its impact. Published in English in 1994, the new *Catechism of the Catholic Church* is far more than a compendium of doctrine. It is a bold, coherent, and compelling account of the hope that has sustained the Church for two millennia. That in itself makes it worthy of serious reporting and analysis. But the *Catechism* can also be called a major cultural event in the Western world. To those who claim that plurality is an absolute in the modern world, the *Catechism* affirms the unity of faith over time and the availability of God's word of truth to all. In a culture convinced that there is *your* truth and *my* truth, the *Catechism* affirms that we cannot live without *the* truth.. At an intellectual/cultural moment in which incoherence is taken to be the bottom line of reality, the *Catechism* proposes Christian faith as a coherent framework for understanding what is, how it came to be, and what its future holds.

   Although the *Catechism* was an international best-seller in the mid-1990s, only in the future will its real impact become apparent. The *Catechism* was a challenge to the process-oriented approaches to religious education that had dominated Catholic catechetics in the United States since the late 1960s, approaches that had produced two sadly illiterate generations of Catholics. Tracking the influence of the *Catechism* on the reform of Catholic religious education is one way to look into the possible future of Catholicism in the United States.

   The *Catechism* is also a powerful populist tool by which parishioners facing dubious preaching and teaching can challenge claims that strike them as questionable. It is thus a further antidote to the perennial problem of clericalism, and an instrument of intellectual accountability of a sort not seen in Roman Catholic circles since the Counter-Reformation.

2. A "Catholic Moment" in the New South? The rapidly changing demographics of the Old Confederacy suggest that Catholicism might be on the verge of great advances in an area where it has long been virtually invisible. While Roman Catholics make up only 3 to 5 percent

of the population of the Carolinas, Georgia, Tennessee, Alabama, Mississippi, Arkansas, and Virginia south of the Rappahannock, prosperous urban areas of the "New South" are 15 to 20 percent Catholic, and the percentage is growing, mainly through immigration. Moreover, the Catholic population at the region's major state and private universities is 20 to 25 percent and increasing. At Duke, nominally Methodist, Catholics are the largest religious group on campus, followed by Jews; Methodists are third. Similar situations obtain at the University of North Carolina, Wake Forest, The Citadel, and the University of Georgia. If a sizable portion of these southern-educated Catholics remain to work in the South, the future upper-middle-class and upper-class elites of the New South are likely to be significantly, even heavily, Roman Catholic.

The booming economy of the New South and the region's increasing influence in national politics also afford opportunities for the Catholic Church. Given the decline of mainline-oldline Protestantism in the region (as elsewhere), the major Christian options are Roman Catholicism and evangelical Protestantism of various forms. And in the future life of the New South, Catholicism has a certain comparative advantage. Catholic social doctrine is a well-developed approach to the tangled moral questions involved in creating the free, virtuous, and prosperous society. Moreover, its natural-law "grammar" gives it more public traction than evangelical Protestantism has in an increasingly pluralistic (and secular) society, given the tendency of some evangelicals to make public moral arguments in ways that seem to preclude the participation of nonevangelicals in the debate. Catholic social doctrine can be engaged by everyone. While evangelical political mobilization in the Old Confederacy during the last two decades has been impressive, the kind of appeals typically mounted by evangelicals may not remain politically viable in the New South.

3. Converts and the high culture. Gary Anderson of Harvard Divinity School, Elizabeth Fox-Genovese of Emory University, Paul Griffiths of the University of Chicago, Robert Louis Wilken of the University of Virginia, Dr. Bernard Nathanson (one of the founders of the National Abortion Rights Action League), theologian and editor Richard John Neuhaus, columnist Robert Novak, historian Thomas Reeves, New York philanthropist Lewis Lehrman, Florida governor Jeb Bush—these are among some of the more prominent men and women who have, in the past decade, been baptized or received into full communion with the Catholic Church. Perhaps the most prominent "revert" is Justice Clarence Thomas

of the U.S. Supreme Court, who has returned to active practice of the faith in which he was raised. It is surely significant for the Catholic future in the United States that many prominent intellectuals and public figures have in recent years joined themselves to a religious community that the modern secular intelligentsia has often regarded as the great enemy of free inquiry. It is also of interest that the ecumenical journal *First Things*, founded in 1989 by Neuhaus (then a Lutheran pastor), has within a decade become the most widely read journal of religion and public life in the country, with a paid circulation of over 30,000 and a core readership of perhaps 125,000. Many prominent converts and "reverts" are linked to *First Things* as authors, editors, or board members.

4. The renewal of devotional life. In the implementation of Vatican II's renewal of the liturgy, attention was so sharply focused on the Mass that more informal forms of piety—the "devotions" that were once a vibrant part of American Catholic life—seemed to drop by the wayside. But after many years of neglect, devotional life has been revived.

   a. *Eucharistic piety.* The devotional practices of perpetual adoration of the Blessed Sacrament and "holy hours" conducted before the exposed Blessed Sacrament have returned to the schedule of many parishes. These practices are intended to promote deeper prayer during the Mass. Where before Vatican II Eucharistic piety was often regarded as a thing in itself, its revival today is clearly linked to the deepening of the Church's liturgical life.

   b. *Marian piety.* The revival of many forms of devotion to the Virgin Mary is doubtless due in part to the continuing phenomenon of reported apparitions of the Virgin. But in many parishes the revival of traditional Marian devotions—communal recitation of the rosary, for example—is unconnected to such paranormal phenomena. Marian scholarship, influenced by John Paul II and by the Swiss theologian Hans Urs von Balthasar, is also being revived. While Marian piety has generally been regarded as a barrier to Catholic-Protestant ecumenism, the insistence by John Paul II that "true devotion to the Mother of God is actually Christocentric" holds out the intriguing possibility of an ecumenical dialogue that moves directly from Mary into the heart of Christian faith.

   c. *New forms of devotional life.* Perhaps the most prominent of these new practices is the "Divine Mercy" devotion begun by Sister Faustina Kowalska, a Polish mystic who died in 1938 and was beatified by Pope John Paul II in 1993. This has become the vehicle by which many

American Catholics have returned to a regular devotional practice. The intensification of devotional life in the 1990s is both another indicator of the inadequacy of the conventional story line—which saw devotions of this sort as a premodern practice that was bound to disappear—and a tale of populist religion waiting to be reported.

5. A new ecumenism? Theologically intense bilateral ecumenical dialogues were one important fruit of the Second Vatican Council and the Catholic Church's entry into modern ecumenism. The Lutheran-Catholic, Anglican-Catholic, and Orthodox-Catholic dialogues in particular were given ample coverage in the years immediately following Vatican II. But the difficulties encountered by those dialogues in recent years have not been so carefully reported. Neither has the "new ecumenism" that may surpass these bilateral dialogues in importance in time.

The Lutheran-Catholic dialogue reached its apogee on October 31, 1999—Reformation Sunday—when representatives of the Roman Catholic Church and the Lutheran World Federation signed a "Joint Declaration on Justification by Faith." The representatives declared that justification by faith can no longer be considered a church-dividing matter, as the two communions share a common understanding of the truths involved in that doctrine. In other words, the core issue that precipitated the Lutheran Reformation of 1517 has been resolved. But ecclesial reunion is not on the horizon, because other issues have emerged over the centuries.

Post–Vatican II hopes for a relatively rapid reunion between Anglicans and Roman Catholics have also been frustrated, as the practice of ordaining women to the priesthood and episcopate in certain Anglican churches has raised questions about the Anglican understanding of apostolic tradition, ordained ministry, and the sacramental nature of reality. Meanwhile, the leadership of world Orthodoxy has not been receptive to the suggestion by Pope John Paul II that Rome and the Christian East could restore unity by returning to the status that prevailed before the Great Schism of 1054. And while there is widespread agreement on the need for some center of Christian unity, Orthodox, Protestants, and Anglicans alike have been slow to respond to the Pope's 1995 invitation to help him think through an exercise of the papacy that could serve their needs.

But as these bilateral dialogues reached various forms of impasse in the 1990s, a new ecumenism emerged, with Roman Catholics in active dialogue with evangelical and Pentecostalist Protestants. This was pregnant with possibility, for evangelicalism and Pentecostalism represent the "growing end" of Protestantism throughout the world. Mainline Protestantism, at least in the developed world, seems to be on an inexorable course of decline, while evangelicals continue to make great strides in North America, Latin America, Africa, Eastern Europe, and Asia.

This new ecumenism is not aimed, at least in the short term, at ecclesial reconciliation, but rather at mutual recognition and cooperation in public life. It is in part an outgrowth of the pro-life movement, where evangelicals and Catholics discovered each other as allies in the trenches. And while it faces profound theological difficulties, the new ecumenism can point to some significant achievements in the 1990s. It has been little reported—understandably so, for it is hard to "find"; it operates more through informal structures than through church bureaucracies. But it is likely to be one of the defining realities of American cultural life in the first decades of this new century, and it could well have a major impact on American politics as well.

6. Catholic intellectual life. This is no longer confined to the campuses of Notre Dame, Boston College, and Georgetown. Several of the converts noted above hold senior appointments at prestigious research universities, as do such other Catholics as Mary Ann Glendon (Harvard Law School) and Robert P. George (Princeton). Perhaps the most notable among the new Catholic intellectual centers is the Washington-based John Paul II Institute for the Study of Marriage and the Family, which has granted 127 master's-level degrees and seventeen doctorates since 1988. The institute seems likely to play a major part in American Catholic moral theology in the decades ahead. A small Catholic college in Texas, the University of Dallas, is widely recognized as one of the nation's finest liberal arts schools; it has been a pioneer in reviving a demanding undergraduate core curriculum in the humanities as the foundation for any professional vocation.

Viewed through the narrowing lens of the conventional story line, the debate over John Paul II's 1990 apostolic constitution *Ex Corde Ecclesiae* and its attempt to revitalize the Catholic identity of Catholic universities is yet another power struggle between liberated Americans and authoritarian "Rome." Viewed through a wider lens, the debate is closely related to the revolt against political correctness on campus, and against the secularist bias that has drained institutions of their religious identities in recent decades. Moreover, the *Ex Corde* debate has forced a shift of considerable consequence in the Catholic university world. During the

1970s and 1980s, universities asked, "How do we disentangle ourselves from the institutional Church?" Today, however confusedly, the question has become, "How do we reclaim our Catholic identity?" Much more is afoot here than is usually reported.

7. An unprecedented encounter with Judaism. The Jewish-Catholic dialogue of the past thirty-five years has been another of the great fruits of Vatican II. The Church has condemned anti-Semitism and reformed its liturgical and catechetical practice to take account of the Christian debt to Judaism; the Pope has called on the Church to cleanse its conscience about historic anti-Semitic episodes and the Holocaust; Jews and Catholics work together to promote interreligious tolerance and a civil public square in America; the Holy See has full diplomatic relations with the State of Israel. That, it is sometimes suggested, pretty well completes "the agenda" as imagined in 1962–1965.

But John Paul II thinks that the real agenda is just now coming into view. That agenda is theological, not social or political, and it goes beyond the achievements of the recent past to raise questions that Jews and Catholics have not discussed for over nineteen hundred years. What does it mean to be an "elect" or "chosen" people? What is a "covenant"? How do Jews and Catholics understand their common moral "border," the Ten Commandments? What is the common content of the messianic hope that Jews and Catholics share? If this new agenda is addressed anywhere it will be in the United States, where the Jewish-Catholic dialogue is most advanced by far, the Jewish population is secure enough to engage in such a conversation, and there are Roman Catholic interlocutors eager to build on recent achievements. Like the new ecumenism, the new Jewish-Catholic dialogue is likely to be most intense in "off campus" settings rather than in official dialogue groups.

8. Liturgy: reforming the reform. Most Catholics in the United States were enthusiastic about the liturgical reforms of the Second Vatican Council. The new question is: is it time to "reform the reform" with a new emphasis on the transcendent, the sacred, and the beautiful? Organizations promoting a "reform of the reform" include the Society for Catholic Liturgy; Credo, an association, mainly of priests, working for more faithful translations of the liturgy from the Latin; and Adoremus, an association of clergy and laity. The way the new liturgical debate plays out will have a major impact on Catholic life in America. Liturgical prayer is not just something that Catholics happen to do when other Americans are reading the Sunday morning papers. *Lex orandi lex credendi*—"what we pray is what we believe"—is one of the oldest and truest theological maxims,

and what American Catholics believe in 2099 will have much to do with the way they pray, liturgically, between now and then.

9. The movements. When theologians speak of the "charismatic element" in the Church, they refer not simply to the "charismatic renewal" with its characteristic behavioral elements (such as spontaneous vocalized prayer, speaking in "tongues," and healings), but also to renewal movements that have emerged through the leadership of gifted individuals. Since Vatican II there has been an explosion of such movements in world Catholicism. That largely unreported fact is beginning to reshape the face of Catholicism in the United States, giving dedicated Catholics communal reference points for the practice of their faith beyond their local parish and diocese.

Among the most prominent of these groups are Focolare, a movement of Italian origin that takes the unity of the human race as its mission; Regnum Christi, a renewal movement of lay leaders (most of them professionals) associated with the Legionaries of Christ, itself a relatively new community of priests; Communion and Liberation, another Italian-based movement with a marked capacity to attract intellectuals; and the Neo-Catechumenal Way, which works with the unchurched and reevangelizes the poorly catechized. The Sant'Egidio Community, founded in Rome by left-leaning Italian Catholic university students in the sixties, combines an active liturgical prayer life with service to the poor and with conflict mediation in the international community; it is widely credited with brokering an end to the Mozambican civil war, for example. Members of L'Arche communities, founded by the Canadian Jean Vanier, work with and live with the mentally handicapped. Then there is the most controversial of these movements, Opus Dei, which has its own unique status as a kind of worldwide diocese.

These groups are pioneering forms of Catholic life that have never been lived before. Some of them include lay men and women, unmarried, who have taken perpetual vows of poverty, chastity, and obedience and who live in community, yet have an active professional life in "the world." Interestingly, some of the new lay renewal movements have proven fertile recruiting grounds for candidates for the priesthood.

In his ease with this unpredictable charismatic element in the Church, John Paul II stands in marked contrast to some local bishops (and some Vatican officials) concerned about where these movements and communities fit in the organizational flowchart. How such groups will fare in the post–John Paul II church remains to be seen, of course. But many of them seem to have achieved enough critical mass to be ensured of a large role in twenty-first-century Catholicism.

10. The seminaries. Seminaries that have welcomed the attempts by John Paul II to revitalize the Catholic priesthood tend to be doing much better than those that have resisted this reorientation. But the story of the priests of the new millennium has only begun to be told. How are these men being prepared, intellectually, for the challenge of preaching and providing pastoral care to the best-educated generation of Catholics in history? How will they help their parishioners cope with the temptations of abundance? What does it mean for the future of Catholicism in America that many dioceses now require seminarians to be at least minimally fluent in Spanish before they can be ordained priests? Will the new immigrants to the United States—the Vietnamese, for example—follow the pattern of previous generations of immigrants in recasting the ethnic character of the Catholic priesthood?

A Culture-Forming Counterculture?

Each of these "new things" in the Catholic Church will have an impact on American public life, for Christianity is an inherently public business. How Catholics pray, how they regard other Christians, how they lead their intellectual lives, how their priests are trained, and the terms in which they understand their dialogue with modernity and whatever follows modernity will shape the Catholic presence in the American public square.

One other aspect of that presence requires a brief look: the Catholic Church as the possible agent of a renewal of American public moral culture. John Courtney Murray raised this issue in 1960, in what remains the single most impressive analysis of the Church's interaction with the American democratic experiment: *We Hold These Truths: Catholic Reflections on the American Proposition.* Murray argued that democracy could be sustained only by a "consensus" on the fundamental moral claims that made democracy plausible, desirable, and worth defending. That consensus had been sustained in the United States since the colonial period by the great churches of the Protestant mainline: Anglican, Reformed/Presbyterian, Methodist. Yet as early as the 1950s, Murray detected cracks in the foundations. The mainline churches were increasingly unable to articulate the "consensus" persuasively, particularly in the face of the secularist/pragmatist challenge associated with Deweyan liberalism. Moreover, these churches no longer formed a demographic critical mass in American society.

Murray proposed that the Catholic community, long held suspect for its "foreign" loyalties, was now best positioned to revive the consensus and thereby reconstruct the foundations of American democracy, because it was the institutional bearer of a way of political thinking—based on a natural-law approach—that was in touch with the true moral philosophy and political philosophy that underlie the American experiment. And those philosophical roots were to be found, Murray further argued, not in the rationalistic individualism of the Enlightenment, but in medieval Christendom and the common-law tradition to which it gave birth.

Some think Murray misunderstood the philosophical roots of the American Founding, and the degree to which the Catholic Church still "possesses" the natural-law-based political philosophy of its patrimony is certainly debatable. But Murray's diagnosis remains prescient. Much of the clamor of current American public life (and no small part of its degradation) has to do with the fact that Americans are losing the ability to debate issues in the realm of the public moral culture in a civil way—a point painfully illustrated by the vast moral confusions in the 1998–1999 debate over the impeachment of the President. Is there a "grammar" that can bring some discipline back into this debate? If so, who is a likely public teacher of that grammar?

The Catholic Church may be. In the social doctrine of John Paul II it has what is arguably the most comprehensive proposal for the free, prosperous, and virtuous society on offer in the world today. That social doctrine has been articulated in terms that are genuinely accessible to "all men and women of good will," as the Pope habitually describes the addressees of his social encyclicals. The interest shown by the national press in the Pope's social teaching may well reflect a widespread yearning for moral reference points as we face the uncharted territory created by the sexual revolution, the post–Cold War world disorder, the cracking of the genetic code and the subsequent explosion of biotechnologies, and the continuous American struggle to build political community out of extravagant diversity.

Moreover, in its pro-life activism since *Roe* v. *Wade* the Church in the United States has developed a considerable capacity for the kind of genuinely "public" moral argument that can indeed be engaged by "all men and women of good will." To say this is to risk derision, for the Catholic position on the morality of abortion-on-demand has long been labeled sectarian. Yet I would challenge anyone to find a single developed Catholic statement on the abortion license whose moral arguments presume belief in the Nicene Creed. The Church has marshaled publicly accessible and adjudicable *scientific* arguments on behalf of the pro-life cause, and publicly accessible and debatable *moral* arguments for the claim that there is an inalienable right to life from conception to natural death. Moreover, in recent years, both the Pope and the U.S. bishops have begun to link the abortion debate to the wider question of the moral foundations of the American democratic experiment.

The U.S. bishops have made their pro-life case in moral terms strikingly similar to those in which they challenged segregation during the 1960s. There, too, public moral arguments rooted in a natural-law concept of justice were deployed—to general approbation. The fact that many now find the same arguments "sectarian" when Catholics address the abortion license (though entirely agreeable when deployed against capital punishment) reinforces the sense that the capacity for serious moral debate has been badly attenuated. Whether the Catholic Church can help lead the country in the recovery of the lost art of public moral discourse at a time when the Church is embroiled in the most divisive debate in the culture war is a serious question.

Is a culture-forming counterculture a contradiction in terms? Not necessarily, as the experience of the Great Awakenings and their subsequent impact on American history suggests. The extent to which the Catholic Church acts as a culture-forming counterculture in the twenty-first century is one of the great stories at the intersection of religion and American public life. And grasping the inherently public character of the Catholic proposal on the life issues is the first, essential step toward covering that story adequately.

KENNETH L. WOODWARD: It's good that George Weigel began with statistics indicating the size and diversity of the Catholic Church in the United States. Numbers really do matter. In attending conferences on American religion I've found that those who most extol the virtues of diversity are likely to come from denominations that are, in fact, the least diverse. The diversity of American Catholicism is attributable in large part to its size: some sixty million Americans call themselves Catholics. And if we are to talk about overlooked stories, my chief candidate is how the Catholic Church has become the farm system for other Christian denominations. If it weren't for disaffected Catholics, there would be half the number of Episcopalians. Without former Catholics, a lot of local, nondenominational "community" churches would have to disband, or might not even exist. Who stays, who leaves and why—these questions have not been thoroughly studied. Nor—and this is my point—have we studied what would happen to some (mainly liberal) Protestant denominations if they could not depend on a steady supply of ex-Catholics.

Large numbers alone, of course, do not create diversity. To have real diversity you also need real unity. What impresses me about American Catholicism—and even more so, international Catholicism—is the degree of unity that the Church has been able to maintain. We all know about disagreements among Catholics, but what is really extraordinary is the manifest unity within diversity. This, of course, is not what most Americans mean by diversity. They are not thinking about diverse social and economic classes, or diverse ethnic communities with different origins and languages. Rather, they are thinking of *ideological* diversity, which is usually limited to the least diverse of categories: race, gender, and sexual preference.

George Weigel's general intention, as I read him, is to demonstrate that the story of American Catholicism has generally been misinterpreted. The old story line, he says, is the conflict between liberals and conservatives. This was the simplistic plot device developed by reporters who covered Vatican Council II. It was wrong then, George tells us, and is even more off the mark now.

Any journalist who covered Vatican II, as I did during its last two years, has to acknowledge that liberals versus conservatives was indeed a much-used category of convenience among the ink-stained brethren. Editors—especially at news-magazines, where space is limited, the writing is compressed, and the need for nar-rative is strong—always wanted to know which side a bishop was on, or which side was winning or losing. These pressures, however, did not mean that this was the only way we reported the council, nor did they necessarily lead to editorial cheer-leading for the progressives. Indeed, I recall that when I was hired in 1964 for the job of religion editor, *Newsweek*'s editor in chief, the legendary Oz Elliott, asked me only one question: "Woodward, can you be fair to the council conservatives?" It was a shrewd query. He knew that a twenty-nine-year-old Catholic was apt to side with those who wanted change in the Church. He knew, too, that the public was cheering the progressives on, and he wanted to make sure my writing would be balanced.

I mention that incident as evidence that, yes, the council deliberations were seen in what George calls political terms. But these categories borrowed from American politics were not altogether inappropriate. The relevant question is: did the council fathers see themselves this way? I would argue that on many is-sues many of them did. The clearest example I can think of had to do with the issue of canonizing Pope John XXIII shortly after his death, which occurred during the council. It was a collection of progressives who pushed for John's canonization; a collection of conservatives pushed instead for his predecessor, Pius XII. In this way, the two popes came to symbolize two broad tendencies, two attitudes toward what the Council should do and say and be. Therefore I disagree with George when he says that this approach was wrong, but I agree with him that it is not the whole story.

If the work of James Davison Hunter and Robert Wuthnow is to be accepted, many religious Americans today self-consciously describe themselves either as con-servatives or as liberals or progressives, and these divisions cut across denomina-tional lines. As a magazine like *First Things* demonstrates, conservative Catholics and evangelical Protestants have more in common with each other in certain re-spects than with their liberal coreligionists.

Perhaps we can agree, then, that the division between liberals and conservatives is useful in some contexts, highly misleading in others. In any case, I think these categories have since been joined by other dichotomous pairs that speak to other kinds of divisions, now that a whole new generation of Catholics has grown up since Vatican II closed. Michael Novak spotted one of those dichotomies long before the council had concluded; I'm thinking of his insight that the council had moved the Church away from an "ahistorical" understanding of Catholicism. (Now, of course, we have a generation and a half of Catholics who have no historical memory of the council, much less of the preconciliar church, and have only a superficial grasp of the essentials of the faith.) For example, I have an eighty-six-year-old neighbor who went to Catholic schools and a Catholic college and is very bright and devout, but who can't believe that the Pope has embraced evolution. "That's not what we were taught" is his constant refrain, and he is talking about what comes from the Vatican, not from the mouths of liberal theologians. Let's agree at least that a lot of Catholics were terribly dislocated by the changes wrought by the council, even as there were a lot of young people—perhaps George Weigel included—who were terribly excited by the possibility of change in an "unchanging" church.

The council brought attention, even celebrity, to a number of theologians who were seen—rightly, in retrospect—as genuine fathers of the council in their roles as *periti*, experts who advised the bishops. One thinks of George's favorite, the Jesuit John Courtney Murray. Almost overnight, theologians like Hans Küng and Karl Rahner and Yves Congar and Henri de Lubac became genuine culture heroes to bright young Catholics everywhere. The conservatives were right: these men were a kind of parallel magisterium, at least for a while. And it was none other than Father Charles Curran who noted wryly: "Now that we have demythologized the magisterium, it is time to demythologize the theologians, beginning with myself."

In a bit of verbal sleight of hand, George suggests that by paying so much attention to institutional conflicts within Catholicism, journalists are guilty of clericalism. But if you have a church that is run by clerics, a structure of authority that is limited to clerics, it does not follow that journalists who report on the institution are thereby clericalists, any more than it follows that newspapers that continually contrast the voice of the hierarchy with a putative voice of "the people" (one thinks here of the *National Catholic Reporter*) are thereby populists.

Moreover, we *do* have bishops who understand the Church in a highly clerical fashion. I recall that when John Joseph O'Connor arrived in New York, he immediately reminded the folks gathered in St. Patrick's Cathedral, including then-mayor Ed Koch, that he was not *elected* to his post as archbishop. O'Connor wanted all to realize that he had been appointed by the Pope, and that it was to the Pope alone that he was responsible. O'Connor was also a military man, and it may have been a military man's way of speaking. But there was no suggestion that day—or on any succeeding day—that he was responsible to the Catholics of New York as well.

George speaks negatively about liberation theology in ways that I would not. He is absolutely right in saying that liberation theology was imported into Latin

America from European universities; I agree that liberation theology was at its source not indigenous. But so what? Theology has always been the province of educated elites. I think that the Pope was uncharacteristically unsophisticated in his criticism of liberation theology. My own sense of the matter is that what went wrong with liberation theology was that it became too abstract, too scholastic. It was supposed to be praxis, founded on the formation of base communities. Anyone who has ever seen parishes in Latin America that stretch for miles, each quarter block teeming with poor people, cannot doubt that something like base communities was (and is) a realistic and practical response. My suspicion is that the reason why liberation theology was condemned was not because of the naïve Marxism of a few academics but because of the threat the base communities presented to the parish system. In any case, the liberationist perspective on the Gospel has, for better and worse, become a permanent addition to the way Catholics think theologically.

On the issue of ordaining women, George says that the real question "was not whether the Church *would* . . . but whether it *could*." That *would* be the real question, perhaps, if the Pope's answer were all that convincing. It certainly doesn't seem to be convincing to very many Catholics. The Pope may be right, but I think he and his successors will have to come up with a more convincing argument on this issue.

I say this as someone who thinks that the Church *ought not* to ordain women but who is not convinced that it *cannot*. *Ought not* because my observation is that religion is already the domain of women. Christianity has always appealed more to women than to men. Women are more likely to go to church than men, and when children get religion, it is more likely to be through the aegis of women—mom, Sister So-and-So, the Sunday school teacher—than through men. I might almost say that the altar and the pulpit are the last bastions of male presence in the Catholic Church. As for Protestant churches, women dominate in the black churches, and they are now the majority in the major U.S. divinity schools. The Protestant ministry—which is not the same, theologically, as the Catholic priesthood—is moving fast in the direction of becoming a female calling.

It may be, moreover, that as a deeply sacramental religion, Catholicism—like Orthodoxy—invests more meaning and symbolism in gender (and sexuality in general) than does Protestantism. Certainly Catholics have a more "organic" understanding of the Church, and these may be some of the reasons why this pope says that the Church is bound by the maleness of Christ's apostles. This, it seems to me, is the kind of issue that journalists no less than theologians ought to explore. I think this pope, together with Cardinal Ratzinger, has not handled the question of female ordination well at all. They have sought by ecclesiastical fiat to answer a question that they have yet to address in a theologically comprehensive—not to mention convincing—way.

George asks why Catholicism isn't doing well in Canada and other prosperous nations while "orthodox Catholic communities are flourishing in Africa." Sorry, but though I think of Africans in a lot of positive ways, I do not think of them as preservers of orthodoxy. Africans are too new to the faith, overall, to be burdened with that responsibility. Orthodoxy is a matter not simply of upholding what a missionary has taught but of living in and with the faith long enough to make it one's own. That hasn't happened yet in Africa, docile as the African hierarchy may be to Rome. And the persistence of tribal beliefs and practices (including mutually inflicted genocide) does not argue well for an "orthodox" African Catholicism.

George recommends that we journalists look to religious groups like the Legionaries of Christ for examples of the future of Catholicism. I can only say that if this is the future—and I have no doubt that it is not—then the Church is in deeper trouble than I ever dared imagine. I am truly astonished that he would look to such a retrograde form of Catholicism as the future of the Church.

He suggests that we look also at the handful of Catholics who have done well in academic life (having made it to the faculty of Harvard University and similarly elite secular institutions) and see in them new hope for the Church. Perhaps. But I must also look at those many other public intellectuals who are Catholic—Garry Wills comes to mind, as does Daniel Patrick Moynihan—but who do not seem at all supportive of the most contentious positions the Catholic Church has taken in the public sphere. Abortion is the obvious test case. George seems to think that the Church's natural-law tradition, its language and grammar, is regaining dominance. I wish I could agree. If natural-law arguments were so obvious and persuasive, then it seems to me that the Church's case against birth control, abortion, and euthanasia would be winning the day. Clearly it is not.

Throughout his paper George argues that a new Catholic conservatism is in the ascendancy and that Catholic liberalism is in manifest decline. Among the evidence he cites is the enrollment at Catholic seminaries: those in liberal dioceses are nearly empty, he says, but those in conservative dioceses are full. I look around and I see something else. I see that there are so few young men studying for the priesthood that many, many dioceses have no seminaries, regardless of whether the bishop is liberal or conservative. Conservative bishops send their men to conservative seminaries, like Dunwoodie in the Archdiocese of New York. These seminaries survive, not because the education is solid, or because conservatism is more attractive, but because conservative bishops trust only a few conservative seminaries with their future priests.

What I worry about is not whether future priests are liberal or conservative but what kind of men are being attracted to the priesthood, and the reasons they have for making the priestly ministry their choice. This is not a problem limited to Catholics by any means. When I was in my twenties, the men who opted for the mainline Protestant ministry were men who might otherwise have gone into medicine or the law. Today people of that caliber or potential do not elect the ministry. The same is true of the priestly ministry in Catholicism. George may be satisfied that they are conservative. I'd be satisfied to know they were competent. Here as in so many other things he mentions, he and I have drawn very different conclusions about what is going on in American Catholicism, and about what is worthy of a journalist's attention—which is why, I suppose, I was given the privilege of responding to his paper.

Discussion

E. J. DIONNE: I'm one of those people who write little marginal notes in books and argue with the author, so you can tell by the number of notes I wrote while George was talking that I found what he said very provocative. I agree with his general point that the "left-right" model doesn't always work. But I have one note here that says, "George replaces the word 'conservative' with the word 'orthodox' and is off to the races." I think that there are a lot of Catholic schools of thought that would not be regarded as conservative by the conservatives, but that do consider themselves orthodox. Some of this is a battle over the meaning of "orthodoxy," but I think that by imposing this framework, George risks reproducing the problem that he criticizes in the first place, and I'd like him to talk about that.

George seems to think that American Catholics are one of the dumbest collections of Catholics in the world. Well, we may be dumb, but we're faithful. Although our church attendance dropped off in the sixties, it's still much higher here than in any other developed country in the world—50 or 51 percent on a given Sunday, I think. Something is going on here that's worth exploring.

The other note that I couldn't resist writing has to do with the Church in the South. I wrote, "Now that the South has taken over the Republican party, George wants the South to take over the Catholic Church." There's an interesting question here. One of the things you find in the survey data is that Catholic political identity changes as Catholics move out of the Northeast and the Midwest. Clearly there is a more conservative Catholic community in the South and also to some degree in the West.

On liberation theology: yes, Marxism itself was a European import, but I do think there were indigenous roots to liberation theology. I would agree with George about some of its problems. When I was covering the Vatican in the mid-1980s, Leonardo Boff was one of the liberation theologians who were condemned. I had an American source inside the Vatican who said, "Boff makes 'Rome' sound like a four-letter word." Liberation theology was part of an internal argument over what the whole idea of a "preferential option for the poor" meant for the Latin American church. I do think there was a political argument there.

Ken Woodward said what I was thinking about women and the priesthood. Obviously, this argument has to be understood theologically. But I think it is not simply a fight over theology; it is also a fight over an understanding of the Church.

I want to end on a note of concord. I think George is right in his core argument about how the terms "liberal" and "conservative" can be misleading. You can analyze this pope's achievement in many ways as a "liberal" achievement, in the conventional meaning of that term. The greatest historical change that took place in Vatican II (and Ken, please correct me if you think I'm wrong) was a fundamental shift in the Church's relationship to democracy, human rights, and religious freedom—in large part because of the work of John Courtney Murray but also many others. I think that in the long run we're going to look back at John Paul II and say that one of his greatest achievements was ratifying that shift. That surely has to be seen as a great liberal achievement

On the new centers of Catholic learning: I have a sense that at places like Notre Dame and Boston College a huge debate is taking place, among Catholics of all stripes, about giving these institutions a more self-consciously Catholic identity. Perhaps in the long run some of the smaller institutions George is talking about will become important, but I think the more important story is this dialogue about the Catholic nature of these well-known large institutions.

NATHAN HATCH: Notre Dame is having a tremendous discussion about what Catholic universities should be. This past May [1999], all the deans at Notre Dame had a two-day intellectual retreat to look at the history and trajectory of religious higher education and what this means. Then the fifty top academic leaders had a similar retreat, where together we tried to say in what ways Notre Dame wants to be a good university and in what ways it wants to be a Catholic university. There's tremendous ferment on those issues among Catholics and also non-Catholics.

GEORGE WEIGEL: And in that sense *Ex Corde Ecclesiae*, this document that we've been trying to get implemented in the United States for ten years, has already won the struggle, because the discussion has shifted. Now we're talking about the fine print. The discussion has shifted from "How do we become Amherst with incense and bells?" to "How do we hold on to a Catholic identity that goes back to the origins of the university in the Western world?" Who invented the university? The Catholic Church.

KENNETH WOODWARD: It seems to me that with 240 Catholic colleges and universities, there is no one-size-fits-all model. Some of them, and I would include Georgetown, clearly aren't Catholic in any traditional kind of way.

GEORGE WEIGEL: I'd like to respond to some things E. J. Dionne said. E. J., I might start bringing a pen to the breakfast table on the days your column appears! I'm as dissatisfied with some of this language as you are. I don't like it when Catholics of a certain disposition use the term "orthodox" as a bludgeon to beat other people over the head with. I firmly agree with James Joyce that the Catholic Church means, "Here comes everybody!" But *the* iron law of religious sociology is that when biblical religion meets modernity, the communities that maintain a firm doctrinal framework and make clear moral demands are the ones that survive; those that can't tell you whether you're in or out because the boundaries have become so porous, that have so lowered the bar of moral expectation that there is *no* moral expectation—those communities die. That's true of both Christianity and Judaism, and of Western Europe as well as America.

I don't know what terminology can best get at this. "Liberal," as you know, has a very specific meaning in the context of post-eighteenth-century theology. It was journalistically reinterpreted during Vatican II to mean anything to the left of the official church position. I'm not satisfied with what I've come up with; I think we are going to have to keep struggling to find the right terms. But let's also remember that iron law. Look at the implosion of mainline Protestantism in America, in the post–World War II period, and the virtual collapse of the great churches of the Reformation in Europe. There has to be some connection between this and the loosening of doctrinal seriousness and moral expectations.

E. J. is right that Catholic practice is much higher in the United States than anywhere in Western Europe and has in fact experienced something of a rebound. But ask any bishop confirming fourteen-year-olds what the condition of Catholic knowledge is among these young people, and you will get one horror story after another. The difference is that E. J., Ken, and I grew up in a more or less intact Catholic culture. The schools we went to, the parishes we were in, the people our families associated with—you just absorbed this stuff through your pores. It was not simply a rational process; the behaviors and certain symbolic realities all got absorbed the way you absorb culture. That is what has broken down over the last few years—the transmission belt. Yes, attendance is about 50 percent on Sunday, but those congregations are getting grayer and grayer. There's a real problem of leakage among young people. I think this does have to do with the fact that the Church in the United States has not figured out an alternative form of enculturation. Balloons and posters, the religious education of the sixties, clearly could not do the job. A more content-serious form of religious education is needed.

As for the history of liberation theology, there's more in the paper than I think Ken gave me credit for. I made very clear in the paper, as I have done in twenty years of writing on this, that there *was* a serious problem in the history of the Church in Latin America and its identification with thoroughly corrupt, undemocratic regimes. That was a very, very serious problem. The Second Vatican Council made it perfectly clear that those days were over, that the Church was to be an active proponent of participation in public life, empowering the poor, defending human rights, and so on. The argument was not *whether* it was going to be that kind of activist church but *how*. Was that going to take place through essentially Marxist categories or through more specifically Catholic categories?

Liberation theology did some very good things. It restored the Bible to the people, as the people's book. It reinforced the notion that the point where the rubber meets the road in the Catholic Church is in local communities, not in the archbishop's house. I think all of that is part of the record and needs to be acknowledged.

E. J. DIONNE: Two things in response. I agree that the issue is about how an institution such as this one deals with modernity. The example of the mainline Protestant churches is always used to say, "This is how you don't do it." The argument is often cast as confrontation versus capitulation, but I think it is more complicated. The question that various sides within the Church are talking about is, What's the right dialectical relationship with modernity?

I agree with you on the transmission problem in the American church. An interesting sociological-journalistic question is, Does the breakdown of this transmission belt have to do more with things that happen inside the Church—Vatican II and the rest—or with the almost inevitable breakdown of the enclosed parochial community, which was created at least as much by discrimination and exclusion as by self-conscious decision?

NANCY GIBBS: That's exactly what I'm curious to hear about, what the impact might be as the voucher debate gathers steam. Suppose that there is a large infusion of non-Catholic children into the Catholic schools; what impact would this have on the schools and on that transmission of knowledge?

GEORGE WEIGEL: Well, it has already happened. The Catholic school in suburban Maryland that my children attended has grown like mad. It has gone from about 280 kids when we started there fifteen years ago to maybe 460, fully 15 percent of whom are not Roman Catholic.

NANCY GIBBS: And that could be 50 percent in another five years.

GEORGE WEIGEL: Five or six years ago we had a number of diplomatic families in our parish, including some from Islamic countries. One of these families wanted to enroll its kids in our school, but the parents didn't want the children to be in religion classes. There was a lot of hemming and hawing about this. No exception had been made for other non-Catholic kids, primarily Protestant. Finally it was decided that, no, if you are a part of this school, this is an integral part of what we do, and no students can be excused from it.

The Catholic argument for "vouchers," or some form of choice, has always been a very public one. It's not difficult to understand. One, the primary locus of responsibility for children's education is parents. Two, education is a public good, and the state has a right to tax people in pursuit of this public good. Where we have disagreed with the position of the courts is in their conclusion that the publicly raised dollar must be spent only in a public institution. Well, our parish school is a *public* institution. It is a doing a *public* job. It is preparing citizens of the United States of America, of many different flavors. But I certainly agree that if we break down the government's school monopoly, this will introduce a vast number of new questions, and there is some reason to be quite concerned about the schools' identities.

ELLIOTT ABRAMS: My question is also about the transmission belt, between what you say is happening or may happen in the Church, and public life. I start with the fact that most of the prominent national politicians who are Catholics seem in no way to be Catholic. The fact that they are Catholic seems to have no impact on their public careers. How does that change so that what's happening in the Church is transmitted in part through these public figures? That "grammar" that you talked about, George, must become a spoken language of living people who are engaged in politics, and that does not seem to be happening at all.

GEORGE WEIGEL: That's certainly true. If one identifies public life with electoral politics, this is a very serious problem. But if in fact we are in, if not a postpolitical time, then a period in which politics—understood in the narrow sense of electoral politics—is going to be less and less important than it was from the New Deal through the Reagan period, then one has to look at other places for indications that some Catholic traction is being achieved. This will mark me as an anthropological specimen, I'm sure, but I think it is a very interesting phenomenon that more than a quarter of a century after *Roe* v. *Wade* the pro-life movement remains an enormous factor in our public life—when it has been told by every sector of the country that it has lost, the battle is over. It seems to me that this effort will eventually have some effect on the legal situation.

HANNA ROSIN: This Catholic revival has the feeling of retrenchment; it feels very insular. It isn't a matter of how a counterculture can change the culture so that when you go out there, there are no longer any liberals. There's Frances Kissling talking to Charles Curran, and nobody else pays attention. *First Things* isn't exactly populist. So how do you go from there to affecting American moral or political culture?

GEORGE WEIGEL: I don't know what you mean by "insular" in this regard. It's certainly not insular if you look at the sense of missionary responsibility in the renewal movements. My daughter has been involved in some outreach activities of one of these movements in which they go door to door and say, "Is there anything you'd like us to pray for?" It's not a sales pitch. This kind of thing is simply unheard of in the American Catholic past, because in the past Catholicism was an enclosed subculture.

MICHAEL BARONE: I'm struck, George, by your view of the growth and the change of American Catholicism in recent years. I see an analogy with the growth and change of American politics in the sense that in this postindustrial time we've become more Tocquevillian, more like preindustrial America. More decentralized, more individualistic than the industrial America in which things were decided by big organizations—big government, big business, big labor, big church.

Maybe there is a connection here. The political parties have their particular institutional strengths and strongholds, such as the ethnic communities of the Democrats or the traditional Episcopalians of the Republicans. One of the consequences of that is that we have seen public policies come out from the hinterlands. For instance, we see crime and welfare in decline in America today. Those policies are almost entirely *not* the product of Washington-centralized bureaucracies or even university-trained experts. The orthodoxy—if I can use that word—in the academy has been more of an impediment than a help. Are we looking at something that resembles the preindustrial church in America?

GEORGE WEIGEL: The period between the 1870s, the First Vatican Council, and 1962, the beginning of the Second Vatican Council, was a unique period of institutional centralization in the Catholic Church, which has always been a much more freewheeling structure, much more Tocquevillian than it looks from the outside. One of the things coming out of this postconciliar period is a return to a more distinctive sense of local church, both nationally and regionally. I don't know whether it is tracking that way because this is happening in society at large and therefore Catholics are reacting to it, or simply because the monolith was in a sense a historical aberration, and once the decision was made to engage the world rather than live inside the fortress with the moat filled and the gates drawn up, all sorts of different things came in.

MICHAEL BARONE: One of the implications for journalism is that it becomes much harder. When you have the big three auto companies and the United Auto Workers in the state of Michigan controlling the economy, you only need four cards on your Rolodex. You need a lot more now to know what's going on in the economy and in public policy.

GEORGE WEIGEL: And much of what is being brewed is not coming from the top of the institution down, but from a lot of populist churning in the pews that eventually is working its way up.

GREGG EASTERBROOK: George, you have mentioned the phrase "Fourth Awakening" and have said the Pope thinks very optimistically about the twenty-first century. This theory is already bubbling up. Robert Fogel of the University of Chicago has a new book called *The Fourth Great Awakening and the Future of Egalitarianism*. He has had an up-and-down reputation as a scholar, but he has been right about a lot of things in the past. Fogel's view is that the United States will become more religious in the next two decades, although he thinks it will be nondenominationally religious rather than any one version triumphing.

MICHAEL CROMARTIE: Isn't Fogel an economist?

GREGG EASTERBROOK: Yes, he writes basically as a conservative economist. We're disgusted with materialism, he says. Typically, in the past, religious movements gave people an escape from the deprivations of life, but this religious movement tries to help them escape from excess. Too much, too high a standard of living, too much daily stress to maintain that standard of living. It's an interesting theory. But he raises this idea that the United States will become a much more religious country—do you think that's going to happen, George?

GEORGE WEIGEL: I'll leave it to others here to say how things are going in their part of the woods. As for the Catholic Church in the United States, I think there is enormous vitality today. It is in fact less divided than it was twenty years ago. There is a kind of élan about it now: the Pope has made people feel proud to be Catholic. That's an important thing. I think the great task of the next twenty years is with young people, to invite them back in, if they have left; to give them reasons to see this as a terribly exciting proposal about how to live your life, a way to human fulfillment.

I agree that the further great challenge is the challenge of affluence. That's one of the reasons why the Church in Germany is such a mess right now. It has too much money and has had for thirty-five years, because it's essentially a ward of the state. There's a sense of comfort if institutional forms are maintained, and deutsche marks are flowing, and we can give seven billion dollars to the Church in the Third World. It doesn't make any difference that the cathedral in Munich has fewer people at Mass on Sunday than my little parish does at Mass on Wednesday morning. Affluence has been a terrible problem in the Church in Western Europe. So far it hasn't seemed to be as much of a problem in the United States; but now we are in a generational shift, we are out of the urban-ghetto church and have become primarily suburban. We'll see how this plays out.

GREGG EASTERBROOK: Well, George, let me rephrase my question. Do you think that what's happening is specific to Catholicism, or is there some larger return to spiritual values in which Catholicism is participating?

GEORGE WEIGEL: I think there is a widespread intuition in the culture as a whole that the materialist/secularist proposal is simply not conducive to human flourishing. Too many people have gotten too hurt not to begin to have second thoughts. I've been deeply struck by the numbers who did not grow up with a serious religious tradition but at age forty-five are trying to get there, because they have experienced a sense of emptiness in their lives. This is a general phenomenon. Where this does not seem to be happening, though, is in mainline American Protestantism. There doesn't seem to be much of a revival going on over there, for reasons that have something to do with doctrinal mushiness and lack of moral expectation.

Let me just point out one other thing in the world picture that I find very interesting. Poland today is a historic experiment of enormous importance, namely: can you build a democratic political community and free economy on the foundation of an intact Catholic culture? This has never been done before, for a variety of historical reasons. The expectation that Polish Catholicism would, like Spanish or Portuguese Catholicism, simply collapse in the face of modernization has not been borne out at all. That is surely due in part to the fact of John Paul II, and whether it will continue to flourish when he is no longer the reference point remains to be seen. I teach in Kraków every summer, and I am deeply impressed by how the first decade of the experiment is working out. Particularly among young people, you find intense Catholic pride, complete commitment to democratic values, and gung-ho interest in entrepreneurial activity.

NATHAN HATCH: I want to pick up this point that you think there's a cause-and-effect relationship between a lowering of moral expectation and a decline in church attendance. If you look at the megachurches in the Protestant community, such as Willow Creek outside Chicago, it's obvious that they are doing extraordinarily well. It seems to me that these gigantic churches offer "religion lite," that they are thriving because they do not require much in terms of formal faith.

JAY AMBROSE: I believe the appeal of the megachurches is more complex than that they may offer worshippers religion lite. Their appeal is multifaceted, I think, but part of it is that they do tie people to a commitment. These are clearly modern, market-oriented institutions, but it seems to me some tend to be orthodox in some respects, and I think many of them do pull people into real engagement.

GEORGE WEIGEL: It seems apparent to me that if an institution cannot tell you what difference it makes to belong to it, and does not have a set of behavioral characteristics that distinguish it and you from the rest of society, it's not going to be terribly attractive. There are a lot of other things to do on a Sunday morning. I'm not sure what else could account for this quite striking decline of the mainline other than the fact that it has taken place behind great theological confusion and a constant lowering of the bar of behavioral expectations. I'm sure that there are other things involved, but that strikes me as the one with the most natural plausibility.

NATHAN HATCH: Two questions. One has to do with the sharp decline of professed religious. The decline of women religious certainly has serious implications for health care. You really didn't deal with the sharp decline of clergy, George, and I think you really have to come to terms with that.

My second point is this: in a sense you historicize the liberal Catholicism of the sixties and seventies, liberation theology and feminism. As one who always worries about culture imposing its values on religion, what do you think about neoconservative political culture in the last fifteen years and how that relates to orthodoxy within Catholicism?

GEORGE WEIGEL: About the decline in women religious: it's true, there aren't going to be many nuns in the United States thirty years from now. The only communities of women religious that are growing are those that have attempted to return to the more traditional practice of religious life. They wear a habit, they live in community, they do more specifically ecclesial forms of ministry. The Catholicism in America that we knew in the 1950s was an enormous institution essentially run by women. Everyone knew that while the pastor was technically in charge, the school principal, a sister, was really the force to be reckoned with. That's gone, and what this will do to the Catholic health-care system (another tremendous set of institutions largely run by women) is a serious question.

With clergy, we are going to have a tough twenty-year period as the median age of the Catholic priests in the United States grows higher and higher. Then we are going to see a better period. There is no secret to why some dioceses produce a lot of priestly vocations today and others do not. When the bishop and the local clergy actively recruit, when they talk about it and encourage it, things happen. If they don't do these things, candidates do not appear. That's in part because of the collapse of the subculture. The subculture could produce vocations before. Nobody had to ask you to consider becoming a priest, because you were surrounded by this stuff all the time. That's no longer true.

On your other point, Nathan, about neoconservative political culture and Catholic orthodoxy: I'm not sure what you are trying to get at.

NATHAN HATCH: Robert Wuthnow talks about certain cultural categories as being the determinants of a lot of religious thought. I guess that's what I worry about.

GEORGE WEIGEL: That may be true for some people, but it is certainly not true of the people who are primarily identified as neoconservative or Catholic. What I write theologically is written out of the great tradition of Christianity. It doesn't have much to do with what I think about marginal tax rates, school vouchers, or anything else. I think what the neoconservative intellectuals in the Catholic world have tried to do is to think through, again, the Catholic "optic" on the American democratic experiment, and then to propose that in a way that can be genuinely engaged by everyone. How successful we've been at that is for others to judge.

GRANT WACKER: I think we ought to be cautious about overstating the collapse of mainline Protestantism. It reminds me of Nelson Bunker Hunt crying "economic collapse!" because resources have dwindled from 6 billion to 5.5 billion. Walk down Fifth Avenue and see those vast churches. Look at the religious affiliation of men and women in Congress. I remember that when Robert Bork was struggling for confirmation, he went out of his way to let his interrogators know that he was an Episcopalian. Clearly he didn't do that because he thought it would hurt his chances. It's still the mark of stability, respectability. If he had been a Jehovah's Witness, I doubt that he would have mentioned it. What

I'm getting at is that even though the numbers in mainline Protestantism may have dropped off, there is still enormous cultural credibility, even normative value. Do you think there would be a similar residual power in old-line, established, more or less liberal Catholicism?

GEORGE WEIGEL: I'll defer to the sociologists among us, but I don't think the decline is from 6 to 5.5. The United Methodist Church today probably has less than half of the membership it had thirty years ago. Ditto for the United Presbyterian Church. Ditto for the Episcopal Church. There have been enormous losses. I'm not rejoicing at this; it doesn't mean a larger market share for Catholics. It accounts in part for the enormous confusion in the public moral culture over the last thirty years. These are the institutions that once carried the moral consensus, and when they get into serious demographic difficulties, there's a big ripple effect.

Liberal theology seems caught in methodological quicksand. Eventually you have to stop talking about believing about believing about believing, and talk about *belief!* Talk about the *content.* Philosophy got into the same pit of solipsism, thinking about thinking about thinking. What's the content of that? What's the truth being engaged? I think the liberal theological project has a built-in *terminus ad quem,* a point beyond which you cannot go. Moreover, I think Chesterton was right that the real drama in either Judaism or Christianity is the drama of orthodoxy. It's the drama of a huge, complex, rich, diverse set of truths. The interesting question is not how little do I have to believe and how little do I have to do to stay in the club. It's how much of this rich, complex, diverse tradition have I appropriated and made my own. The liberal theological project somehow got into this "how little do I have to believe and do" business. That is, ultimately, boring. And as many have noted, boredom is a most underrated factor in human affairs.

KAREN DEWITT: I belong to St. Matthew's, which is the big Catholic cathedral in Washington, but I go to Foundry Methodist Church because I find more intellectually stimulating sermons there than at St. Matthew's, where it seems to be the 1950s again. So I want to ask, what is Catholic culture nowadays? Also, that enormous vitality you say you see in the Catholic Church, how much of that is just the general sweep across society of that Fourth Awakening, whether it's a twelve-year-old whose parents are not religious looking for some kind of moral structure, or a forty-five-year-old who makes a six-figure-plus salary and wonders, "Is this all there is, and then we die?"

GEORGE WEIGEL: Karen's question is an obviously crucial one for the next two decades. Absent the religious subculture, what transmits belief? I think it finally will be worship. *Lex orandi lex credendi* is where this all starts and stops. Despite the confusions of the past thirty years, Catholic liturgy remains an experience of the sacramental, of the extraordinary that lies on the far side of the ordinary—bread, wine, water, salt, oil, on the other side of which is God, passionate and loving.

KAREN DEWITT: So it will be the Mass.

GEORGE WEIGEL: I really think that is what carries the Church, forever and ever.

Can the Jews Survive America?
A Conversation with Jack Wertheimer and David Brooks

JACK WERTHEIMER: Why, one may wonder, should we give equal consideration at this seminar to Jews, a small minority constituting roughly 2.5 percent of the American population? According to the best estimates, there are approximately five and a half million Jews in this country, hardly a numerically significant population.

I would offer a twofold answer. First, Jews play a disproportionate role in several key sectors of American society. For a variety of social and cultural reasons, Jews have been drawn to high-profile occupations such as the professions, the media, academia, and certain entrepreneurial endeavors. (I should note that historically they have played a negligible role in other economic sectors, including heavy industry.) The reasons for this Jewish overconcentration in a few types of work are complex. Anti-Semitic discrimination kept Jews out of certain economic spheres, and so they tended to take greater risks in emerging, if initially peripheral, occupations. Jewish cultural values have also played a role, especially the emphasis Judaism places on textual study; Jews tend to pursue a higher education and then are drawn into fields that value such learning. There are also social considerations: long constrained in their occupational choices, Jews responded to the easing of occupational restraints with the explosive drive of a people that has much pent-up energy. (All these patterns have characterized Jewish occupational pursuits in other countries, too, during the modern era.)

Second, Jews are deserving of our attention because they serve in some important ways as a model ethnic and religious minority. In recent years, I have enjoyed a number of opportunities to speak at a variety of college campuses and have been struck by the level of interest in the American Jewish experience displayed by Muslims from the Balkans, Korean Americans, Hindus from the Indian subcontinent, Christians from the Caribbean, and other recent immigrants who attended my lectures. When I asked these students why they were interested in Jews, they responded forthrightly, "Because we are struggling with many of the same issues." Members of other minorities identify with the great dilemma facing contemporary American Jews: how do they, as Americans with strong religious and ethnic traditions, strike a balance between the drive for individual socioeconomic and geographic mobility and the desire to maintain a distinctive group culture and cohesiveness?

This is not a new dilemma. The very first Jews to arrive on these shores in the second half of the seventeenth century already confronted an important aspect of it. The question they faced was: how does a religious/ethnic minority organize itself in the United States? During the Middle Ages and beyond, Christian states in Western Europe and as far east as the Byzantine Empire, and also Muslim rulers around the Mediterranean basin and in the Middle East, had required Jews to maintain and support separate communities. External coercion, then, imposed internal Jewish unity and organization. Such a system satisfied everyone's needs. Jews oversaw their own internal affairs; they collected taxes from amongst themselves and turned those tax revenues over to the government. Governments, in turn, were required to devote relatively little attention to Jewish communities, which relieved rulers of a burden. They therefore granted a good deal of autonomy to Jewish communal leaders.

Jews who arrived in colonial America (the first ones came in 1654) had to decide how they were going to organize themselves. Coming from lands in which governments *compelled* them to be members of a Jewish community, they were faced with a radically unfamiliar ethos: American voluntarism. Initially, they developed a model in which the synagogue served as the center of all Jewish communal life. Indeed, the half dozen colonial synagogues monopolized virtually all Jewish goods and services, including the cemetery plot. A Jew who wished to be buried in a Jewish cemetery had to be a member in good standing of the synagogue. And if his or her membership dues were in arrears, then the heirs would have to pay those dues before the community permitted interment in its cemetery. Philanthropy and charity were funneled through the synagogue, as were such ritual-related services as the preparation of kosher meat and the baking of matzoh. The synagogue, as provider of all these services, then used its monopoly as leverage to convince Jews that they had to be members in good standing.

In a sense, these early Jewish immigrants tried to transplant to America the coercive form of community they had known in Europe. But American voluntarism soon triumphed: synagogue monopolies collapsed rapidly once new congregations were founded to compete with existing ones. There then ensued a great proliferation not only of synagogues but also of many other kinds of Jewish institutions, for social welfare, education, cultural pursuits, recreation, and fraternization. Each successive wave of Jewish immigrants established its own set of such institutions. In this way, over the course of the nineteenth century, Jewish communal life evolved from a highly concentrated and coercive system to one marked by fragmentation and institutional anarchy. The pressing challenge facing Jewish leaders at the start of the twentieth century was to bring some order out of this chaos.

Two Common Denominators

The solutions they devised are still with us. Early in the twentieth century, a Jewish attorney in New York named Louis Marshall created an organization called the American Jewish Committee. Marshall realized that Judaism itself was not what unified Jews; rather, religion *divided* Jews. He suggested that there are only two ways to organize Jews, two workable common denominators: all Jews have a sense of responsibility toward fellow Jews who are impoverished, and all Jews have a concern for fellow Jews who are victims of anti-Semitism. And so Louis Marshall founded an organization that would concern itself with these two matters, especially with combating anti-Semitism. But no sooner did Marshall announce his new approach than other organizations sprang up to meet the same needs.

Around the same time, American Jews began to develop something quite remarkable to deal with social problems. Local Jewish communities established federations of philanthropy in order to centralize the fund-raising efforts of Jewish agencies. By the end of the twentieth century, nearly one hundred and eighty federations existed in North American cities or regions, each serving as the central collection, allocation, and planning agency for local Jewish needs. Every federation runs a single fund-raising campaign and then, through a hierarchical and committee-driven process, determines how those funds should be dispensed. A central umbrella organization coordinates the work of the North American federations.

This aspect of Jewish life in the United States rarely gets reported, because it is a complicated and largely local story of how money is raised and dispensed. Yet it is through the federated system that a great deal of policy in the Jewish community is made, since allocation decisions force the community to define its priorities and ultimately its agenda.

The other concern unifying Jews, the desire to combat anti-Semitism, gave rise to several new organizations early in the twentieth century: the previously mentioned American Jewish Committee, the American Jewish Congress, and the Anti-Defamation League (ADL). Each has implicitly said, We are the ones defending the Jews; therefore we are the ones who speak for the Jews. Initially these organizations were involved mainly in community-relations work, improving relations between Jews and their neighbors and combating anti-Semitism. But as time went on, and particularly during World War II, the organizations embarked on a more comprehensive program. They came to believe that anti-Semitism is a symptom of other social ills. They therefore determined that both self-interest and a commitment to the improvement of society required the Jewish community to fight all forms of discrimination.

Over the years, the agenda of the Jewish community-relations agencies broadened, first to encompass housing and employment discrimination and eventually, in our day, to stake out a "Jewish" position on virtually every conceivable public-policy question. Church-state matters were a natural, of course, but then other kinds of questions came into play. What is the position of the Jewish community on the environment, on vouchers, on gun control? Jewish organizations developed a mechanism to address all these issues. Of course, there is something quintessentially American about all this: one way to participate in American society is to take positions. But there is also something quite strange about such an approach. Why, one may wonder, should Jews try to speak *with one voice* about so many complex questions of social policy?

Jews as a Religious Group

Thus far I have been speaking about the ways Jews have organized themselves as an ethnic community, but of course Jews also constitute a religious minority. American Judaism has conformed to American models. Like their Protestant neighbors, Jews in this country have spawned a multiplicity of religious movements that have begun to call themselves "denominations," a very Protestant category. These include Reform, Conservative, Reconstructionist, and Orthodox Judaism, and also a movement for Jewish Renewal, Humanistic Judaism, and so on. Interestingly, each movement has created institutions that parallel Protestant denominational infrastructures—an organization unifying congregations, another one for the clergy, and denominationally oriented seminaries to train rabbis and cantors. American Judaism has also become very congregational. Not surprisingly, many of the same problems that beset Protestant denominations today, such as the increased blurring of denominational boundaries, are affecting Jewish denominations too, in part because of the strength of congregationalism and the extent to which the individual synagogue decides on its own policies. Here again, the proliferation of congregations with highly independent policies very much mirrors the American scene.

The early forms of Orthodox, Conservative, Reform, and Reconstructionist Judaism all emerged out of ethnic synagogues, and represented the responses of particular immigrant waves to the challenge of adaptation. Reform Judaism was initially the movement of religious accommodation founded by Jews who came from German-speaking lands in the middle of the nineteenth century. The Conservative and Reconstructionist movements reflected the needs and aspirations of people who came from Eastern Europe at the turn of the twentieth century. The case of Orthodox Judaism is a bit more complicated, because some Jews in each of these other groups identified with Orthodoxy. But Orthodoxy was primarily molded by immigrants who arrived just before and after the Holocaust. There has also been a class dimension to these movements. Until quite recently, one could assume that Orthodox Jews were the poorest, Conservative Jews were in the middle, and Reform Jews were the wealthiest. I'm not certain that this pattern has totally broken down yet, though one could certainly find rich Orthodox Jews and poor Reform Jews.

Fundamentally, then, each of these movements sought to accommodate to American society while maintaining some fidelity to Jewish traditions. While the solutions they devised differed, the underlying assumption was that if you do not accommodate to American society, you are lost. And until recently, these accommodations seemed to work very well. Since World War II, Judaism has been treated with great esteem and regarded, as Will Herberg famously put it, as an equally valid component of America's "triple melting pot"—on a par with Protestantism and Catholicism. But do these strategies of accommodation work today? And is the struggle for acceptance and esteem the major challenge of *our* time?

Let's address these questions by backtracking to the organizational arrangements of Jews as an ethnic community and as a religious community. A decade ago, the federations of Jewish philanthropy probably reached a peak of their power and authority. At that time they collectively decided to levy a tax on every single Jewish community to help underwrite a billion-dollar loan to Israel to be used to help resettle Jews from the former Soviet Union. The federations raised that staggering sum, a billion dollars, within three years. Today, ten years later, the federation system is struggling to hold together. It has been renamed, it has new leadership, and it has very little national presence at this point. Here we see the centrifugal forces of American society at work. New organizations are established, new individuals step up and say, "We know better," and every centralized system seems to break down. That is the case in the federation world today.

Fissures of a different sort are growing in the public-policy arena. In this regard, the Jewish community is riven by a left-right split comparable to that dividing other segments of American society. Moreover, a number of Jewish groups have questioned the wisdom of trying to speak with one voice on environmental matters or other issues far removed from Jewish self-interest. Some are also challenging the *content* of these policy pronouncements: to what extent, they ask, do they reflect traditional Jewish teachings? Finally, some also question whether those who say they speak for the Jewish community reflect the actual views of most

Jews. The upshot of this debate is a recognition that there is less consensus than had been long assumed.

Religious polarization is also increasing. The American media have reported on the various controversies in Israel over the question "who is a Jew?" Little has been written, by contrast, about similar controversies in the United States. But the issue is no less divisive here. The difference is that in Israel the question has political and legal ramifications, whereas in the United States differing groups of Jews simply don't recognize one another as Jews. In truth, there is no agreement within the American Jewish community on who is a Jew. Some continue to embrace the traditional rabbinic definition that a Jew is a person born to a Jewish mother, whereas others consider it sufficient if either parent is a Jew. There is also no agreement on the requirements for conversion to Judaism. Moreover, there is not even agreement on the nature and limits of Judaism. The one group that the Jewish community will unanimously read out of Jewish life is the movement of Messianic Jews, "Jews for Jesus"; but Jewish Buddhists, who call themselves "Jew Bus," are patted on the head and told they are terrific. Yet both represent forms of religious syncretism.

Even more than in the civic arena of Jewish life, the religious sector is riven over these kinds of issues. Each area of dispute points to a weakening of consensus among American Jews about crucial contemporary issues. Without such consensus, it is hard to maintain institutional coherence.

Fighting an Obsolete War

Perhaps the central challenge now confronting American Jews is to determine whether the strategies that served them so well in the past can address contemporary needs. To what extent does the Jewish community continue to fight the last war? Does it grasp the radically different reality of the current battle? The last war was a struggle for social acceptance, for an end to discrimination, and for the legitimation of Judaism as a respected religion. In 1951 the president of the Jewish Theological Seminary, Louis Finkelstein, made the cover of *Time* magazine, in large part because he was a leader in the campaign to win respectability for Judaism. I believe that battle has been won. Jews have achieved respectability, and Judaism is treated with a great deal of acceptance within American society. The issue now is whether Jews who have integrated so well can maintain themselves as a distinctive group. To what extent can they survive as a religioethnic group if they do not define limits to their community and establish boundaries to acceptable behavior?

One of the symptoms and also causes of the fuzzy boundaries is the rapid upward spiral in rates of intermarriage between Jews and non-Jews. Like many other religious and ethnic groups in this country, Jews have witnessed a dramatic surge in intermarriages over the past thirty years. As a consequence, the rituals and outlooks of many other cultures are being absorbed into American Jewish life. Jews are eager to integrate Asian, Native American, and other religious and cultural practices into their Judaism; this religious syncretism makes it increasingly difficult to discern what remains distinctively Jewish about the religious rituals or world view of many Jews.

Two symbolic battles that took place in recent years shed light on some of these conflicts. One was a minor skirmish fought in 1997 at Yale University, when five Orthodox Jewish undergraduates sued the university on the grounds that they were compelled to live in coed dormitories in their freshman and sophomore years. Since such arrangements were at odds with the sexual comportment expected of Orthodox Jews, the students asked to be exempted from the dorm requirement— and the fees. When Yale refused, the students sued the university.

The overwhelming response of the Jewish community was to stigmatize these five students for their "ghetto mentality." If you really want to live that way, they were told, go to Yeshiva University. Lost in the fray was a recognition of how much Jewish life had changed in this country. Here were students, after all, who had made it to Yale, an institution that like so many others of its type had imposed strict quotas on Jewish admissions until fifty years ago. But the students felt themselves so at home at Yale that they took action to sue the university. Taking for granted their own social acceptance, they waged a court battle to protect their right to be different, to stand out, to resist the powerful culture of the campus with its attendant sexual morality. Significantly, they found allies in both Protestant and Catholic circles, not only at Yale but at other institutions as well. But fundamentally they were fighting for the right to live according to the distinctive requirements of the Jewish religion, as they understood it, rather than capitulate to the powerful dominant culture. Compared to their Jewish predecessors a half century earlier, they waged a very different kind of battle for acceptance, one that stresses how Judaism *differs*. Not surprisingly, they won scant support in the Jewish community, which is still preoccupied with fitting in, with social acceptance.

The second symbolic battle I wish to mention has evoked far more debate than the Yale case, and that is the brewing battle within the Jewish community over school choice, vouchers, and the like. The background of this new debate is the remarkable growth over the last forty years in the number of Jews who enroll their children in all-day Jewish schools. Almost 40 percent of children receiving a Jewish education today are enrolled in these all-day schools. That is a staggering figure, which needs some qualification. First, we must note that some Jews never enroll their children in *any* Jewish educational program, and so the 40 percent does not relate to the total population of Jewish children. And second, all-day Jewish schools now begin in preschool and continue at least through lower and middle school, with a movement building to extend that education through high school.

What makes these Jewish day schools remarkable, and I believe different from Catholic parochial schools, is that in many of them, the day is divided equally between religious education and general education. In Catholic schools, from what I have read, usually just one period a day is devoted to religious instruction. And so Jewish children in day schools receive a much more intensive religious education. The point here is that parents feel secure enough to send their children to these schools, even though they still want those children to become doctors, lawyers, and dot-com-ers, no less than do other upwardly mobile parents. They feel that these vocational goals are possible even though their children are attending Jewish schools. (The five Yale students, we should note, all attended Jewish day high schools, and that did not prevent them from winning acceptance to a prestigious university.)

As the population of Jewish day-school parents continues to grow, and as those parents stagger under the burden of paying both steep taxes for public schools their children do not attend and high tuition fees at day schools, more and more are coming to see vouchers and other plans that help parents afford school choice as an attractive if not financially necessary option. This, in turn, is prompting some reconsideration of Jewish policy positions on matters of church/state separation.

This is a remarkable development in a community that has long been a great supporter of the public school. Jewish advocates argued for much of the twentieth century that public schools are the instrument by which American society brings together a great diversity of children so that they can learn about one another. Where else will young people learn to respect Jews if they do not befriend them in public schools? Yet a growing number of Jews feel secure enough to send their children to intensely Jewish schools instead of to public schools because they no longer consider winning respect to be the most crucial issue facing Jews.

Having succeeded in gaining acceptance into American society, Jews in this country must now confront new and perhaps harder questions. How distinctive are they prepared to be? How out of step are they willing to march? Where will they draw boundaries between themselves and their neighbors? Given the wide diversity of the Jewish community today, there are no consensus answers to these questions. But as a small religious and ethnic minority, America's Jews face no more pressing set of questions.

DAVID BROOKS: At the beginning of the twentieth century my mother's grandfather moved into the Lower East Side of Manhattan and became a kosher chicken butcher. It was always a matter of pride in my family that when the kosher chicken butchers in his area set up their collusive price arrangement, he was the one who got to hold the pot of money. Everybody chipped in a few thousand dollars, and if you broke the price rule, you lost your two thousand. Apparently my great-grandfather was the most honest of the colluders! He married a German Jew, which was an immediate step up. Then, as soon as he could afford to, he moved uptown, out of this vibrant Jewish community, and eventually ended up in the South Bronx. There he spent all his money on real estate, which was not a good move.

When I was growing up in New York City, Anglophilia was one of the dominant moods in my house. This was a popular assimilationist impulse for Jews; the phrase was, "Think Yiddish; act British." The Jews gave their kids names like Irving, Norman, and Milton, which seemed very English, though we now think of them as Jewish. The English way—all that nobility, all that grace—seemed like a most admirable thing to us striving, vulgar Jews on the Lower East Side. My pet turtles were named Disraeli and Gladstone. Disraeli is the perfect Jew for this mentality: he was proud of his Jewish roots, and yet he got to be Lord Beaconsfield.

So I was all set to carry on the family tradition of assimilation. I voted Republican, I married a Protestant, and I went to work at the *Wall Street Journal.* But a couple of years after we were married, my wife decided to convert to Judaism, certainly with no pressure from me. She got very serious about it, to the point of deciding she wanted to become a rabbi. She has studied very hard and knows a lot of Hebrew. Our kids go to Jewish day schools where 50 percent of the day is devoted to Jewish instruction. I now live in an incredibly Jewish household—really despite myself.

There are three services every Saturday morning in our Washington synagogue. The one in the main sanctuary with rabbis feels a bit like a Protestant service. The rabbis use microphones, which the other two services would never use. There's a choir on high holy days. The other two services are newer, and these we go to on alternate weeks. The Havurah ("fellowship" in Hebrew) started in the early seventies, and it was very much a sixties thing. It's lay led. No rabbi. No authority. A woman can read from the Torah, and my wife now does. In the middle of the service there is a forty-five-minute seminar, where they talk about the Torah portion for that week; the leader conducts a Socratic dialogue. Nearly everybody is very knowledgeable, and the discussions are usually quite sophisticated. But whenever the Torah grates against pluralism, they draw back and start doing intellectual gymnastics, explaining why it doesn't mean what it seems to mean. This happens when it says "our enemies will be vanquished," for instance, or whenever there's an imputation that there is one true way.

The third service is called "Traditional Egalitarian." It's huge. On high holy days there are maybe five hundred or more present at this service. Even on ordinary Saturdays the group is very big and very vibrant. I'd say 70 percent are in their twenties to mid-thirties. It's a very rigorous service, more rigorous than the Havurah. While the Havurah reads only a third of the Torah portion, the Traditional Egalitarian reads the whole thing. They say a particular prayer and then repeat it. These youngish people are really impressive in their knowledge of faith and scripture. They too have a seminar thing in the middle, but it's much more therapeutic than the one in the Havurah. It's a bit jarring. There might be a discussion, for instance, of why vegetarianism is really the ultimate in Judaism. One woman wrote a short story that had Isaac talking to the grave of Abraham, saying, "You know, we never really communicated since that day when you held the knife"—very New Agey. It's as if you're in an Orthodox shul and suddenly the Oprah Winfrey show breaks in.

What we see in these two services, the Havurah and the Traditional Egalitarian, is a return to something more serious, but it's a funny kind of return. In some ways it's rigor without submission. It's the idea that you can bend the rules to fit your sensibility.

I differ from Jack a bit in saying that this return to serious Judaism is not distinctly Jewish but has been caused by intellectual pressures in the outside world. I would say that educated people, whether Jewish or non-Jewish, share a similar trajectory. Remember *The Organization Man*, *The Lonely Crowd*, all those books from social scientists in the 1950s? The main thrust of them was that society had become too orderly, too group oriented, too passive, too conformist. John Hewig drew a distinction between customary and reflective morality. Customary morality was sort of what you inherited; it was based on long-established rules, deference to eternal maxims. Reflective morality was based more on conscious deliberation. It was the moral directives you figured out for yourself. The assumption was that reflective morality was better. This went down well in popular culture, with the beats and the hippies—go your own way, find your own spiritual destiny.

In many ways that cultural force walked through an open door and has triumphed. Now it's better to be seen as unconventional than conventional. It's better to be called a nonconformist than a conformist. It's cooler to be a rebel than an obedient foot soldier. In this sense individualistic pluralism is the foundation for people both in the Havurah and in the Traditional Egalitarian group, and probably for all members of the educated class since the boomers. In the 1970s, of course, that sort of "breaking free," that desire for emancipation from the traditional, led to the rise of the New Age movement. By the mid-1980s the New Age had cooled down a bit, but Robert Bellah and his associates tell in their book *Habits of the Heart* about a woman whom they took as representative of a sort of spirituality that was out there. This young nurse named Sheila described her religion as "Sheilaism." You custom-designed your religion to fill your needs. "It's just trying to love yourself and be gentle with yourself, you know, take care of each other," she explains. Robert Wuthnow found a daughter of a Methodist minister who called herself a Methodist–Taoist–Native-American–Quaker–Jewish–Buddhist. She's a Jew Bu and then some.

These self-created religions were unsatisfactory for several reasons. In the first place, you might find there was no real self to discover if you kept digging down; maybe it's only for social contact that the self is created. Second, the self-religions didn't really help you much with the transitions of life: birth, death, marriage. Third, they made it very hard to pass your faith on to your children. The organized religions are really good at that and know how to structure things, which the self-religions didn't. And finally, the self-religions never gave you something to hold fast to—you were always experimenting. The Book of Samuel has a great sentence that represents what people long for: "Moreover, I will appoint a place for my people Israel, and I will plant them that they may dwell in a place of their own and move no more." That sense of moving no more is important.

So there has been, I think, in American society over the past ten years, a return to order, a return to community. In contrast to the social critics of the fifties who were saying, "We need less order, less group conformity, less community," today's are saying, "We need more community, more order, more civil society." Robert Putnam wrote "Bowling Alone," that famous essay about the loss of civil society, in 1995. What 1950s or 1960s intellectual would have taken the loss of participation in bowling leagues as something to be worried about? Bowling leagues would have seemed like absurdities that we should get rid of—sort of bourgeois, small-minded parts of Middle America.

We see every day that the main project in the political sphere is the restoration of authority, community, compassionate conservatism. And I think that vibrant movements like the Traditional Egalitarian and Havurah groups I described are the religious component of that same project. One of the striking things in these new movements is the emphasis on the Talmudic scholars of Judaism. They are looking for intellectual authority figures. In an earlier age they would have been talking about Freud or Marcuse, but now it's Maimonides. The tremendous emphasis in both of these services—and I may be overstating this, because it is true to some degree for all Judaism—is on a return to the past, a sense of the linking of generations, a desire to preserve the great chain of rituals and traditions. The *New York Times* had a great headline: "Religion Makes a Comeback (Belief to Follow)." The discussion was about whether, with rituals coming back, there is also belief. It was an open question.

Two final points. First, it could be that the political cleavage in the future will be, not Catholic versus Protestant versus Jewish, or anything like that, but a split between the orthodox of all faiths who are interested in fighting these cultural issues and the ambivalent who don't want to fight. Second, I wonder how long the mixture of orthodoxy and flexibility can last. When a circuit rabbi in Montana named Gershwin Winkler was asked, "What kind of shul do you run?" he replied, "It's 'flexodoxy.'" It's an expressive term. This urge for orthodoxy and this desire for flexibility—how long can they coexist? Can you worship God rightly if you insist on deciding for yourself which of the Bible's teachings you will follow? Can you establish ritual and order if you feel that you must continually experience new things? Can you be tightly bound to your community and still feel part of the larger diverse America?

I can imagine a future generation saying to us, "You know, you are all caught up in your ambivalences. You are divided against yourself. It makes you tepid. It gives you no fervor. Enough with being both a modern, liberal person and a religious person. We are going to go whole hog—well, maybe not in Judaism—all the way in one direction or the other and be pure."

I have this scenario: after my whole family spends a hundred years trying hard to be assimilated, my wife reverses the whole process just like that. I have this vision of my kids out there in Hebron. The whole return will have fulfilled itself.

Discussion

ROBERT SHOGAN: First I want to express my appreciation for both the presentation and the response. Jack Wertheimer struck a chord with the question "who is a Jew?" I was raised Jewish—both my parents were Jews—but eventually I drifted away. I married a Catholic woman. And since I was Jewish and she was Catholic, together we became Unitarian.

You spoke about the forces that compel Jewish unity: the desire to help the less fortunate and the desire to fight anti-Semitism. It seems to me that those motivations are waning. More Jews are better off, and anti-Semitism seems to be at least in ill repute. While both of these earlier motivations still play a part, it seems to me that the singular force behind Jewish unity today is the existence of the state of Israel. What is the effect when people who want to assimilate and want to maintain their identity have what amounts to loyalty to a foreign state?

JACK WERTHEIMER: I don't think the issue is one of loyalty to Israel in the sense of *patriotism*. American Jews have convinced themselves that there's a complete convergence of interest between Israel and the United States, and that is the case they have made all along. They don't want to think about any serious divergence of interest between the two nations. Certainly, in the current era of good feeling, American Jews perceive strong agreement between the Clinton and Barak administrations.

The evidence seems to suggest a waning of zeal about Israel among certain populations of Jews, especially younger ones. The generation that lived through the 1967 and 1973 wars identified wholeheartedly with Israel as an embattled and endangered population. Last year one of my undergraduates asked me, "Professor, how long have you been teaching?" I told her I began teaching full time in 1978. Her response was, "Oh, that was the year before I was born!" This sense of Israel as an embattled population understandably has less resonance with the young people of today, who cannot recall the time when Israel was in mortal danger.

As for the decline in anti-Semitism and its effect on the Jewish social conscience: survey research indicates that there is no necessary contradiction between being involved in social and civic issues and being involved in "particularistic" Jewish issues. It's not either/or: those involved in Jewish issues tend to be more involved in their local communities—which leads me back to some of David's very interesting comments. I don't think we really disagree about there being a climate within American society that very much influences Jews as well. That climate is reflected in bookstores, where there are huge sections on religion and mysticism. Jews are certainly a part of that larger world.

I want to pick up on this question of "flexodoxy"—I'd never heard the term before, and I love it. But I have a problem with that approach to religion. We live in a time when people in many faith communities are paying greater attention to religion, and in new ways. They are motivated by highly individualistic preoccupations. To put matters crassly, they are asking, "What's in it for me?" Some people attend religious services because they find it enriches their lives. I worry about their ability to go beyond themselves and realize, "That's what brings me into the institution in the first place, but the institution still stands for certain things. To what extent am I prepared to buy the package?"

Sociologists who have studied modern churches have found that congregations do much better when they communicate a clear message of basic expectations rather than say, "Come, we're inclusive, we will accept you as you are, no matter how you live your life." This literature on churches is now being scrutinized by people in the Jewish community who want to make a similar case. It's not enough to attend synagogue services because it makes you feel good. That's part of the motivation, but to what extent do you have a commitment to the core values and expectations of the institution—even if some do not necessarily make you feel good? I think this is a challenge to religious and institutional life that crosses religious boundaries.

DAVID BROOKS: It's a bit more problematic than that, because modernity *happened.* The apple of knowledge, the apple of individualism was offered to us, and we took it. It's not going away. It's harder now to go back to the sense of immersion in the group, to a suspension of individual judgment.

Just one thing about Israel. Jack mentioned that it is no longer as embattled. It's also a much richer country, so why should I give them money? I think the other thing that's coming across is that the Israelis themselves are much more ambivalent about our assistance. There's a much greater sense among them that "we don't need your help." Zionism is definitely a waning force in the synagogue I was mentioning. The one service that is not so vibrant is the most Zionist; in the other two, Israel just doesn't loom large in the discussion.

LARRY EICHEL: I want to explore the voucher issue in the Jewish context a little more. In Philadelphia we have a very competitive mayor's race going on. The Republican candidate is Jewish; he sends his children to Jewish day school, and he is advocating vouchers on a limited basis. His Democratic opponent is African American and Seventh-day Adventist, and he has tried to make the Jewish candidate's support of vouchers a very big issue, primarily to appeal to Jewish voters. Despite the increasing use of Jewish day schools, Jews as a group are more opposed to vouchers than any other segment of society, mostly for the old church-state reasons that we are all familiar with. Is a strategy like this wrong headed?

MICHAEL CROMARTIE: Peter Beinart has an article on Jewish schools in the October 1999 *Atlantic Monthly,* so let's get Peter's opinion on this.

PETER BEINART: My strong sense is that the opposition to vouchers really is waning. In the Conservative movement, where there was strong opposition to vouchers, there's a real and growing change, and even in Reform circles a significant minority is in favor of vouchers.

I have a question about Modern Orthodoxy: do you think it is moving more to the right or to the left? The Modern Orthodox are the ones who have had the Jewish schools all along. Their congregations are basically well educated. And it seems to me that if indeed the Conservative movement is becoming more traditional, then you can see your way toward a synthesis that might bring the community together in a new consensus about how to deal with questions like vouchers and the role of women. One of the things that struck me about the Yale Five was that they did not refer to themselves as Modern Orthodox. They said, "We call ourselves *yeshivaish.*" They wouldn't have anything to do with the Modern Orthodox movement at Yale. I found this encouraging, in that it suggests there may not be as much of a difference between the kind of Conservative you're talking about and Modern Orthodoxy.

JACK WERTHEIMER: Modern Orthodoxy—and this is a very narrow part of the story—was a sector of the Orthodox world that in the 1950s and 1960s believed that the future belonged to them. Its leaders were the spokesmen for Orthodox Judaism. As time goes on, they are coming more and more under siege. The world of Orthodox Judaism is moving to the right; it is now driven far more by people who really want to remove themselves from the rest of the Jewish world. The burning question in the Orthodox world is, to what extent can the Modern Orthodox reassert themselves?

On the voucher question: the issue is a very complicated one in the Jewish community, in part because there is still a great deal of nervousness about taking care of one's own. What has turned opinion around more than anything else is not whether vouchers would be good for Jewish day schools, because most people understand that the amount of government funding that would come to these schools under current plans would be just a fraction of the tuition they charge. When day-school tuition runs between $8,000 and $18,000 a year, the kinds of vouchers now available, running around $2,000, would not be a major factor. What seems to be turning Jews around is a much greater interest in vouchers among inner-city populations, specifically minorities. These are the traditional allies of liberal Jews, and so suddenly Jews have to pay new attention to vouchers because their traditional allies are telling them, "This is really good for inner-city kids."

GEORGE WEIGEL: I'd like to revisit the Yale incident to suggest that what was going on there was not simply a request to "respect our morality." It was a statement: "Don't impose your morality—which is in fact a negation of morality, a kind of debonair nihilism—on everyone." If that is indeed what's going on, if parts of the American Jewish community may be beginning to recognize that lifestyle liberty is in fact a new kind of totalitarianism, I wonder if there isn't a parallel in what we conventionally call church-state relations but I would rather call the religion-and-public-life realm. What began as an intention to make room for genuine pluralism has in time turned into a new establishment, the establishment of an ideology that is absolutely unable to give kids reference points from which they can deal with the pressures of a consumerist society. Is there a rethinking in the Jewish community about church-state issues?

JACK WERTHEIMER: Only in some sectors. I think that the orthodoxy of strict separationism is still very strong. I don't agree with it, but I understand it.

There is a fear: what's going to happen to a small non-Christian minority in a land that is overwhelmingly Christian if this wall of separation is breached? American Jews historically were not as obsessed with church-state questions and were far more open to breaches in the wall of separation than they are today. I don't see evidence of a really strong turnaround on these issues. Rather, more Jews today are open to a reconsideration of selected issues, to some small breaches in the wall.

GEORGE WEIGEL: In the history of the twentieth century, it seems very clear that a society constructed by people who believe that tolerance of other religions is a religious obligation is much safer for Jews than an utterly secularized environment. An intensely religious country has historically been the best place for Jews.

JACK WERTHEIMER: I agree with your point of view, but I've had many conversations with Jews on this issue, and what they always trot out is the marginalization they experienced as kids when religion intruded in public schools: "Let me tell you how uncomfortable I felt at Christmastime when we all had to sing those Christian songs." My response to this tale of woe is to ask, "Did you survive it?" "Oh yes, I did, and I felt more strongly Jewish because of it." But these people want to shield their children from that kind of experience even though they survived it intact, and were actually strengthened by it.

MICHAEL BARONE: Well, I think Jews are still voting against the czar. The experience of czarist Russia was that of a church united with the state that actively persecuted people, that had public policies of forced conversions. I take this to be one of the reasons why American Jews are so sensitive about the matter of conversion. If a bunch of Baptists want to convert me, it doesn't bother me. They can't compel me to convert, so what's the threat? The threat comes when you are going against that background of czarist Russia, which is the ancestral home of most American Jews. You look at it through that template and you see Newt Gingrich and Dick Armey as the vanguard of the Cossacks. When I talk to forty-something, fifty-something, eighty-something Jews in well-established Jewish neighborhoods across the United States, again and again I hear people voting against the czar.

ELLIOTT ABRAMS: I'd like to ask a question about faith. One could, I think, handle everything Jack described sociologically, politically, institutionally, without much reference to religious faith itself. Is there much knowledge about whether, for example, the people in David's Traditional Egalitarian service actually are people of deeper religious faith? Do they like that service because they like the singers?

Or do they like it because somehow it is more deeply spiritual? To what extent—
if at all—is there a revival of Jewish religious faith?

JACK WERTHEIMER: That's hard to say. We can observe from the outside that people are engaging in a particular religious ritual. The question is whether they believe that the ritual is important to God, not only to themselves. "I fasted on the
Day of Atonement, and now I feel a sense of catharsis" is a very different statement from "I fasted on the Day of Atonement, and I believe my fasting and prayer
make an impression upon God." We do not know whether people believe in the
religious efficacy of the rituals they perform.

It's very difficult to know whether we're actually seeing a great increase in faith
rather than just good feeling. What complicates the matter is that the whole language of faith and spirituality is not the natural language of Judaism. The natural
language of Judaism is one of actions and ritual observances. There's a lot of wig-
gle room, traditionally, about faith, about debating with God, about God's actions,
so it's really hard to know how much people believe and how important their belief is to them. I think the greater emphasis is on some of the things we have mentioned, like community, a sense of continuity, the link that rituals and traditions
provide to our ancestors.

E. J. DIONNE: Before I make my comment, I'd like to thank George Weigel for the
wonderful phrase "debonair nihilism." When he said it, I could see an ad in *Cigar
Aficionado*!

Part of the problem we're trying to get at here goes back to George's point that
a belief in tolerance, rooted in faith in God, is a strong bulwark against oppression. I believe that's true. However, historically, we Catholics have not always
thought that tolerance was taught by God. Indeed, we have tended to be much
more for tolerance in societies when we were in the minority than when we were
in the majority. We are not exceptional in this way. I think that's why this conversation is so difficult. In a way people who are defending an orthodox position, especially in America, are people deeply affected by liberalism—liberalism in the
broadest sense, in the sense that the *Wall Street Journal* editorial page, too, is liberal.
We really don't want to let go of that. In the Jewish community, because of the
history of oppression and because liberals were tied to the forces that opposed it,
there is an enormous and understandable reluctance to give it up.

So we're stuck with the quandaries that David Brooks described, with flexodoxy (a wonderful term), and I think that anyone who is religious is struggling to
balance this notion that what he or she believes is indeed the truth with a deep desire to preserve tolerance. That's not an easy thing to do. Dwight Eisenhower was
laughed at when he said that "our government makes no sense unless it is founded

on a deeply felt religious belief—and I don't care what it is." But in fact what we are hearing now from certain kinds of conservative or orthodox people is, "Everyone must belong to an orthodox, demanding religion that insists it has the truth, and I don't care what it is."

DAVID BROOKS: None of us here are going to the Christian Coalition meeting this year, apparently, because it's going on right now, but in past years it looked like Ratner's with the number of rabbis who were up on the platform. There seems to be a natural alliance of people who are orthodox in their religion, whatever that religion is. The Yale Five got tremendous support from Christian conservatives.

E. J. DIONNE: The religious situation in America was well described by a Jewish friend of mine who is principal of a Quaker school. He told a group of parents, "This is a place where Episcopalians teach Jewish kids to be Quakers." I think that what David said about Jews, that to some extent they model themselves after Protestants, is true of all Americans. When I was covering the Vatican, people there used to tell me this all the time, with great unease or displeasure.

JACK WERTHEIMER: The Protestant model has been dominant in many areas. Take education as an example. The Protestant model is that we all attend public schools to receive our general education, and we get our religious education separately in Sunday school. A hundred years ago, Jews totally bought the Protestant model. Jewish day schools are in fact a reflection of a greater openness on the part of Jews to the Catholic model of schools, where religion is an integral part of the curriculum.

JODY HASSETT: I want to go back to an earlier point about a sense of obligation. Last year, Abe Rosenthal was chastened by certain religious leaders about his series of *New York Times* editorials on the persecution of Catholics and Protestants that is going on in various countries today. While the Jewish community certainly has quite a track record when it comes to defending the oppressed, the poor, and ethnic minorities, where is the sense of obligation toward others oppressed in the name of religion?

JACK WERTHEIMER: I believe the Jewish community has a pretty strong track record on this, too. Both Abe Rosenthal and Michael Horowitz have been leading voices in the campaign against the persecution of Christian minorities. There are other examples. Officially, at least, the Jewish community mounts campaigns to raise sums for the victims of disasters, such as Muslims devastated by the earthquake in Turkey. I know of no serious disagreement within the Jewish community about this. You can say there are elements of self-interest at work: Jews want to show the world that they are not concerned only about their own, that they reach out, just as they want others to be of help in times of crisis for Jews. Still, there is a track record of considerable aid to victims of catastrophe, regardless of their religion.

KENNETH WOODWARD: Most of the Jewish people I run across in my line of work have almost no religious background and are in no way religious, though they're pretty predictable in terms of where they stand on things. When I look at Unitarians, I find they are half to three quarters Jewish. Ethical Culture is something like 98 percent Jewish. When Mata Amritanandamayi, the Hindu goddess, comes to town, the people who are organizing the event are all Jewish. We've already mentioned the Jew Bus. How many people are so far out of the faith that they're Jewish in name only? Where is the religiously committed Jewish population?

DAVID BROOKS: It hasn't been mentioned but it should be, that for every person like me there are four or five others who intermarry and just drift away from Judaism. Elliott Abrams has written a book on the danger this presents. It seems to me there really are two mindsets: that the czar is the greatest danger, and that the anticzar, the lack of any religious context, is the greatest danger.

JACK WERTHEIMER: A bipolar movement is occurring in the Jewish community. A sizable faction, perhaps the majority, is drifting away from Jewish life, while a large minority is intensifying its involvement with Jewish activities. The challenge lies in devising ways to enlarge that minority. Jews who are really not terribly interested in religion *per se* but who nonetheless still feel ethnic and communal ties have enormous difficulty transmitting that bond to the next generation.

MICHAEL BARONE: Just to put a few data in line: in the 1930s you have 4 percent of the American electorate Jewish, and 20 percent Catholic. The corresponding figures for today are more like 2 percent and 28 percent. I think we'll be looking at a different Jewish community twenty or thirty years from now—smaller numbers, a smaller percentage of the population, more tradition minded. There will be less what I called voting against the czar. I don't mean to use that as a demeaning phrase. The Irish voted against Sir Robert Peel for a hundred years. The South voted against General Sherman for a hundred years. Experiences that go deep to the heart and really change people's lives are passed down in families and continue to influence behavior for a long, long time.

What are American Jews going to be like in forty years? What should we look forward to?

JACK WERTHEIMER: The answer depends on where the respondent stands ideologically. In the Orthodox world today, the assumption is that the only Jewish group that will survive is the Orthodox; we can write off these other populations. More liberal Jews have convinced themselves that there's going to be such a wide diversity of Jewish expression forty years from now that we should be open to all options.

I daresay nobody around this table worries whether there will be Catholics in this country in forty years, or whether there will be evangelicals, or even mainline Protestants. Their continuance is taken for granted. Jews do worry about this; they are always convinced that they are on the verge of extinction. But whether this small minority will be able to muster the resources to perpetuate itself is not an idle question. Jewish communities in Europe were obviously decimated by the Holocaust, but there were still hundreds of thousands in them after World War II. Now those communities have drastically shrunk, largely through assimilation and intermarriage. There's reason to be concerned. When Jews contemplate a 52 percent rate of intermarriage for Jews who married between 1985 and 1990, they wonder, Will the offspring of these interfaith marriages be raised as Jews, and if not, what does that portend for the future of the American Jewish population?

DAVID SHRIBMAN: Jack opened his remarks with a thoroughly unremarkable comment about Jewish overrepresentation in certain professions and in certain areas of American civic life. But I wondered what the reaction would be if Patrick Buchanan made the same comment. Why is it no big deal when Jack says it but a very big deal when Buchanan says it?

JACK WERTHEIMER: Because Patrick Buchanan makes it sound as if there's a conspiracy. When I said it, I tried to offer an explanation, which has to do not with a conspiracy but with the unleashing of a group with a lot of pent-up energy.

DAVID BROOKS: When Buchanan says it, he means there is a monolithic or cohesive Jewish group in the media. When Jews say it, they know that . . . well, there were two Jewish guys on a desert island, and there were two synagogues. When the rescuers asked, "Why do you have two synagogues?" the answer was, "That one I wouldn't go to." Every group says things about itself that other people can't say.

KENNETH WOODWARD: Pat Buchanan also seems to suggest that Jews in public policy positions are sending other people's kids to war to get killed because they are more concerned about Israel than the United States. That kind of argumentation is really poisonous to society. The achievement of Jews—and particularly Eastern European Jews in this country—is an astonishment, unequaled in human history. Second-caste people from a third-rate society becoming, many of them, the top people in the top society. Astonishing.

Does God Belong on the Stump?   4
A Conversation with Stephen Carter,
Charles Krauthammer, and Leo Ribuffo

STEPHEN CARTER: "Does God belong on the stump?" is really an issue for God to decide, I suppose, and not for us here present. But that is part of the point I want to make. Those of you familiar with my work know that I am a great believer in an active role for explicitly religious voices in our public life. People are sometimes made uncomfortable by those voices, or are irritated by them, or are just unpersuaded by them. In principle that is no different from the reaction we may have to any of the other voices we hear in politics: they may irritate us or make us uncomfortable, or we may find them unpersuasive. Religious language by religious people in public life has long been an important part of the republic, and I hope it always will be. But when we get to the area of electoral politics, there are some differences and some problems. I want to talk about two aspects of this.

First, the aspect that is most on people's minds is so-called God talk by the candidates themselves. Some months ago Governor Bush said that the philosopher who had influenced him the most was Jesus Christ, and more recently, Senator Lieberman has made frequent references to his faith and its importance to him. Speaking to a black religious group in Detroit, he said that religion was an indispensable part of the morality of a people. A lot of people have been wondering, isn't it unusual to have so much talk about religion in the political arena? Yes, it is unusual—because it tends to happen only in election years.

In every election cycle we rediscover the fact that candidates talk about their religious faith. I remember in 1992 candidate Bill Clinton, Bible under his arm, speaking about his faith in one interview after another, not just to religious groups but for a lot of different audiences. I think he said much more about his faith than the candidates are doing today. In both the 1988 election and the 1980 election there was a lot of God talk. In 1976 candidate Jimmy Carter helped us to discover, on the national scene, the meaning of the term "born-again." You can go back as many elections as you like and find this pattern repeating itself.

But there are some problems with it. One is that for me as a voter, if a candidate wants to speak about his religion, that suggests to me that he wants me to think that religion is a relevant criterion, that I am learning something about him because I am learning something about his religion. The information I would like to be getting is, "This is an important part of me. It helps form who I am, and therefore, when I reason about the world and about important issues of public policy, my religious faith is a part of my reasoning process." I think that a candidate who is going to talk about his own faith owes us more than just saying, "Isn't it neat that I'm a religious guy?" That candidate owes us at least some discussion of how his faith affects his thinking about public issues, because only in that way can we judge its relevance. Now, one might object that to make candidates tell us how their faith affects their reasoning gets far too deeply into the personal, protected sphere of religion. If that is so, then they shouldn't talk about it in the first place. The candidate who says his religious faith matters ought to give us some idea of *how* it matters.

It seems to me that this year's candidates have not been saying much about how their religion actually affects decision making. It may seem an odd choice, but I remember, for example, that in 1968 Richard Nixon talked on more than one occasion about how his Quaker upbringing affected his views on a variety of issues: war and peace, civil rights, and so on. Now, in retrospect there may be reason for some skepticism about what he said, but my point is that, whether or not he was being forthright, at least as a candidate he was trying to articulate *why* he thought his faith was relevant. He wasn't just saying, "I want you to know that I'm a person of faith."

If religion is real, if it has bite, it changes who we are. Through our encounter with the historical and lived traditions and experiences of our faith we are different people than we would be without that encounter. And in making us different, faith opens a world of radical possibilities. I don't mean *radical* in the usual political sense; I simply mean that faith opens up the possibility of looking at things in ways that are sharply different from the cultural norm. This suggests that, unless the candidate is a member of an extraordinarily *convenient* religion, there will necessarily be times when, if elected, he or she will feel a tension between duty to faith and duty as a public official. I'm interested in how the candidate would try to resolve that tension. Some may say, "I can fully wall off the demands of my faith and conduct myself as a public official entirely apart from my religious values." This is one kind of claim that could be made. But I'm more interested in hearing the candidates try to speak frankly about where some problems might arise and how they would work through them.

In 1960, when John Kennedy gave his famous speech in Houston, he tried to diffuse the anti-Catholic issue. "On public matters," he said in an often-quoted line, "I do not speak for my church and my church does not speak for me." People sometimes forget what he said later in that speech, that if a conflict arose between his public duties and his private conscience and he could not satisfy both, he would resign the presidency. Now again, as with the story of Nixon, the issue is not whether we believe him or not; my point is that he felt it was important— if his religion was relevant—to deal with that issue, to talk to us about how he would resolve a conflict. My view is that "I would resign the presidency" is probably too quick and easy a way out. What I am interested in is where the tension arises. And again, if candidates would rather not go into that, then why do they talk about religion in the first place?

Let me suggest why they do so. This point will also help to explain why the Lieberman candidacy has been so spectacularly successful, why, far from raising a wave of anti-Semitism as some had feared, it has raised a wave of adulation among all sorts of people. I think that one reason why candidates try to impress us with their faith without relating it to any particular issues of policy or governance is that they sense—correctly—that we as voters are hungering for some sign of strength of character, of virtue, that is hard to articulate, and religion serves as a proxy for that. So candidates who want us to know how religious they are are really trying to convince us that they are moral, upright people, people who are tied to a sense of the good that is larger than the day-to-day strivings of life. That national longing may be reflected in the fact that for the last forty years every elected president has been either a Southern Democrat or a fairly conservative Republican. A lot of voters seem to sense that affiliations can teach us something about the character of the candidates.

Now, I said that I had two points to make about the use of religious language in electoral politics. The first had to do with candidates talking about their faith. But there is another kind of God-on-the-stump issue having to do with organizations and clergy that endorse candidates or work for candidates on the grounds that candidates A and B represent something closer to their religious vision than candidates C and D. That too is a very old tradition in American political life. In the nineteenth century, activism of this kind was fairly common. But I do think there are problems with it, problems that we should take seriously.

In a little essay published about fifty years ago, C. S. Lewis wrote in opposition to the establishment of a Christian party in England. The essay is entitled "A Meditation on the Third Commandment," and it nowhere quotes or identifies the Third Commandment because Lewis felt he was writing for a literate audience that would know what that commandment was. In this essay he opposes the establishment of a Christian party on a number of grounds. The one that most interests me at the moment is that he felt a Christian party would be an oxymoron. Why? Because if it were truly Christian, he said, it would preach the entire gospel—even the hard parts—and therefore get no votes. If it were truly a party wanting to win, it would craft a kind of modified gospel, emphasizing some parts, omitting or muting others, compromising the purity of the faith in order to prevail in the election, and then it would not be truly Christian. He thought this would be a very bad thing. I agree that it is a very bad thing, and it is what tends to happen. A kind of radical energy can lead, say, clergy into political involvement out of a genuine desire to accomplish a particular goal; but when religion touches politics, politics touches back. The energy gets dissipated and, for lack of a better word, co-opted. Think for instance of the radical energy of the black clergy of the fifties and sixties, in the early days of the civil-rights movement. A lot of the clergy who were leaders of the movement had a fairly radical vision for restructuring American society. That vision has largely vanished from the rhetoric of leading black clergy today, in part because of their incorporation into the Democratic Party as part of the power base.

Similarly, the radical energy of the white evangelical clergy from the eighties and early nineties—a different radical vision, to be sure—has largely vanished from the rhetoric of a lot of leaders. By 1995, when the Christian Coalition issued its "Contract With the American Family," this ten-point public platform of the Christian Coalition had barely a word of explicitly religious language in support of any of the ten points. A lot of critics at the time said, "Well, they're just hiding their true purposes; they're not telling you what they really think." For C. S. Lewis, that's the point. The fact that involvement in electoral politics suddenly makes you feel you have to hide the ball a little, or talk about something a little bit different, translate it into a different language—C. S. Lewis says that is a bad thing. The desire to win the election leads to a muting of certain messages and an emphasis on others, and in the end a secularization or co-optation of radical religious energy.

Some say that this kind of co-opting is one of the glories of democracy, that our political system has done a wonderful job of bringing into the mainstream all sorts of radical forces. Maybe that's true. But while it may be a glory of democracy, it's a problem for religion. The prophetic voice, the voice of the outsider, is lost when religious groups are involved in actual activism on behalf of candidates.

CHARLES KRAUTHAMMER: My assignment is to respond to Professor Carter, but there's very little that I would disagree with in his lucid and nuanced presentation. I think he made a strong point when he talked about how the prophetic vision of the churches that had been involved in the civil-rights struggle, and of the evangelicals who were involved in their own struggles in the late seventies and the eighties, has been leached away by being co-opted or assimilated into political parties.

The great danger of too close an association between religion and politics is not that it poses a threat to our politics or our political freedoms but that it poses a threat to religion. The temptations of corruption that accompany the acquisition of political power are the real problem. The classic example, which lasted for a millennium, was the corruption that occurred in the papacy when it exercised not just spiritual but also temporal power.

On the other hand, at a time when Senator Lieberman's candidacy and to a lesser extent some of the remarks of the Republicans have elicited complaints about too much God talk, I would like to make the case *for* this kind of speech, the invocation of religious ideas in politics. It is rather astonishing hypocrisy on the part of liberals to complain vociferously when George Bush invokes Jesus or when members of the Christian Coalition engage in politics. After all, the great and glorious victories of liberalism in this nation have been civil rights and the antiwar movement, and those struggles were heavily influenced and supported by the churches. You can almost say that some parts of the civil-rights revolution were operated out of the churches, and of course Martin Luther King always invoked spirituality and a vision of the transcendent in justifying his cause. For a more recent example, recall that when the Catholic bishops issued their letter on nuclear war in the early 1980s, we did not hear a lot of complaints from the left about the involvement of clergy in politics. But when the Catholic clergy speak out on abortion, we do hear loud complaints about the mixing of religion and politics.

What we have—and this seems so obvious that it is almost not worth noting— is a double standard. Why were people on the left so slow to criticize Senator Lieberman for doing in a major way what the Republicans have been doing in a more minor way? There was about a month of silent acquiescence to Lieberman's God talk before the Anti-Defamation League issued a statement and then others, sort of in embarrassment, joined the chorus—a muted chorus, I might say, hardly the full-throated attack one would have heard had the God talk come out of, say, Dick Cheney's mouth.

I think that people on the left would answer that Lieberman is different because he speaks for a minority in religion, so that the threat of imposition on others is not there. This of course contrasts with similar talk emanating from Christians. That is a psychological explanation for why many have been silent about Lieberman's God talk, but it's not a very logical one. I don't think that America, either in its history or in its spirit, is a nation of ayatollahs. For a hundred and fifty years, until the secularist revolution of the early sixties—when school prayer was disallowed and many other secular reforms took place, including the ACLU's stealing of the Christmas crèches from the town square—our republic existed with a heavy involvement of religion in public schools and public life. It was hardly a period where minority religions were in any way suppressed or forced into acquiescence with the majority. In fact, you could almost argue the contrary, that it was a time of flourishing for minority religions like Judaism, and that the secularized climate of the last forty years has seen an alarming decline in the adherence of Jews to their own religion.

About thirty years ago Robert Bellah wrote a brilliant article on America's civil religion. In this distinctive American faith, the God is the God of the Founders. He's Jefferson's Creator, who endows us with unalienable rights; he's Washington's Author, who guides the affairs of the nation; he's Lincoln's Lord, whose judgment even in civil war is just and righteous; and he is the inspiration for Martin Luther King, whom God took to a mountaintop to see the promised land. This is a particular kind of God, a nonsectarian God. There is a sense in America of Providence, a Creator who is involved in American history, who inspires the American experiment, and who does not pick and choose among eras. This inclusive, nonsectarian God enjoys a kind of legitimacy in American public life that the more narrowly construed sectarian God does not.

I remember a House debate on school prayer in the early eighties in which Representative Marjorie Holt said, "This is a Christian nation." It was a very late-night session, and Barney Frank, who had been asked to come in and preside, stood up and said, "If this is a Christian nation, why is it that a poor Jew has to get up at three in the morning to preside over the House of Representatives?" The God of the American civil religion enjoys widespread legitimacy. Every inaugural address—with the exception of the perfunctory two paragraphs that constituted Washington's second—has a reference to the Almighty, or God, or Providence, but only one makes a reference to Christ or Jesus or any other more denominational divinity, and that exception was the address of William Henry Harrison, who spoke of the Savior and Christ. (I would only note that he took sick soon after his inauguration, and thirty days later he was dead!)

Lieberman speaks of this God of the American civil religion in a way that I think appeals, as Professor Carter indicated, across denominational lines. I'm impressed by the support he gets from denominations that people had assumed would harbor some suspicion of a Jew in such high office. I think it's because he has spoken of religion in general as a guide, has spoken of God as this inclusive American Providence, that his religious stance has been accepted as legitimate.

In 1984 Justice Brennan was trying to explain why he thought crèches on public property should be disallowed but "In God We Trust" on coins as well as the statement at the opening of the Supreme Court, "God save the United States and this honorable court," should be permitted. His answer was that the latter things were merely "ceremonial deism," emptied of its meaning by repetition over the years. In other words, an empty religiosity was permissible in public life. That's how he squared his circle of being against the crèches and not against "In God We Trust" on the coins.

I think Justice Brennan was wrong. To say that this God of American civil religion is an empty idea is to say that King's invocations of the God who took him to the mountaintop, the God whose righteousness flows down mightily, is a trivial or empty notion. It's not. I think it's central to the American experience. Invoking it in politics not only is legitimate but ought to be defended because of what it gives and adds to American life.

LEO RIBUFFO: There's nothing the candidates have said this year that could not have been said by Eisenhower, FDR, or for that matter Washington—with one possible exception. I'm going to do what historians do: put this in probably deeper historical context than you want, by referring to the religious faith of various presidents, civil religion, and religion broadly speaking as a factor in American politics, broadly conceived. I see a good deal more conflict than Charles Krauthammer does.

Keep three things in mind at the outset. First, Americans have always had a propensity to put together their own versions of religion, no matter what the orthodoxy of the broad religious stew. Second, presidents are people, too. There were some who were seriously interested in theology (Jefferson, Adams, Carter), at least one with a great knowledge of the Bible but skeptical of orthodoxy (Lincoln), devout believers and practitioners (like most of the Republican presidents of the late nineteenth century), believers who nonetheless thought there were better ways to spend Sunday than in church (Truman, Reagan), and even a world-class womanizer who was a spiritual searcher (Lyndon Johnson). And keep in mind, third, that presidents are people who want to win elections and therefore don't want to offend religious groups in general.

The controversy over the religion of the Founders could be clarified if we could decide what we mean by the Founders. The American Revolution was won by an odd coalition. It was supported disproportionately by deist Enlightenment figures on the one hand and early evangelicals, the heirs to the First Great Awakening, on the other. It seems to me that the Constitution reflects a compromise between those groups. Lieberman said that the First Amendment was not intended to protect people from religion. Well, it might depend on which of the Founders you asked. Some surely would have believed that it *was* intended to do that. This is the exception I referred to earlier.

Of the deist-influenced Founders, Washington was among the most conventionally religious and started our tradition of civil religion, adding to the presidential oath, for example, "So help me God." The least conventional was Thomas Jefferson, who said that he was a true Christian, by which he meant a follower of the ideals of Christ stripped of the mythology. Jefferson was a founder of the Democratic Party, which from the outset was more religiously diverse and more secular than its Federalist, Whig, or Republican foes.

When Jefferson became president, a Second Great Awakening was in progress, which by the 1830s or 1840s made the United States a predominantly evangelical Protestant country. But deist ideas still floated around, affecting among others Abraham Lincoln, who was accused by the evangelical preacher running against him for Congress in 1846 of being an infidel. Lincoln answered in a Lincolnesque way: he never denied the truth of the Scriptures (though he never affirmed it either), and he always showed respect for what he called "religion in general." Of course, he became the great theologian of the United States, being tested during the Civil War. I would say that, though there's a linkage between God and the United States from the outset, many of the earlier figures doubted that God was unambiguously blessing America. But as we move toward the present, that kind of skepticism diminishes.

Lincoln's party tended to be less reflective about religion than Lincoln himself. From the beginning the Republicans were the preeminent party of white Protestantism. They were also the preeminent party, in the mid- to late nineteenth century, of anti–Roman Catholic nativism. But of course they sought votes, and so there were interesting mixes. In 1896 William McKinley, a much underrated man, ran against the Democrat Populist William Jennings Bryan—the most devout pair of nominees ever! McKinley was supported by a powerful nativist movement, which he courted. Then he made a Catholic his attorney general and for the first time invited a Catholic to appear at the inauguration. When McKinley died in 1901, it was a Victorian Christian death. To the doctors he said, "It is useless, gentlemen. Let us have prayer."

McKinley was the last unambiguously evangelical Protestant president until Carter. Religion had been changing in the late nineteenth century, with Protestants splitting between theological liberals and theological conservatives. A minority of the theological liberals promoted the social gospel, explicated by such significant theologians as Walter Rauschenbusch. And it is indirectly from the social-gospel movement that Gore gets his sense that he tries to live every day asking, "What would Jesus do?"

The so-called Progressive era before World War I is sometimes characterized as our Fourth Great Awakening, though its three presidents would not by current standards be considered evangelicals. Theodore Roosevelt apparently doubted the divinity of Jesus. William Howard Taft certainly did, as a proud Unitarian, and that was a minor issue *sub rosa* in the election of 1908, though to his credit Bryan did not try to use it against Taft.

Wilson is one of the most misunderstood religious figures. A theological liberal uninterested in doctrinal issues, he was essentially a social gospeler and used that in his election campaign. In 1911 he gave an address called "The Bible and Progress," presenting the Bible as the "people's book of revelation" to spur reform, and roughly a million copies of this address were distributed when he ran for president in 1912. Though he didn't mull over theological issues, there is no question that he saw God directly guiding the United States and guiding Wilson himself. But instead of an era of Wilsonian progress, the twenties were a time when two to five million Protestants joined the Ku Klux Klan, most as casually as they would join the Elks. Perhaps one of those members was President Harding.

By the standards of the day, in 1928 Hoover did not behave badly in his campaign against the Catholic candidate Al Smith. As a Quaker, he was religiously tolerant "by blood and conviction." Yet there is no question that the Republican Party used religious bigotry against Smith. Both conservative and liberal Protestants opposed him, and it was not always simple bigotry, though sometimes it was. On the other hand, the Democrats tried to win votes by presenting their party with its Catholic candidate as the party of tolerance.

Franklin Roosevelt can be seen as the founding father of the modern version of religious pluralism—tolerant civil religion. With the exception of Newt Gingrich, everyone in public life seems to have forgotten how much Franklin Roosevelt talked about religion—religion as tolerance, religion as belief. He advocated, before the term became popular, respect for the "Judeo-Christian tradition." And religion is truly all over the place in Roosevelt—as much as in Eisenhower and Reagan. Except for occasional references to godless communism, we get much less of that under Truman. He said that he left religion to Mrs. Truman. This is not simply so. He also claimed to have read the Bible twice by the age of twelve, and he continued to read it regularly all his life. Every day he said a prayer he had composed in his youth, asking God to help him be a good person. He was a Baptist who took very seriously the separation of church and state.

World War II began what we have come to call the Fifth Great Awakening. Claims of church and synagogue membership rose from about 40 percent in 1940 to roughly 70 percent by 1960, and the fitting symbol of this was Dwight D. Eisenhower. Although he looked back in misery to what he called the "goddamn" West Point chapel service, Eisenhower believed that as president he needed to set an example. He composed his own prayer for the inauguration. After the inauguration (he refused to do it beforehand), he was baptized in the Presbyterian Church. He liked to begin cabinet meetings with a prayer, but occasionally he forgot, so after a few minutes he might blurt out, "Goddammit, we forgot the prayer!" Nothing in this should be condemned as hypocrisy—he was trying to advocate religiosity as a way of calming the country. It was under Eisenhower that "In God We Trust" became our national motto and "under God" was added to the Pledge of Allegiance. And Eisenhower is also known for something he said about religion in 1952: "Our form of government makes no sense unless it is founded on a deeply felt religious belief—and I don't care what it is!" Everybody always laughs at that quotation, but a higher-brow version of it was advocated by Will Herberg's *Protestant, Catholic, Jew*—those were equally valid ways of being an American. Eisenhower intuited that if we take religion too seriously, we are going to fight about it, and he didn't want religious fights.

Those criticizing this broad civil religion included the great Jesuit John Courtney Murray, who grumbled that the fifties were a time of "religion in general, whatever that means." They were also a time of considerably more religious conflict than is usually remembered. While many—perhaps most—fundamentalists softened into Billy Graham–type evangelicals and anti-Semitism steadily declined, conflicts between Protestants and Catholics rose—fights over McCarthyism, over school aid, over the fact that Catholics thought their patriotism undervalued by Protestants.

This was the context in which Kennedy ran for president in 1960. It is commonly said that religion was an *issue* in 1960; I think it is more accurate to say that it was a *factor*. After Kennedy skillfully deflected the question, it was not discussed in the way of the so-called missile-gap crisis or Castro. The Kennedyites weren't stupid. Like Al Smith, but more successfully, they presented their party as the party of tolerance. Nixon grumbled that this put him in a "predicament." But whether out of residual Quaker decency or out of political prudence, Nixon did nothing to encourage bigots, nor did he seek a public endorsement by Billy Graham, who by then was well on his way to becoming the national pastor. The standard interpretation is that Kennedy's religion cost him a million and half votes.

The "Judeo-Christian" civil religion of the fifties and the assassination of the first Catholic president permanently changed the boundaries of religious debate in the public square. No longer could anyone run for national office and say, "My religion is better than yours." They were all equal in the political marketplace.

Religion was relatively muted in the 1964 campaign between the half-Jewish Episcopalian Barry Goldwater and the womanizing religious seeker Lyndon Johnson. Johnson was a religious eclectic, baptized in the Disciples of Christ denomination but a lover of liturgy and ritual who often attended Episcopal or Catholic services. Some nativists feared that he might convert to Catholicism as his daughter Luci did.

It was Richard Nixon, not Carter or Reagan, who brought an overtly partisan religiosity back to the White House. He was a Quaker, raised with substantial doses of evangelicalism, and by the time he was an adult he had put together his own religious mix of Norman Vincent Peale's positive thinking plus Billy Graham's evangelicalism. It might seem incongruous, but it was no more so than most Americans' versions of Protestantism. Nixon accepted Graham's open endorsement in 1972, held religious services in the White House, and used religious connections to underscore support for what he liked to call "square America."

After Nixon's fall, it's not surprising that in 1976 the United States had the most devout pair of presidential candidates since McKinley and Bryan in 1896: Carter and Ford. Recently journalists have said that religion hasn't been discussed so much in politics since 1960. It's not surprising that journalists would want to forget their coverage of the campaign of 1976; at a time when religion-related issues were more central to politics than at any other time since Prohibition, journalistic coverage was stupid, stupid, stupid, and woefully ignorant. Carter was shrewd: he understood that the evangelicals were a growing constituency; he understood that he could appear as a cultural conservative as against a man married to the scarlet woman Betty Ford; he understood that evangelicalism gave him an affinity with many evangelical blacks. On the other hand, he had to balance these considerations with his position as standard-bearer of the more cosmopolitan and tolerant party.

Carter was a sophisticated lay theologian, a born-again Baptist, mostly liberal in his theology, and seriously influenced by neoorthodox theologian Reinhold Niebuhr, who warned that individuals and nations should beware of the sin of pride. Yet he was presented over and over as a holy roller from Hicksville. And that partly explains why he appeared in *Playboy*. The official explanation was that he was trying to explain the sin of pride to the ungodly. In fact, he was trying to show a cosmopolitan audience that he was not just a hick. There was an uproar of unimaginable proportions. The wisest response in my view came from Martin Luther King, Sr.: to Carter's remark that he had lusted in his heart, King replied, "They can't kill you for looking." Carter's famous "malaise" speech is, in fact, an interesting Niebuhrian attempt to call Americans back from their pride and their greed. All it did was reinforce what Hamilton Jordan called the "weirdo factor."

The New Christian Right mobilized against Carter, but much to his credit he would not exploit his evangelicalism, and in 1980 he made religious references much less frequently than in 1976. He was clearly disgusted by what he considered a theological politicization of politics. Unlike Carter, Ronald Reagan had no doubt that God blessed America, no matter how much he tested us. And Reagan had no doubt that evangelicals should be courted. His alliance with the Christian Right should not obscure the fact that he very much fitted the general American religious temper of the 1980s. He was a fairly standard religious eclectic: Catholic father, Protestant mother, raised in the Disciples of Christ, over the years interested in Billy Graham, Bible prophecy, Baha'i, astrology, and the Shroud of Turin.

To put it another way, he was the New Age equivalent of Dwight D. Eisenhower. Keep in mind: *presidents are people, too!* And if they seem bizarre, they often reflect the bizarreness of their country.

By the time Reagan left office, "religion in general, whatever that means" had a high public cachet. It was fashionable as opposed to weirdo to proclaim oneself a born-again Christian, as more than 40 percent of the population in the polls said they were. Among them was George Bush. A little noticed factor of the 1988 campaign, when Bush ran against Dukakis (the most secular candidate at least since Stevenson), is that a religious issue was raised, but not by Bush. Some bigots pointed out that Dukakis was not in good standing because he had not married in the Greek Orthodox church and had in fact married a Jew. But the issue had no legs—a good sign.

In the years since the Dukakis defeat, the Democrats have tried to recapture the support of "people of faith," and Gore's choice of Lieberman is clearly part of this effort. The whole enterprise, it seems to me, is tricky both politically and ethically. As was the case with Al Smith and Kennedy, clearly the Democrats are trying to take advantage of Lieberman's religiosity and ethnicity without making the substance of his religion an issue, and they are also trying to present theirs as the more tolerant party. As Nixon might have put it, this puts the Republicans in a predicament.

How should those of us with no vested interests in the outcome of the campaign look at this? So far, there's little sign that Lieberman's religion will be either an issue or a factor. But I hope the press will stop discussing it! Okay, we know he's the first Jewish candidate; we know where Jews stand on civil religion; we know he can go to war on Saturday—fine! Stop it there! Too much discussion of Lieberman's religion, I think, may make religion as an issue a self-fulfilling prophecy. In other words, let me end with my ambivalence. As a historian I would love to know more about the religion of the candidates. I would love to ask George W. Bush, who described Jesus as his favorite philosopher, whether he meant that in the sense of Rauschenbusch or Niebuhr. But as a citizen, I think I'll wait for his memoirs.

Discussion

CHARLES KRAUTHAMMER: In London there's a troupe that does all of Shakespeare's plays in an hour and half. I must say, they might envy Professor Ribuffo's tour of American history in twenty minutes. At one point I disagree. This notion of "religion in general" is easy to ridicule, particularly when presented in the context of Eisenhower's famous alleged remark. I would argue that the Founders *do* make the point that sectarianism is impermissible in a pluralistic society. They would surely be against the sectarianism of some of those who promote religion in public life. On the other hand, I think it's hard to make the case that they were anything but in favor of "religion in general" as opposed to irreligion.

Interestingly, what triggered the complaints about Lieberman's religiosity was his statement about morality being grounded in religion. That is not something he made up. It's an allusion to the farewell address of Washington, in which he said, "Reason and experience both forbid us to expect that national morality can prevail in exclusion of religious principle." So the statement was not a recent invention during a God-talking moment of a candidate; it is rooted in American history. The last point I would make is that I'm always intrigued when I hear Gore say he asks himself what Jesus would do, because I wonder how you would say in Aramaic, "Open the strategic petroleum reserves!"

STEPHEN CARTER: Regrettably, I don't have any anecdotes as good as the ones my fellow panelists used! I agree with virtually all of what both Charles and Leo said, but with some minor differences. First, I don't want the press to stop talking about the religion of the candidates unless the *candidates* stop talking about the religion of the candidates. The point that "politicians are people too" is one with which I strongly agree. But politicians are very carefully scripted people; they make their living in part by deciding day to day which parts of themselves to open to our scrutiny. Candidates who believe that it's important for us to understand aspects of their faith are inviting scrutiny. When, for example, Reagan at least seemed to flirt with the elevation of creationism over evolution, that was a perfectly legitimate subject for inquiry by the press because Reagan himself had opened it up by his comments—musing, offhand, unscripted comments, to be sure, but nonetheless comments he himself had made publicly.

I also want to say something about the civil religion because it relates to the Washington statement about morality and religion that Charles just quoted. John Adams said things like that, and other people made similar comments in that era also. I think that the religion-in-general point actually is relevant to this question of the link between religion and morality. There's something a little bit Burkean about it. Edmund Burke's view of religion as a stabilizing, civilizing force didn't ever assume that everybody had to *share* in the religion, or that the people who shared in it were better than the others. It was just that when you looked at a great mass of people and asked what it took for that great mass— or for a single person—to be good, Burke's answer was that we've never found anything better than religion. Now, when he said religion he was really speaking of the Anglican Church, but he didn't seem to say much about how particular religious *doctrine* made people good. It was simply the connection, the belief in something greater that transcended human striving, that made people good. It wasn't an argument—and I don't think Washington meant, or Adams meant, or Lieberman meant—that you can't be good without a connection to religion. The point is simply: at the margin, when you look at the next person to come along, which way is it safe to bet?

ADAM WOLFSON: Stephen Carter mentioned that religion was acting as a proxy for character in the current campaign. I had a more cynical thought: when religion acts as a proxy for character, it enables the candidate to wink and nod in a certain direction and suggest things without actually saying them. In the case of Lieberman, the religious display is a way of saying, "We are not the party of Clinton anymore." And in the case of George W., what he says about his faith lets him nod in the direction of the Religious Right without actually addressing the issues they care about. This is how the candidates stay in the middle.

On the issue of civil religion: Charles Krauthammer made a point about what God we want in the public square. I think he said that in the case of Lieberman, it was a nonsectarian God. My question is, to what extent does a vibrant civil religion with its nonsectarian God depend on sectarian beliefs? Can you have a nonsectarian God without a vibrant sectarian religion? Do the religious allusions in the speeches of Lincoln and Martin Luther King mean anything to a public that has been secularized over the last thirty or forty years?

CHARLES KRAUTHAMMER: To take your second part first: that's a very interesting question. I think the answer is that yes, the civil religion requires a public that has its own sectarian God. The people can then have this sort of coterminous belief in the civil religion, which would be strengthened by the fact that they begin by believing in a God of a certain kind. The counterexample, perhaps the way to suggest a proof historically, is the French Revolution. The civil religion of Rousseau was not rooted in sectarian religion; it was radically rationalist, extremely anticlerical, and extremely antisectarian, and it didn't survive. Rousseau is the one who invented the idea of civil religion, and it failed utterly, because it didn't have an underpinning of more traditional, more historical, more rooted religion. A more complicated belief system is required to have a civil religion than to have a religion in which you learn catechism or songs in the cradle.

On your first point, about religion as proxy for character: I think the God talk is legitimate; there aren't grounds for attacking it as a violation of American principles. But personally I'm suspicious of it, in the same way that I'm suspicious of any other kind of talk by candidates about their private lives, their families, their tragedies and histories. I think it's almost always done cynically, and it does not reflect on the real character of the candidates. There are exceptions, of course, but in general I would see a candidate's deployment of religion in the same way that I see a candidate's deployment of other privacies: as generally cynical and not very informative. In principle, however, I would never criticize a candidate for speaking about religion.

STEPHEN CARTER: First, on civil religion: I agree that it rests on the underlying presence of a lot of religious traditions, or at least a lot of different denominations. And I think it is very important, for the following reason. A lot of contemporary political philosophy aims very explicitly at trying to craft the common language with which we can conduct debate in the public square. It strikes me that civil religion has served one part of that function by trying to bring together strands of a variety of different traditions, to track their commonalities into something that is recognizably and substantively religious. However, in an era where there are forces aggressively seeking a more secular society, I'm not sure civil religion can serve that function anymore. It begins to look peculiar.

This leads me to the proxy point. Some of the religious appeals by candidates, some of the rote language, like ending speeches with "God bless all of you and God bless the United States of America," is an attempt to appeal to civil religious sentiment, but it's falling into a different era. Today a lot of the energy of those various religions is dissipated. In surveys, very high numbers of people will strongly identify themselves as religious. But by any measure of religious participation or of religion's affecting people's daily lives, the numbers fall off quite dramatically. My friend Robert Wuthnow at Princeton is fond of saying that the Norman Rockwell image of two white parents sitting with their children in church on a regular basis applies to only 7 percent of the American populace today. It's not an era of great religious participation, so appeals that might in an earlier era have been thought of as part of the civil religion now seem more cynical. A lot of us doubt whether it matters as much whether candidates say that stuff or not. And that's where my proxy suggestion comes from.

But even if your more cynical interpretation is right, if the God talk is a way of saying "I'm with you" to some conservative Christians, or of saying "I'm not like Clinton," that still seems to be a perfectly legitimate function for rhetoric of this kind.

LEO RIBUFFO: Civil religion, it seems to me, comes in different versions, ranging from a general religiosity to "God is unambiguously on our side," with those like Carter and Niebuhr in the middle saying, "Well, maybe, maybe not." I think the different versions of civil religion have different consequences. As to whether the candidates should be asked about their faith and whether they are using it as a surrogate for high character: sure. Nonetheless, I think they should be asked about religion-related issues, such as abortion and the Hollywood-and-violence thing, without being pressed to go back to the specific theological base of their views. I realize I sound a little bit like Seymour Martin Lipset in 1955, saying that some issues are too hot for the public square, but I think that trying to explain theology is not going to work. I would love to see a nice conversation on TV with the candidates discussing their religion, as Bill Moyers did with Carter, but I don't think that's what we would get. I think we'd get the religious version of Bernard Shaw to Michael Dukakis: "Your wife has been raped! What are you going to do?"

MING HSU: I have a two-part question regarding what Professor Carter said about the prophetic voice that's needed and potentially lost in an elected position. First, it seems like a fascinating paradox: the prophetic voice by definition is going to be unpopular—serving, as in the Old Testament, as a corrective to the rule of kings—but it is necessarily associated with an elected position that draws on a majority in a democracy. How can those two functions be embodied in one person—in this case, the president? Second, if there are multiple prophetic voices, then what do you do? For example, if elected officials such as senators and representatives come from different faith backgrounds—especially when it's not just Judeo-Christian faith but Buddhist, Hindu, and other faiths that aren't monotheistic—how do you reconcile those potentially conflicting prophetic voices?

STEPHEN CARTER: Let me make it very clear that I don't expect a prophetic voice from political leaders. I think it would be unreasonable to expect that. The prophetic voice I have in mind is very much the voice of the outsider, one who stands apart from electoral politics. What's striking about the prophets of Israel, with minor exceptions, is precisely this standing outside the corridors of power to try to correct what the ruler is doing. So I think the prophetic voice can come not only from the obvious sources, such as Martin Luther King, but also from people who, without any effort to turn this to partisan advantage, either for themselves (I want to win the election) or for a party (this is God's party over here), simply want to call the nation to a better way. That's the prophetic voice that I think should be an honored and important part of our national life.

Now, the prophetic voice may be unpersuasive. And there are always multiple voices, since even these faith traditions themselves are not by and large univocal. That's fine. It means that most of the prophetic voices will not prevail. But prevailing and surviving are two different things. The prophet will usually not win, not in the short run, and that's fine. Prophets by and large are not people with short-run horizons. In the long run, one of the reasons why I cherish the separation of church and state is as a tool to preserve religious liberty by preventing that great, enormous force of the state from interfering with the development of religious voices, religious truth, and religious communities where the prophets are nurtured. The more religious communities attempt to look a lot like everything else in the culture, the less prophetic they will be able to be. So the prophet is not one who seeks power, whether for himself or for someone he may anoint, but rather is the one who simply tries to persuade people to change. Multiple prophetic voices? Great. The more the merrier. Sometimes they'll be ignored, and occasionally they'll prevail, and it seems to me that that's exactly the way it ought to be.

TERRY MATTINGLY: *New York Times* columnist Maureen Dowd made the comment that the whole Clinton era has essentially been a fight between people who are pro-Woodstock and those who are anti-Woodstock. I would argue that the third great triumph of liberalism, after civil rights and the opposition to Vietnam, is the sexual revolution. I wonder whether you all think Lieberman simply got a pass on a lot of this because his God is not interested in judging the sexual revolution or the hottest issues involved therein, such as abortion and homosexuality. He's basically with the lifestyle left on those most divisive, pro-Woodstock issues. So what's threatening about his God?

CHARLES KRAUTHAMMER: I think this fits the pattern of giving a pass to the left. And on the issue of separation of church and state, the left gave a pass to the civil-rights movement, to the antiwar movement, and as I mentioned to the Catholic bishops in their opposition to the Reagan nuclear policy. So it applies across the board; I don't think it's specific to issues of personal morality. But I do think that in Lieberman's case it explains part of the pass. The other part of it, and the reason why many people who are *not* lifestyle liberals—such as evangelicals—have admired him even though he is, as you say, soft on those issues, is that he speaks to a kind of religiosity/piety that is nonsectarian but elevated, and is generally missing in public life. Lieberman promotes it unabashedly and with pride, and I think that appeals across the spectrum.

STEPHEN CARTER: I agree with most of that but would add another small point. In the same way that religions and religious institutions can have political parties and partisan fights, so can ideologies. And so, to the extent that there is a genuine, principled view that says certain kinds of religious conversations do not belong in the corridors of politics, that principled view has become the captive of the Democratic Party and its interests. Therefore, that principled view tends to be asserted only if the *Republican* Party and its interests are being furthered. One of the reasons I really admire the ADL's Abraham Foxman is that he has been consistent on this issue without regard to whose oxes are gored. Not everyone is consistent in that way.

MICHAEL CROMARTIE: It did take a while, though, for the ADL to express concern about Senator Lieberman's use of religion in the campaign.

STEPHEN CARTER: Well, it did, it did. And I understand the kind of struggles they had over that issue. Anyway, I do think that part of the pass has to do with the simple point that the candidate in question is a Democrat and not a Republican. Again, I'm a registered Independent, so I have no horse in this race, but I do think that this is a simple line along which a lot of people divide. Law professors at the leading law schools tend to go overwhelmingly Democratic, overwhelmingly liberal. Most of them are giving Lieberman a pass because—and this is exactly what they say—they don't want to do anything to hurt Gore's candidacy. They'll say that quite explicitly.

LEO RIBUFFO: I think the main reason Lieberman is getting a pass is that no one wants to appear bigoted. I think in addition that he represents moderation, which is the flavor of the month. But I wouldn't give him a pass. I wonder who gave him the title "Conscience of the Senate." It seems to me that if you believe in anything like political principles, the Senate has two consciences: Teddy Kennedy and Jesse Helms. A word about the Clintons: theological conservatives do not consider them religious, but they are. They are theological liberals with some twists. And Hillary believes in the literal return of Jesus.

MARK O'KEEFE: Both Bush and Gore advocate more government collaboration with faith-based organizations. Are any of you concerned that the state could corrupt the independence, creativity, and integrity of churches?

STEPHEN CARTER: Yes. I don't think that the various charitable-choice initiatives as they are called raise any constitutional questions, nor do I think that school vouchers, applied to religious schools, raise any constitutional questions. But religious groups that are eager to get their hands on this money should think long and hard before becoming, in effect, another set of interest groups feeding at the public trough. Quite apart from the problem of what that says about the nature of religion and where it places its reliance, consider a scenario like this: members of an inner-city church want to start a church-related school and really do something about their neighborhood. So they take public money and build a school, and it flourishes. A lot of neighborhood kids attend. It becomes a big part of the church's ministry. Then a new administration takes over in Washington, and suddenly the money comes with regulations, some of which are inconsistent with what they preach. Well, they can't afford to run the church's school without the money. Are they going to close it down? The time to think about that is *before* rushing to take the money in the first place.

CHARLES KRAUTHAMMER: I agree completely. The real danger with taking down the wall is less to political liberty than to the faith-based organizations themselves. I think they can easily become dependent and then easily sacrifice their beliefs in order to stay alive. The only thing I would add is that I sort of marvel at the invention of the term "faith-based organizations." I think they used to be called "churches"! It's a triumph of language equal to the substitution of the word "investment" for "government spending."

RICHARD CIZIK: I agree that the Religious Right's identification with the Republican Party was part and parcel of its diminished influence. It probably stepped over some other lines by appearing to endorse candidates. Yet my concern about this election, with all the talk about religion, is that what is being said is not really helping people make the judgments they need to make. Amid all the conversation about Senator Lieberman's religion, for example, it seems to me that Al Gore is getting away without truth telling on White House scandals. No one seems willing to call him to account. Nor is anyone interested either in Bush's and Gore's differing views on implementing "charitable choice." What evangelicals want from the candidates, more than we want Jesus to be their political philosopher or for them to ask "What would Jesus do?," is to have them speak essential truth.

My question to you who write publicly about this issue—I was at a White House meeting the other day in which the President invoked your name, Professor Carter—is this: If such fundamental questions that ought to be asked at this election time (i.e., how a candidate integrates faith with policy making) are ignored or go unanswered, what does that say about the real influence of religion on our country and its politics?

CHARLES KRAUTHAMMER: I think the historians will agree that the effect of Lieberman's candidacy and the buzz about religion he has created has been to deflect from the Democratic nominee the issues hanging over him from the current administration, his own actions with fund-raising, and the taint of the Clinton era. I think that was undoubtedly part of Gore's calculation in choosing him. But I would say in defense of Lieberman that he is saying things today about his religion that he said yesterday and the day before. It is not for him an invention or a tactic. It has tactical effect, but I think he speaks with conviction and principle now in just the same way he has spoken in the past.

TIM SHAH: I'm not sure the distinction between civil religion and sectarianism is very neat, especially in a society where the gatekeepers of ideas are not friendly to the idea of allowing any sort of religious meaning to enter the public sphere. It seems to me that the civil religion of the Founders that Charles Krauthammer eloquently described is quite a substantive set of ideas. It includes not just an image of God benevolently presiding over the affairs of the United States, but also the idea that there is a direct connection between our natural rights and God, that those rights do not exist unless we understand them as coming from a transcendent, divine source. Even Kennedy in his 1960 inaugural address gave assent to that. If we lose that connection, our health as a society will suffer. Now it seems to me that someone who tried to make that point today in the public sphere would certainly be called sectarian. Precisely insofar as one tried to invoke the traditional American civil religion, one would be considered sectarian.

CHARLES KRAUTHAMMER: In fact, that's what Lieberman did; he was quoting from Washington's farewell address, where he made precisely that point, rooting morality literally in religion. But Lieberman was not attacked as sectarian; he was attacked as someone who was promoting religion against irreligion. That attack is less supportable than an attack on an openly sectarian comment would be.

LEO RIBUFFO: I don't see the animosity to civil religion in the broad sense that others do. My own preference would be, not from politicians but from others, *more* religious contentiousness, more fighting over religious basics. In that sense, I think it's just horrendous that Bob Jones III is written off as a bigot. He is someone who seriously believes Catholicism is wrong, and he is trying to bring Catholics to what he considers the true faith—which would have been the position of just about every Christian between Saint Paul and the theological liberals of the thirties. I don't want to say that I'm opposing God talk or journalists' writing about God talk. I just don't think people running for office are the best people to talk about religion.

STEPHEN CARTER: I think that in the end we won't find the answers we seek simply by analyzing what the Founders and the Framers thought about the appropriate role of religion or the extent to which our institutions rest on it. We can certainly learn from the wisdom of the past and from the errors of our noninfallible Founders, but I don't think it is by understanding *their* view of the relationship of religion and free institutions that we will come to the right answer. What strikes me as important today is to figure out what *we* think about it, to make arguments on either side resonant in *our* terms. That's not something I would do as a constitutional scholar; that's for me as a citizen to do.

How the Faithful Voted
A Conversation with John C. Green and John DiIulio

JOHN C. GREEN: The results I will report are from the third of three surveys we have done funded by the Pew Charitable Trusts in 1992, 1996, and 2000. Their purpose is to measure the influence of religion on voting behavior more precisely than surveys typically do. Since we've done these surveys the same way three times, we can compare the behavior of religious groups over time with some confidence. In the spring of the election year, we take a large sample—this time it was a random sample of 4,004 adult Americans—and ask them a large number of religious questions. Then we go back after the election to ask these people how they voted. The postelection surveys tend to be fairly brief. Although we try to contact all the people we interviewed in the spring, we are able to resurvey a little more than one half of them. In this case, we contacted 2,363. Our report covers the two-party vote only.

In table 5.1, we divide adult Americans into fourteen religious groups. The first two are white evangelical Protestants and white mainline Protestants, with the classifications "evangelical" and "mainline" based on denominational affiliation. We have found that denominational affiliation is very important to voting behavior. While it may not be the best way to define these groups in religious terms, in social and political terms, denominational affiliation is very important. Each of these large categories is broken into two parts, more observant and less observant based on church attendance. The more observant are those who claim to attend worship once a week or more often. This definition puts some people who attend fairly frequently in the "less observant" category, along with some who by their own admission rarely or never attend. We separate out black Protestants; we believe that the black Protestant churches represent a separate religious tradition. And politically, as we'll see, black Protestants are very different from white Protestants. We also separate out Hispanic Protestants and Hispanic Catholics; although these groups are not really separate religious traditions, they differ politically from their non-Hispanic coreligionists. Roman Catholics are also divided into more observant and less observant. Then there are some smaller groups: we broke out Mormons, "other Christians," Jews, and "other non-Christians." Finally, there is a large category we call "secular" voters. These persons lack a religious affiliation but may have religious or spiritual values.

We measure religious affiliation as precisely as we can, and try hard to reduce what are called "social desirability" effects. Many people think it's good to be a member of a religious group and may claim an affiliation even if they don't really have one. Church attendance tends to be similarly overreported. The result of our method of measuring religious affiliation is that we typically come up with fewer mainline Protestants and fewer Roman Catholics than other surveys. For a fair number of people in those traditions, the affiliation is purely nominal. Under our measures, these people end up in the "secular" category. This approach produces better relationships between religion and politics. Of course, surveys are statistical artifacts. These are best thought of as *estimates* of how these various groups behave. They are not written in stone.

Table 5.1. How Religious Groups Voted in 2000

	Bush	Gore	
White Evangelical Protestants			
More Observant	84%	16%	=100%
Less Observant	55	45	=100
White Mainline Protestants			
More Observant	66	34	=100
Less Observant	57	43	=100
Black Protestants	4	96	=100
Hispanic Protestants	33	67	=100
Roman Catholics			
More Observant	57	43	=100
Less Observant	41	59	=100
Hispanic Catholics	24	76	=100
Mormons	83	12	=100
Other Christians	28	72	=100
Jews	23	77	=100
Other Non-Christians	20	80	=100
Seculars	35	65	=100
ALL VOTERS	49.8%	50.2%	=100%

* Two-party presidential vote: minor-party votes excluded.
Source: The Third National Survey of Religion and Politics, conducted by the University of Akron Survey Research Center in Spring and Fall 2000 (Total Weighted N=2,363).

Our numbers have an additional problem. We broke out some very small groups, such as Mormons and Jews, just because we thought they were interesting. But these small groups may include only a few dozen people, so one needs to view such figures with caution. Some of these smaller groups show such distinctive voting patterns that we suspect we would get very similar results if we surveyed hundreds of their members.

Table 5.1 shows that 84 percent of observant white evangelical Protestants voted for Bush. This is a striking increase from our 1996 survey, when this group voted 70 percent for Bob Dole. Less observant white evangelical Protestants did not vote as strongly Republican, just 55 percent. But in our 1996 survey, Bill Clinton and Bob Dole broke even in this group, and some other people's surveys showed Clinton winning this group. So less observant white evangelicals returned somewhat to the Republican fold. There are similar patterns among white mainline Protestants: 66 percent for Bush, up from 58 percent for Dole in 1996.

With Roman Catholics, a pattern continues that had been developing all through the 1990s: more observant Roman Catholics voted more Republican, less observant more Democratic. The Catholic community is indeed divided in political terms.

In contrast to their white counterparts, black Protestants voted overwhelmingly for Gore: 96 percent. Of course, African Americans generally vote Democratic, but the black Protestant church is the strongest Democratic component of the African American community. Hispanics voted for Gore as well, particularly Hispanic Catholics, at 76 percent. Hispanic Protestants were a little more divided but still gave Gore 67 percent of their votes. With blacks and Hispanics, there was not much of a percentage change from 1996, but turnout increased.

We broke out the Mormons because they're so solidly Republican. In most surveys, they turn out to be the most Republican of all religious groups, more so than observant white evangelicals. Some other smaller groupings are broken out in the survey also, and they all voted Democratic. Finally, there is the "secular" bloc, which voted—as in 1996—about two-thirds Democratic.

Table 5.2 is more interesting from a political point of view. Here we show each of these religious groupings as a percentage of the Bush vote and the Gore vote. This gives us a sense of the relative weight of these groups in the presidential coalitions of the two major parties. More observant white evangelical Protestants were clearly the dominant religious category in the Republican coalition. In our numbers, almost a third of the Republican votes came from this group. That's up from 1996 and has been growing all through the 1990s and indeed since the 1980s. If one adds in the less observant, who are less Republican and less numerous, then a full two-fifths of Bush's votes came from white evangelical Protestants. Mainline Protestants also contributed to the Bush column, but they're distinctly junior partners in the Republican Party. Not very long ago they would have been the distinctly senior partners. Roman Catholics also contributed; all together, about one-fifth of the Republican votes came from Catholics. The other groups didn't contribute a whole lot to the Republican column.

The Gore coalition was more diverse, as Democratic coalitions tend to be. The largest group was black Protestants, who contributed almost one-fifth of Gore's votes. But notice that the secular category contributed about the same, almost one-fifth. Roman Catholics, interestingly enough, provided about the same proportion of the Bush vote as the Gore vote, a little over one-fifth. Other minority groups tended to support the Democratic coalition, and if you add them together they are a fairly significant bloc. The Democrats had some problems with white Protestants: in our survey, the Gore vote among white evangelicals was the lowest proportion of that group that the Democrats received in the 1990s, lower than Clinton in 1996 and in 1992. This year Democrats had some similar problems with white mainline Protestants.

Thus the survey shows some old patterns and some new patterns. Religious traditions do indeed matter in politics, very much as we've come to expect. What we see that's new in 2000 is a polarization of some key groups. Observant white evangelical Protestants are voting more Republican than they have in the past,

Table 5.2.   How Religious Groups Voted in 2000

	Bush Vote	Gore Vote	Total Vote
White Evangelical Protestants			
More Observant	32%	6%	19%
Less Observant	8	7	7
White Mainline Protestants			
More Observant	10	5	7
Less Observant	11	8	10
Black Protestants	1	19	10
Hispanic Protestants	1	3	2
Roman Catholics			
More Observant	12	9	10
Less Observant	8	11	9
Hispanic Catholics	1	3	3
Mormons	3	†	2
Other Christians	1	3	2
Jews	1	5	3
Other Non-Christians	†	2	1
Seculars	11	19	15
ALL VOTERS	100%	100%	100%

† Less than one percent.
Source: The Third National Survey of Religion and Politics, conducted by the University of Akron Survey Research Center in Spring and Fall 2000 (Total Weighted N=2,363).

balancing out the strong Democratic vote among black Protestants and Hispanics.

JOHN DIIULIO: Political scientists in general did not fare very well in the 2000 campaign. We were the big losers. Our very econometrically sophisticated "it's the economy, stupid!" models had generally predicted a walkaway Gore victory, not the fifty-fifty split that we got, and so I am especially glad to have a fellow member of the tribe doing a very interesting and cogent analysis that may help to redeem our credibility a bit.

This is a very good piece of survey research, using 2,363 randomly selected adults. I agree that the data analysis by Professor Green and his colleagues suggests what they say it suggests. Nonetheless, it's always important to remember what statistical analysis of this kind is: it's about drawing inferences about large populations from small samples. The inferences are only as good as the samples, and the samples, even when you have a nice big group, are not always perfect. A second thing to remember about statistical analysis is that it has three rules: disaggregate, disaggregate, disaggregate. John has done a very good job of disaggregating these data denominationally. The most interesting finding, I think, is that the more religiously observant people voted for Bush and the less observant voted for Gore.

There are three slightly contrarian points that I would like to make. First, I think that peeking out from behind certain of the data here, from behind the religious variable in the analysis, is a race variable. Research by my University of Pennsylvania colleagues Ram Cnaan and Byron Johnson and by others who have studied the contemporary life of black congregations suggests that there is probably as much variance in patterns of religious observancy among black Protestants as among whites. It would appear, therefore, that almost all self-identified Protestant blacks, whether they are weekly churchgoers, twice-weekly goers, or not-very-often goers, voted for Gore. From this I think we can conclude that race, not just religion or degree of religious observancy, was at least in part predictive of the vote. I don't mean to imply that Professor Green suggested otherwise. Both he and I will explain to anyone who cares to hear that after a hundred years of this kind of research by social scientists, we can agree on the fact that it's a multivariate world.

Second, I would agree wholeheartedly that religion was unusually prominent in the 2000 election. Three of the four top candidates seemed unable to remain mum on the Almighty. Only Mr. Cheney was able to do that. The first candidate to give a powerfully faith-friendly speech was Vice President Gore in May 1999, when he called for an expansion of the "charitable choice" provision of the 1996 welfare-reform law. Around that time, he talked repeatedly about religion and about his own faith as a born-again Christian. I thought he seemed fairly sincere, and he said it quite often, at least as often as Bush.

Why then were more religiously observant people in general, and Gore's fellow born-again Protestants in particular, so much more inclined to vote for Bush? For the same reason that blacks, despite Bush's appeal to compassionate conservatism, were inclined to vote for Gore: namely, that party identification, independent of both religion and race, continues to be a major determinant of voting behavior even in this age of independent voters, fewer yellow-dog Democrats, fewer rock-ribbed Republicans, and lots of split-ticket voters. Blacks are disproportionately registered Democrats, while highly religious whites tend to be disproportionately Republican. So while religion was certainly an important factor, there are other mediating variables here, especially of race and party ID, but also such things as ideology, positions on issues, and indeed the state of the economy. I would be very interested to learn whether the data on congressional voting would show a similar pattern of religion—mediated or not by these other variables. I suspect that it would, though not quite as strongly. That's the nice thing about an empirical question: you can get data and find out.

Finally, Professor Green's paper reminded me of a question I had long had about the electoral significance of groups like the Christian Coalition. While the media have often written about such groups as if they were a huge factor in mobilizing white evangelical turnout and deciding elections, I've never actually seen any good evidence that these groups did more than essentially increase the winning margins of essentially conservative Republican candidates who, given the usual turnout in voting, would have won anyway. So I don't know the answer to the question, Would the white evangelical vote be as one-sided and cohesive as it now appears to be were it not for the Christian Coalition and other such groups? I suspect that it probably would be, but I do not know.

The first interesting question about elections is of course who won and who lost, but what most interests us academics is the broad voting trends and what they imply about the attitudes of voters, the operation of the electoral system, the fate of the political parties, and the direction of public policy. Just as we're beginning to recognize that religion has a much stronger influence on volunteering behavior than we had realized before, so we're also beginning to understand better that religion has a powerful pull on voting behavior. I think that Professor Green's analysis gets us much further down that path of understanding.

Discussion

ROBERT SHOGAN: John Green, could you speculate about the effect of the third or maybe the fifth man in the campaign, Bill Clinton?

JOHN GREEN: In looking at the other items in this survey, we saw clearly that the country had ambivalent views toward Clinton. A lot of other survey research has demonstrated this as well. Even among groups that voted Republican there was a general appreciation of Clinton's job performance, and even among groups that voted Democratic there was a generally negative view of his personal behavior. Among white Protestants, particularly the less observant ones, the personal problems of President Clinton seemed to be more important.

ROBERT SHOGAN: Among the *less* observant?

JOHN GREEN: The less observant. It wasn't that they were necessarily more troubled about Clinton's character, but their troubles with it seemed to influence their vote. Although the more observant evangelical Protestants and even Catholics didn't care much for the president either, their voting behavior can be explained by a lot of other things. But with these less observant people, the character issues seemed to make a difference. I think that some of the character questions about Vice President Gore seemed to make a difference also.

RICHARD OSTLING: The polarization you described as being greater in 2000 than in 1996, was it also greater in 1996 than in 1992?

JOHN GREEN: Yes, the religious polarization that we highlight does seem to have been increasing all during the 1990s, election by election, usually by just a few percentage points.

FRED BARNES: Why didn't Gore's appeal to religious voters work?

JOHN GREEN: Many of the white religious groups that Gore was trying to mobilize had over the 1990s become increasingly Republican, and so there was a perceptual screen there. I think the Clinton problems and Gore's association with the Clinton problems made it difficult for a lot of these religious persons to respond to Gore's religious appeals. Although Al Gore is actually a very religious man, most people did not know that about him. Then his faith suddenly appeared on the radar screen, and it surprised a lot of people, including journalists. I remember getting a number of calls asking, "What is this all about?" People seemed to see it as something odd. In that sense, George W. Bush had an advantage; the partisan cues worked in his direction—well, at least with whites. His expression of faith didn't seem like something new, and anyway people think that Republicans tend to be this way. Bush had similar problems with black Protestants and with

Hispanic Christians. He simply was not as credible, even though he made tremendous efforts to appeal to them.

JOHN DIIULIO: That May speech by Gore was a bold speech for a Democrat, at least as bold as Governor Bush's speech in July. In it Gore said what role he thought religion should have in public affairs. But as the Democratic convention drew nearer, there was a fight, apparently, about whether even to keep the language favoring charitable-choice expansion in the party's official talking points. Finally they agreed to keep it, but the point was somewhat watered down. Gore had a problem in that his appeals were episodic and rather sketchy; he was never able to flesh out the implications, even when Senator Lieberman was nominated and it seemed like a perfect moment to put flesh on the bones of these sentiments. It never happened.

LARRY WITHAM: One interesting thing that came out of the election post-mortems in GOP circles was that the Republicans didn't get as much of the white evangelical vote as they had hoped. By one reckoning, the turnout had been 19 percent of all voters in 1996 but was only 15 percent in 2000, and so the Republicans lost potentially six million conservative evangelical voters. There were two explanations. One was that their electoral strategy required setting priorities, so they didn't go out to the states with a lot of white evangelicals and pump them up. But by not trying to secure those votes, they lost six million of them. The other view was that the Jim Dobsons and the Christian Coalition certainly didn't deliver this time, but maybe they never really could.

JOHN GREEN: In terms of the folks who did show up at the polls, the Republicans did well among both evangelical and mainline Protestants; it would be difficult—though possible—to do better. But I think there is some truth to both of the points you suggested. Many states where white Protestants are common were not considered competitive in 2000, so there wasn't as much pressure to turn out the vote. Alabama didn't matter; Texas didn't matter. In our data, we have some evidence that turnout among white Protestants was down a little. Black Protestants were way up, but white Protestants were down a bit. There's a strong regional component in this pattern. Florida aside, there was not a lot of competition in the South.

I think that the organizations of the Christian Right, the Christian Coalition and other groups, were quite active and reasonably effective, though not as effective as in 1996 or 1994. Even if they didn't bring any new people to the polls, they certainly certified to their constituency that George W. Bush could be trusted.

Early in the campaign, particularly in the primaries, there were some serious questions as to whether white evangelicals would stay with Bush. He seemed to be too moderate, and in fact was being advertised in many circles as very moderate. But he did manage to do very well in this voting bloc. So I think the Jim Dobsons and the Pat Robertsons, if nothing else, succeeded in certifying George W. Bush to this community. By the way, I think a similar thing happened in the Catholic community; a lot of priests and lay leaders went out of their way to indicate to their followers that Bush could be trusted.

MICHAEL CROMARTIE: John, isn't there an untold story here as to how Bush got Christian Right leaders to keep a low profile during the campaign?

JOHN GREEN: I was absolutely amazed that those leaders actually worked quite hard for the Republican ticket and didn't make the kind of headlines they have typically made that would disillusion other voters. Yes, there is a good untold story there.

TERRY MATTINGLY: Does your survey form include specific questions about social issues, such as sexual freedom and abortion rights?

JOHN GREEN: Yes, we had batteries of questions on abortion, gay rights, a whole range of social issues.

TERRY MATTINGLY: Do you have tabulations by those issues?

JOHN GREEN: Not in these results, but we'll soon make them available.

TERRY MATTINGLY: At the height of the Lewinsky affair, the *New York Times* columnist Maureen Dowd said that the country was divided into two groups, those who opposed Woodstock and those who liked it, and that this was a sexual-morality cultural divide. Did you see evidence of this in your survey?

JOHN GREEN: I think there is a cultural and moral divide in the United States, though not quite as simple as Woodstock versus traditional values. The most controversial issues like abortion are in some ways the least significant part of that cultural divide. Throughout the South and the West and around middle-sized cities, there is a much more traditional view of sexual behavior, family relations, and the public role of religion than in major metropolitan areas, where there is a much more cosmopolitan view. That tension underlies to a substantial degree what we saw in the election. A very interesting survey on this issue was done by Richard

Morin and Claudia Deane of the *Washington Post*; it documents this divide more fully than we do.

MICHAEL CROMARTIE: The authors of that survey are here today. When did you do the survey, Rich and Claudia?

RICHARD MORIN: [In 1998 and 2000.]

CLAUDIA DEANE: The *Washington Post* published it on September 30, 2000 ["Among These Voters, Values Matter—but Vary Widely"].

JOHN DIIULIO: Let me add something on the cultural-divide question.

MICHAEL CROMARTIE: Were you at Woodstock, John?

JOHN DIIULIO: Nobody from south Philadelphia was at Woodstock—Democrat or Republican! Let me try to be a little bit of a contrarian. That's a wonderful map that the survey results provide. But there's also a state-legislatures map and a may- ors map and a governors map. With eighty-plus thousand elected officials, we've got lots of elections in this country. My, my, how interesting things get when peo- ple who voted one way on that particular Tuesday in November seem at midterm election two years later to vote for members of Congress whose stance on con- troversial moral questions looks very different. Now, I'm not saying there is not a divide—I think you would have to be more than a little out of it to think that there's none—but I'm suggesting again that there are reasons to be a bit more cir- cumspect about how deep it is and how much of a driving force it is.

BOB JONES: There was a lot of analysis of the surge for the Democrats among white suburban voters, particularly in the industrial states. Given your survey num- bers, that seems a little counterintuitive, since those suburbs are strongholds of the evangelical megachurches and the white mainline Protestant churches. I'm won- dering if you think the white Protestant vote would look different if you could break out suburban versus rural or urban.

JOHN GREEN: Yes. There are regional and size-of-place distinctions in our data. Gore did better among all these groups in suburbs and Northeastern/Midwestern states than in the rest of the country. So it goes back to John's point about a mul- tivariate world. Let me add another variable: gender. There is a gender gap even among the most observant white Protestant evangelicals. I think gender was a par- ticular factor in the suburbs of the Northeast.

STEVE WAGNER: The thing that struck me when I examined the exit polls was the degree to which what you call secular voters—those people who also think the country is morally on the right track—coalesced around Al Gore. Do you detect an emerging political identity among secular voters?

JOHN GREEN: Yes, I do. Throughout most of the 1990s, secular voters largely voted Democratic in reaction to what was going on with religious voters in the Republican Party. Like all these other groups, secular voters are diverse in many respects. But one thing they tend to have in common is very liberal positions on sexual and family issues. In recent times, there does seem to be something of an identity developing among at least some secular voters; they really see themselves as something apart. Of course, secular voters don't have institutions to nurture and maintain that identity.

JODY HASSETT: In the last week or two, we've seen a split among evangelicals between the pragmatists—who are parsing Bush's language when he talks about the fact that the country is not ready for overturning *Roe* v. *Wade*, and who are taking the long-haul, incremental view—and the purists who want him to review his predecessor's executive orders, to get that office on faith-based organizations set up in the White House, to make things start to happen right away. Any thoughts on that?

JOHN GREEN: It's hard to tell how the voters themselves view this, but if you look at the leadership, there has always been this gradient between the pragmatists and the purists. Lots of evangelical and other religious leaders were very pragmatic in 2000, figuring that, for all his faults, Bush was better than Gore. I see this breaking down, in terms of expectations postelection, very much according to preexisting lines. The hard-core pragmatists think that Bush ought to be given time and that only so much can be achieved. The hard-core purists never went along with the strategy—they were induced to be quiet during the campaign, but they never bought into it. Now some of the pragmatists are falling away—they're moving toward expecting a lot more, having less realistic expectations. This presents the president and the Republicans with some interesting problems, because they are going to have to deliver on some things fairly quickly to keep the new pragmatists—not to mention the more purist groups—in line. But this is very common in American politics: people coalesce around a candidate, he wins, they divide up the spoils and become discontented.

MICHAEL BARONE: You've taken these surveys now in three successive elections. Which of these groups is growing larger as a percentage of the electorate and/or population, and which is growing smaller? Which is the wave of the future?

JOHN GREEN: Evangelical Protestants appear to be growing. When we first did this survey in 1992, using the same kinds of measures, evangelicals made up slightly less than 25 percent of the adult population. By 2000 they were just over 26 percent. That's not a huge increase, and it may just be the result of sampling problems, but since these are fairly big samples, it may represent growth. We also see continuing decline in mainline Protestants and some decline in white Roman Catholics over that period.

MICHAEL BARONE: What about seculars, the second-largest group?

JOHN GREEN: They seem to be edging up as well. Again, we're not talking about huge changes here. Of course, the Hispanic population continues to grow. There are more Hispanic Catholics, but there are also more Hispanic Protestants, something a lot of people don't realize. We don't see much growth in the "other non-Christian" category, among Muslims or people of Eastern faiths—a little increase, but not a dramatic one.

MICHAEL BARONE: So the two growing groups seem to be the ones that politically are among the most one-sided in their preferences: evangelical Protestants and seculars.

JOHN GREEN: That's what our figures show.

GERARD PERSEGHIN: Why didn't Hispanic Catholics vote like the rest of the Catholics?

JOHN GREEN: I think a lot of it was ethnicity. Hispanics are largely new immigrants, and new immigrants do not identify as strongly with their coreligionists in the United States as they do with their own heritage. I suspect that the message of the Catholic Church on issues like abortion does not come through as clearly in the ethnic churches as in other congregations, while the messages on social welfare resonate more with those communities. It's interesting that Hispanic Protestants, not just in this election but also in previous ones, are somewhat more Republican. It may be that the more conservative messages of the evangelical clergy somehow get through. But they don't get through all that strongly, because Hispanic Protestants vote more Democratic than their non-Hispanic counterparts.

MARY LEONARD: Professor DiIulio, to the extent that evangelicals have a political agenda, how do they expect it to be advanced through Bush's proposal on faith-based action?

JOHN DIIULIO: I really don't know. I don't know what their expectations are. One thing I would say is that there are different communities within the evangelical community. There are liberal evangelicals, and even liberal evangelical organizations, as well as what are conventionally thought of as conservative evangelicals. I think that when then Governor Bush talked about what he intended to do, he made it pretty clear. What he said won't satisfy all evangelicals, but there was a lot in it that should please most of them.

JOHN GREEN: For many evangelicals, the expectation is pretty straightforward, I think: that religious institutions will be honored and will have an important place in public life. When you get beyond that kind of general symbolism, though, I think there are some real disagreements. A lot of leaders we talk to in the evangelical community are deeply suspicious of charitable choice; for good, historic, evangelical reasons, they don't want entanglement between religion and government.

MICHAEL CROMARTIE: For theological reasons.

JOHN GREEN: Yes, theological reasons. Others are just champing at the bit; they want federal money, and they really think they can do a tremendous amount of good with it. They think they can really take care of alcoholics, for instance, and troubled youth.

CARLYLE MURPHY: Do any of you have details about President Bush's faith-based plans?

THOMAS PRATT: I might be able to shed a little light on that since we, Prison Fellowship, have a major project in Texas as a result of Governor Bush's office of faith-based activity. He wanted a unit in the governor's office that would encourage faith-based organizations of repute and capability to take on some aspects of the state's social responsibilities, such as operating prisons and offering drug treatment. You had to meet certain requirements, of course. We run a prison outside Houston. We chose to do it without government money, so we were not beholden. But we had to pass muster with regard to constitutional issues. We had to spend time with constitutional lawyers, with the ACLU, with the unions, and so on, to get the lines straight. We've been operating there for about three years. We operate in two other states under the same set of rules, and in those cases the states provide dollars for the programs. It is possible to do this. You do have to watch the lines and have them set before you get started.

KARLYN BOWMAN: Do you think we have a deeply or closely divided electorate? I'm thinking here of the work of Alan Wolfe in which he finds that people of different stripes nonetheless have a lot in common.

JOHN GREEN: It's clear that the country is deeply divided over the choice of president, and that probably reflects disagreement about the future direction of the country. I'm not sure, though, that this reflects deep-seated social divisions. Many of these groups that in our data would appear to be warring with one another actually get along pretty well and have a lot in common. One of the great lines from Alan Wolfe's book *One Nation After All* was that the culture war is "within us." For a lot of the groups in our survey, that statement seems accurate. They have contradictory views. A few of them, notably black Protestants and more observant evangelicals, have less of a conflict. But for a lot of the other groups, the choice for president was tough because their values pull them different ways. While they may disagree with their neighbors, they don't hate them. Most people wanted the election to go away so they could get back to regular life, which is really pretty good these days.

JOHN DIIULIO: If you look at the electorate as a whole and try to divine from the data what you might say about the degree of polarization according to race, region, religion, and so forth, the picture gets murky pretty quickly. Remember the "new progressive coalition" that Clinton brought us in 1992? In 1994 that was gone and there was a new voting bloc of "angry white males," who in 1996 had been replaced by "soccer moms." Now we are on the verge of "religious identity politics." These things have a remarkable volatility in American politics. Perhaps in the year 2004, given a different set of economic and other issues and different candidates with different positions, the Catholics might turn back and become once again more reliable Reagan Democrats. What's important is the fact that you must look at religion continually to explain political outcomes.

JOE LOCONTE: We hear quite often that African Americans, particularly churchgoing African Americans, are one of the most socially conservative population sectors. But this doesn't seem to be reflected in these election results. Is there something going on in that community? Are they becoming less concerned with some of these social issues? Stephen Carter in his latest book accuses the African

American leadership of being utterly co-opted by the Democratic Party and sacrificing its prophetic voice.

JOHN GREEN: In our data, church attendance and other measures of religious commitment have essentially no effect on the voting behavior of African Americans but tremendous effect on their attitudes. Regularly attending black Protestants have more conservative views on abortion, on gay rights, on traditional morality in general, but this social conservatism is not connected to their votes. I suspect there are two reasons for this. First, there are issues of racial justice and civil rights that trump that connection. Second, African American leaders offer a very consistent message to their followers that the Democratic Party is superior to the Republican Party. In this last election, we saw that mobilization reach new heights of effectiveness. It's interesting that back in the 1950s, most evangelical Protestants in the South voted Democratic because of class reasons, although they had the same conservative views on morality that evangelicals have today. There were other issues that connected them to the Democratic Party. I think there is a potential for conservative or Republican votes in the African American community *if* Republicans can get around the issue of race. I know that George W. Bush tried hard to do that, but the election results show that he was very unsuccessful.

JOHN DIIULIO: I think there is no question at all—and I'll invoke the name of George Gallup, who has more good kinds of data on these subjects than journalists and academics have generally noticed—that African Americans are, by every measure, the most consistently religious people in America, and they hold strongly what would be considered conservative views on a whole range of social issues. Then why don't they vote with the more conservative party? One reason, I think, is that the Republican Party is still identified as an antigovernment party. Government is not a bad thing in the African American community. It's not all good, either, but there are very few libertarians in the African American community. And here comes the interesting dynamic that we'll watch over the next several years: candidate Bush put out a message that was consistently targeted to say what I think was in his heart about the poor children, youth, and families in urban neighborhoods. He made every effort to get that across at the Republican convention in my hometown, Philadelphia; his speech was extraordinary in that regard. Then came the ninety-two-to-eight split. It's a bad thing, and those within the Republican Party who say, "Well, let's not think about this anymore," are making a terrible social, moral, and political mistake. I think the African American electorate is saying, "We heard this and we didn't believe it, but maybe now we'll know you by your works."

RAMESH PONNURU: Could you give us a breakdown of age among these religious groups? How relevant is age?

JOHN GREEN: In the South, younger evangelicals are becoming more Republican and older evangelicals are less Republican, reflecting generational change. Outside the South, there doesn't seem to be much of a pattern by age.

GEORGE WEIGEL: Let's discuss the candidacy of Senator Lieberman. Publicly, at least, it seems that the ancient prejudice of anti-Semitism simply doesn't exist at a national level. Was there anything to suggest that Lieberman's Jewishness was an issue in the campaign?

JOHN GREEN: I've seen no poll evidence—ours or others'—that it was.

GEORGE WEIGEL: This would not have been the case forty years ago.

JOHN GREEN: Yes, I think it is a big change. Of course, it's possible that there is some deeper anti-Semitism that we are unaware of, and maybe in another context it might rear its ugly head. But certainly, on the face of it, there does seem to be a change. Interestingly, our evidence suggests that Joe Lieberman probably helped Al Gore with a lot of people, including conservative Christians.

HILLEL FRADKIN: Professor Green, you mentioned that evangelicals hope to get respect for their churches from this administration. How much of their political outlook at this point stems from this sense that they are held in disrespect and want to be vindicated in the public mind?

JOHN GREEN: Within the mass public and particularly among political activists and elites, evangelicals feel severely put upon. They particularly dislike journalists, but I think college professors are only slightly behind. They see all of the cultural elites as being very hostile to them. I speak to a lot of different religious groups on these sorts of issues, and I generate the most suspicion among evangelicals. You get the sense that they're thinking, "You all don't respect us, you don't understand us, and because of you, the powers of the earth don't treat us as they should." Now, I suspect that a lot of other religious groups feel the same way. But part of what makes it especially difficult for evangelicals is that when they talk to people outside the evangelical community, the reaction usually is disbelief. "You're the biggest religious tradition in America! Your values dominate huge sections of our society! How can you feel discriminated against?" But nonetheless they really do. It's a serious thing.

HILLEL FRADKIN: So this is "religious identity politics"? What you just said suggests that it wouldn't necessarily be tied to the actual positions people have on sexual matters or family matters but rather to a sense of themselves as a group that wants respect like any other group.

JOHN DIIULIO: I'm trying to think of a term for this new variable, this sort of religious Rodney Dangerfieldism—"I don't get no respect." Where surveys ask, "Do your views on this, that, or the other issue set you apart from most people you know, most people in your neighborhood, in your state, in your country?" the response is likely to be "no, it's fine," until you get to the "cultural/academic/media elite." There aren't many evangelicals visible in those institutions. How many Assemblies of God folks have been cabinet secretaries lately? It's interesting to see in the coverage of Senator Ashcroft how the fact that he doesn't dance is received quite differently from the fact that Joe Lieberman doesn't drive on the Sabbath or somebody else doesn't do something else because of religious scruples. It's an odd thing. Evangelicalism is a religious tradition that causes people to say, "My goodness, isn't that odd," and yet 47 percent of the American people, according to Gallup data, define themselves as born-again Christians.

JOHN OMICINSKI: Does the split in the Catholic vote make those votes irrelevant, so that politicians don't have to deal with them?

JOHN GREEN: No, it makes them especially valuable, because these groups are more likely to be moved.

JOHN OMICINSKI: Have they been moved in the last few elections?

JOHN GREEN: The more observant Catholics have been moving—let's say creeping—in the Republican direction, and the less observant have been creeping in the opposite direction. We hear a lot about "swing voters." The middle-of-the-road Catholics are the swing voters, and politicians spend a lot of time trying to appeal to them because they can be moved. In this election, the Catholic swing voters split pretty much down the middle: the more observant moved to the Republican side and the less observant to the Democratic side. Forty or fifty years ago, when Catholics were a very reliable voting bloc for the Democrats in the Midwest and Northeast, Republicans didn't spend much effort on them at all, because there weren't very many votes to be gained. But now Catholics are very much up for grabs, and a lot of effort is spent on trying to persuade them.

JOHN DIIULIO: I think that's exactly right. It's interesting that non-Hispanic white Catholic voters have a perfect record of voting with the winner in the last four or five elections. They are the bellwether voters. Republicans were hoping they were reliably Reagan Democrats, but they're not. The fact that they are split, or nearly split, probably means that both parties will try to do more vote hunting in that segment of Catholic voters in elections to come.

JOHN OMICINSKI: Besides the Baptists, what other denominations are in the evangelical category?

JOHN GREEN: The Assemblies of God, other Pentecostal denominations, the Presbyterian Church in America (not to be confused with the Presbyterian Church USA, which is a mainline church). The one that does confuse people is the Evangelical Lutheran Church in America, which is not an evangelical church. But other Lutherans, the Missouri Synod and the Wisconsin Synod, *are* evangelical. Another big piece is nondenominational churches, the fastest growing part of the evangelical community.

MICHAEL CROMARTIE: Tell us again what a "less observant evangelical" is. I thought the very essence of evangelicalism was fervency.

JOHN GREEN: It's a person who is affiliated with one of the denominations we classify as evangelical but who claimed to attend church less than once a week. So if you were a Southern Baptist who didn't show up at church every week, we would categorize you as a less observant evangelical.

MICHAEL BARONE: With Jewish voters, there seems to be a pattern emerging. My theory has been that it has really been fear of Christian conservatives that has moved Jewish voters toward a very heavily Democratic, very anti-Republican kind of feeling. They are voting as they did sixty years ago, which is not true of most of these other groups. It's as if Roosevelt was on the ballot again against some *goy.*

JOHN GREEN: I think there's a lot of truth to that. In some of our surveys, we find Jewish political activists who in terms of their issue positions would seem to fit better in the Republican camp, but who report to us that the involvement of the Christian Right in the Republican party is deeply troubling to them. Part of it is the church-state issue—they are really worried about that. But it's also broader. There is a cultural element. The Christian Right would certainly favor more conservative cultural policies, and many Jews would not, because they are culturally liberal.

HILLEL FRADKIN: Right after the election, some polls showed that younger Jewish voters were more Republican this time around than their elders by some significant degree.

JOHN GREEN: I've seen reports of those surveys, but our numbers are too small to show that. An interesting study in Philadelphia showed a Republican trend among younger Jewish voters.

GEORGE WEIGEL: Within the white vote, can one say, on the basis of your data and other data, that going to church is the single most effective predictor of voting behavior?

JOHN GREEN: I'm not so sure I'd go so far as to say it's the single best, but it is certainly one of the best predictors.

TIM SHAH: Is religiosity a good predictor of voter turnout?

JOHN GREEN: Church attendance and other measures of religious behavior are very strongly correlated with voter turnout, and that's true in all religious traditions. It seems to have to do mostly with social connectedness. People who go to places of worship frequently are more connected socially and are more likely to vote.

JOHN DIIULIO: One of my colleagues at Harvard, Sidney Verba, published a book called *Voice and Equality: Civic Voluntarism in American Politics.* He wasn't looking for religion at all, but he discovered that, lo and behold, just what people had found with respect to religious institutional affiliation and volunteering. Especially among Latino populations, there was this interesting effect that people who were associated with a church were more likely to register and more likely to turn out to vote. Why was that? Well, church is a place where people learn certain skills, such as how to join together in a common cause, or how to write a letter to a congressman. They learn language skills also. That's important to watch because I think, especially with this growing population of Latino voters, that the mediating role of the local church is going to be a nontrivial factor, not only in whether those populations get to the polls, but also in what they do when they get there.

How Should We Talk? 6
Religion and Public Discourse
A Conversation with Jean Bethke Elshtain
and William McGurn

JEAN BETHKE ELSHTAIN: Let me begin with a brief autobiographical note. I didn't start out with the intention of thinking about religion and politics. I grew up as a Lutheran in a little village in northern Colorado. When I got to undergraduate school I was a deist for about two weeks. It didn't work; I just didn't quite get the point of deism. Then for a while I decided I was an agnostic, a very *anguished* agnostic. When I got to graduate school the issue really was forced upon me, for two reasons. One was that in working through the canon of Western political thought I realized that something peculiar was going on with the texts of Hobbes and Locke and others: a lot of their scriptural referencing was eliminated from the editions we would read. It was as if the scriptural texts were completely unimportant to the arguments these political philosophers were making. And in the case of Hobbes, sometimes a whole last half of the book was left out, the section that Hobbes calls "The Kingdom of Darkness." That contains Hobbes making a theodicy argument, political theology quite explicitly, but it was considered unimportant. Furthermore, such apparently "minor" figures as Augustine and Aquinas and Luther and Calvin didn't appear *at all* in the canon of Western political thought as I was taught it. In political science the emphasis was on people's preferences. Values were considered entirely subjective; there was no rational warrant for people's values. But if we knew their preferences, we could concentrate on those and figure out what motivated them. That outlook dominated empirical political science. At the same time, on the normative side we find an approach that left out the religious questions. All this seemed odd to me.

Then I got involved in feminist issues. There I was confronted by one wing of feminism—and I don't mean this as a blanket criticism of feminism in general—that was very powerful during the late sixties to mid-seventies. It was a radical separatist wing that engaged in vicious attacks on religious traditions and on people who had religious views. Much of my reconsideration of some of these issues, then, was entirely defensive. I wasn't so much concerned on my own behalf, because I wasn't sure where I was on many of those questions, but I was thinking of all those unnamed men and women who were trying to live decent lives, to do right by their families and their communities, to live with some dignity, and who were sustained in that by their faith; suddenly they have opprobrium heaped upon them. I decided that I needed to rise to their defense. That was considered a dangerously heterodox thing to do—that and my insistence that men were not necessarily ontologically tainted creatures all slated to become rapists!

Then my first book came out: *Public Man, Private Woman*. The book is a reconsideration of the tradition of Western political thought with feminist questions in mind. One of the reviewers suggested that there was some closet religious conviction at work in it. So at one point I said, "What the heck? Maybe it would be better to start dealing with these questions explicitly." That's the circuitous route by which I came to these issues. I worked in political science departments for twenty-two years until the University of Chicago Divinity School decided I belonged in their midst, and I'm happy to be there.

That's the full disclosure statement, and now I'll move on to my theme. Americans are rightly associated not only with rights talk but also with God talk. American culture and politics are indecipherable if you sever them from the panoply of religious conviction. It's also the case—and none of this is new news to anybody—that much of our political ferment, both historically and currently, flows from religious commitments. Sometimes this happens directly. At other times it happens through a kind of translation process whereby people turn convictions deriving from religion into civic commitments that appeal to others who don't necessarily share their religious beliefs. The vast majority of Americans continue to profess belief in God—though it's not always clear exactly what that means—and an extraordinary number claim membership in a church or a synagogue or a mosque, though the number who attend regularly is much smaller. Without this feature we just wouldn't have American political and civic life as we now know it.

Tocqueville's great book *Democracy in America* helped to capture the tone and texture and temperament of a fledgling republic over a century and a half ago. One of the things that most intrigued him was that in America one found both separation of church and state and a rich intermix of religion and politics. When Tocqueville wrote his observations on the Jacksonian era, he proclaimed that religiously formed and shaped convictions brought a tremendous energy to the American democratic enterprise. He realized that the associational enthusiasm he saw around him derived substantially, if not largely, from these religious convictions.

What Tocqueville was observing in operation is what we now call civil society. Discussions about civil society have been out there for a decade now, inaugurated, some claim, by Robert Putnam's famous "Bowling Alone" essay, now a *Bowling Alone* book in which Putnam lays out more of the data behind his conviction that there has been a turn in America away from associational activities—clubs and political parties and bowling leagues and the like—toward private, individual pursuits. When we talk about civil society we're talking about the many institutions that human beings create to sustain work and family life, to promote domestic peace and security, to propagate their faith, and to attain various other ends and purposes. For Tocqueville, this associational enthusiasm was the heart of the American democracy.

What he was observing—although he didn't put it in quite these terms—was the connection between confessional pluralism and social pluralism. Confessional particularities usher in the social and civic manifestations of these faith commitments. Confessional pluralism is what we usually call freedom of conscience, freedom of religious belief; social pluralism refers to the maintenance and accommodation of a plurality of associations, many of them in order to foster religion or to make religious belief manifest in institutional forms. Tocqueville was most interested in what he called the "habits of the heart." These determine what drives people, what makes up their individual and collective identities. And for him this social pluralism, derived mainly from confessional pluralism, was essential.

Tocqueville was a Catholic whose family had narrowly escaped complete devastation during the Terror, so he understood—and he has a long discussion of this—what happens culturally when a people's religion is violently wrenched from them. It is not a pretty picture, he says. Why? Because this wrenching out of a religious tradition enervates and depletes a culture. It destroys the intermediary associations that help to give people social power when they're confronted with the power of the state. When those are wrenched away, people don't become more robust democratic actors; instead they become more available for mobilization by the nation-state apparatus, which is certainly what had happened by the time of Napoleon.

Tocqueville also observed that in the United States the Constitution didn't require that people relinquish the communal dimensions of their faith, the external signs of their faith commitments, as the Napoleonic Constitution had, for example, demanded of French Jews. In order to be full citizens, the French Jews were told, they needed to forsake a lot of what made them distinctive—their characteristic dress, their dietary regulations, Hebrew schools, all the public markers of their confessional difference. And just to underscore the point, Napoleon called the meeting to decide many of these issues on a Saturday, so that the leaders of the Jewish community who wanted to attend in order to help to pave the way for equal citizenship had to violate the Sabbath to do so. This is a point made in an essay by Michael McConnell. That, Tocqueville said, is not what the American Constitution requires of people. Americans are free to make their faith commitment socially explicit.

Tocqueville also said that you couldn't understand the extraordinary civic currents rushing through the United States without being aware of the Christian insistence that all persons are equal in the eyes of God. Once people take this idea seriously, he said, the logic of it will start to manifest itself politically. It may take a long time to work out, but he was convinced that, for example, slavery couldn't last. The manifestation of that religious conviction required communal institutions and the communal expression of religious faith.

With regard to one other claim Tocqueville made, it is harder to argue for his complete prescience: he thought that religious conviction would restrain some of the striding individualism and the ambition that an energetic, prosperous, commercial republic would generate. Religious notions of covenant, stressing mutual accountability and the responsibility of persons one to another and before God, would help restrain what he called the "excessive and explicit taste for well-being" that human beings acquire in an age of equality. Religion would help to forestall a slide into a world totally dominated by self-interest. Here he put a lot of faith in Catholicism because of the strong ecclesiology of the Catholic tradition, the strength of its sacramental and liturgical tradition, its language of solidarity. Tocqueville reported on some labor rallies he had attended where a priest got up and addressed working men and women, championing the rights of the poor to organize. This sort of thing would play an ongoing essential role, he thought, and help to check the rushing tides of individualism. He also hoped that over time religious conviction would help to prevent people from falling into what he called indifference, a lack of concern about one another. If taken seriously, the religious obligation to love and serve your neighbor would counteract this indifference and have a salutary civic effect.

[In 2001,] USA Today published a report on contemporary America religiosity that said this: "Where once a community of believers shared a common vocabulary, many feel free now to define God by their own lights." That is a lot of lights. If you define religion that way rather than providing some barriers to the rush of libertarianism and individualism, religion becomes part and parcel of the individualist cultural project. We each have our own little individual light rather than a communal calling, a membership, a form of covenant and solidarity. This notion better comports, obviously, with individualism and also with a kind of indifference, a kind of "Whatever" attitude. The USA Today piece quotes Bishop Wilton Gregory, vice president of the National Conference of Catholic Bishops, who in response to the finding that people are much more comfortable with spirituality or religiosity than religion said, "Well, what do they mean by spiritual? That they watched two episodes of 'Touched by an Angel'?" A question I would pose is whether we'll see the loosening or loss of religion in a robust sense in favor of a kind of spiritual individualism that much better comports with the rise of libertarianism in this country, on both the right and the left.

One of the worries of people who argue strongly in favor of pluralism is that too much power is reposed in centers of power, and there is not enough power at the periphery. We can find that argument in all sorts of political thinkers, many of whom were not religious. Hannah Arendt often made this point about the importance of animating the peripheries. She was thinking not just of the state—though especially that, given that she was a German Jewish refugee from Nazi Germany—but also about the centers of corporate and other power. Defenders and theorists of democracy have argued for a long time that in the absence of strong social institutions, strong formative institutions other than the state, it will be very difficult over time to sustain civic freedom. That freedom requires that people have concrete ways of manifesting their civic identity. It's not just an abstract thing; it's the notion that there are things I can do, there are all sorts of mediating possibilities available to me, to enact my civic membership.

Most of us, when we were taught the scope of Western history, were taught that liberal constitutionalism forced a regime of toleration on religion. Faith communities, we learned, were paradigmatic instances of what are now called "sectarian groups" that, if they had their own way, would immediately oppress other people or start killing one another. There is obviously some historical support for the argument that religion represents a potential menace, and that if it's not held in check it can get out of hand. But if you look at instances of the persecution of believers around the world today, you see that much of the danger now comes from overweening state power that routinely violates religious freedom, rather than from religious believers intolerant of the faith of others. And of course if you were to do something as unseemly as a body count, the non- or antireligious ideologies of the twentieth century would win hands down.

Why do people always return to the Inquisition and the wars of religion in any discussion of toleration? Part of it, I think, is the degree to which Locke's famous "Letter on Toleration" has seeped into our understanding of things. It's worth going back once in a while and rereading that great essay, considered a signal turning toward religious toleration. Of course, Locke argues that atheists and Catholics are *not* to be tolerated, they're not part of the deal: atheists because you can't trust them to keep an oath, since they don't have a higher power to help enforce it, and Catholics because they're going to be loyal to some power other than the magistrate, so you can't trust them either. But for everybody else you have toleration.

There's a price to be paid for this toleration. Locke insists that, as a precondition for civil government, very sharp lines must be drawn not just between church and state but also between religion and politics. Fine. But then he extends that logic to say that religion belongs in one sphere, politics/government in another, and you can be a citizen of both realms so long as you don't ever attempt to blend the two. In the religious realm you can answer God's call and do what your faith requires (if you're a Protestant, that is). But when you step out of that domain you enter the civic realm, and then your religious convictions cannot figure directly anymore. Your civic fidelity is pledged to the sovereign, to the magistrate. So religion is seen as a potential danger to the civic realm, and that's why we need this rigid line between religion and politics. Religion becomes irrelevant in a public sense. It is privatized; it's reduced to the subjective well-being of each individual practitioner.

The 96th American Assembly held in March 2000 produced an interesting document called *Matters of Faith: Religion in American Public Life*. The American Assembly was founded by Dwight Eisenhower when he was president of Columbia University. It's run out of 475 Riverside Drive in New York, which is sort of the heart of liberal Protestantism in America, but they did ninety-five of these assemblies over almost fifty years without touching on the question of religion in American life. Fifty-seven men and women attended this one, representing something like sixteen different religions. I will quote four sentences from this document:

> We reject the notion that religion is exclusively a private matter relegated to the homes and sacred meeting places of the faithful, primarily for two reasons. First, religious convictions of individuals cannot be severed from their daily lives. People of faith in business, law, medicine, education, and other sectors should not be required to divorce their faith from their professions. Second, many religious communities have a rich tradition of constructive social engagement, and our nation benefits from their work in such varied areas as social justice, civil rights, and ethics.

This suggests, in an understated way, a logic for engagement in the civic realm, or suggests at least that we need to develop some terms of engagement. A view still very dominant in the academy—I hear it all the time in political philosophy—and associated with the work of the important political philosopher John Rawls, is that your religious convictions need to be translated into a strictly secular civic idiom if you're going to base any argument on them in public life. You have to make that translation or you'd better stay quiet. Part of this position is an insistence that there is a single vocabulary that is standard, and that arguments have to be made in these terms. There's a single vocabulary of political discussion, a single understanding of authority. Fortunately, since all this is mostly on the level of political philosophy, there aren't many people who are going to take it seriously, but it is very dominant in the academy. Certainly it has made its way into jurisprudential thought; I've seen law-school articles that extend the logic of it to suggest that religious institutions be pressured to conform to what democracy looks like, and what one-person-one-vote looks like.

Let me mention a couple of religious responses to this and to the whole tradition that I'm associating with John Locke. The first I'm calling "full-bore Christian politics," which is the belief that the fullness of your religious belief and commitment and witness has to enter the public sphere, and precisely on religion's terms. When you go public you're obliged to make the whole thing *present*. That can lend itself to the notion that there's a Christian position on almost everything. One of my worries about this position is that it can court parody. Is there really a Christian position on term limits? Certainly there is such a position on war questions, on issues of abortion and euthanasia, on the kinds of questions that are at the heart of what theologians call "anthropology," the understanding of the human person. If issues concerning the common good are at stake, then a person with religious convictions is obliged to bring those convictions to bear in a very energetic way. But on a lot of other issues, contrary to "full-bore Christian politics," there is not a "Christian" position.

Another strong view in this area is the one associated with Stanley Hauerwas: the view that Christians signed on to a rotten deal when they agreed to the regime of liberal toleration, and so when persons with religious convictions engage politics, they are bound to do so on the world's terms. Having accepted a lousy deal, now they're going to have to perpetuate it, to accept civic peace on those terms. The essential worry is not what happens to politics but what happens to Christianity, to the Church. I call this "radical dualism"—the Church is the Church, and what happens to the world is not a central concern.

My own position is rather complicated and difficult to articulate, and is compatible with the tradition of Catholic social thought. Let me just outline some of its guidelines. When you're thinking about the form that religious convictions should take when they enter civic discourse, you have to ask yourself certain kinds of questions. What are the stakes? Who are the key players? What areas of social existence are touched upon here? Is this a question of the common good or some other kind of question? Your response to questions like these should determine the way in which you engage, and your understanding of what it is you're doing when you engage.

WILLIAM MCGURN: The role of religion in public discourse is a subject that I'm particularly interested in as an editorial writer and as a practicing Christian who does not believe his job is to proselytize in print. Much of this question is considered to be a clash about how we conceive of God. In Jean's latest book, *Who Are We?*, she makes the point that without a strong anthropology there is no sturdy rationale for drawing and defending limits in regard to human dignity and human rights. That really cuts to the heart of what we're considering here: in terms of this kind of debate in the public square, it's not so much how we view God as how we view man.

Having returned to America from abroad, I'm struck by the realization that in the United States, despite our interaction with many different religious groups, we tend to talk in rather abstract terms of "Christians," or "believers," or "faith-based communities," and "nonbelievers." In other cultures they don't use such broad terms. We're not just Christians—we are Southern Baptists or Methodists or Irish Catholics or Hispanic Catholics. In public discourse the culture you're addressing really does determine a lot of your choices of language and framework and references.

When I was an editorial writer with the *Far Eastern Economic Review* I lived in Hong Kong. I had no political rights there, absolutely none; yet Hong Kong was the freest place in Asia, I think, at that time. Its government was very hospitable to a wide variety of religious expressions. This seemed similar to the dress code in our office: national dress. For a white guy from America "national dress" meant a suit and tie, but it was very different for a Muslim from Pakistan or a Singaporean. What people wore was considered a very natural expression of who they were, just as their religious expressions were considered natural and not proselytizing.

In the publication that I worked for, we were trying to articulate a set of beliefs and principles about Asia that were not necessarily just a reflection of an American view of the world. This meant that we were really thrown back on first principles. In a debate over human rights you may find that your opponents don't believe in human rights—they believe the concept is an example of Western romanticism. If you use these terms—human dignity, inherent rights, equality, and so on—that we Americans all agree to here, they have no resonance. They sound like Western bleatings, because though you think you're appealing to a universal standard, that standard is not accepted here. They're highly charged words. A lot of people in other countries don't believe in democracy. The whole notion of human rights, individual rights, the notion that the individual has a right not to be crushed by the community—I wouldn't say that these things are all disrespected, but they're certainly not taken for granted. You have to argue for them. You have to go back to first principles. And where there's so much disagreement on religious expression, you're left with an anthropological vision of man.

I also have a domestic example of the importance of language. In my state of New Jersey a year or so ago there was a move to have schoolchildren recite fifty-five words of the Declaration of Independence, the part that begins, "We hold these truths to be self evident . . . they are endowed by their Creator with certain unalienable rights . . . to secure these rights governments are instituted." You would think this wouldn't be a contentious thing. Well, it ended up being very contentious, and eventually it was defeated. There were three main types of opposition. The feminists opposed it because women didn't have the vote at the time when men prepared it; women were not equal citizens then. Some African Americans opposed it because of Jefferson's affairs with his slaves and because of slavery itself. A third group was concerned about introducing the word "Creator" into the classrooms. So there were three sorts of opposition to this, our founding document, which one might think would constitute the lowest common denominator of acceptable language.

The people who opposed the recitation of these words from the Declaration of Independence ended up on the side of Stephen Douglas, who viewed the Constitution and Declaration in the same way. In his first debate with Lincoln, Douglas said, "I believe this government was made on a white basis. I believe it was made by white men for the benefit of white men and for their posterity forever, and I am in favor of offering citizenship to only white men forever." So the irony is that a lot of these groups came down on the side of Stephen Douglas as opposed to Abraham Lincoln and Martin Luther King. This is a dangerous place for people to go. If you do not accept any religious authority on which to base the view that there should be equality of races and genders, and then you exclude the constitutional basis also, your position has no basis. It's a very vulnerable position.

Discussion

MICHAEL CROMARTIE: I'm struck, Jean, that neither you nor Bill mentioned natural law. Did you intend to?

JEAN ELSHTAIN: There's a natural-law basis, obviously, for constitutional thinking and for the Declaration. The presupposition that all human beings have access to reason, to certain sorts of standards, the warrant for which we can articulate in language—that's definitely part of the backdrop here. When people sit down to reason together on some issue, they might not come up with absolute unanimity, but they should be able to arrive at some commonality on how people are to be treated, or at least how they are not to be treated.

The Universal Declaration of Human Rights has two categories or parts. One is the positive things that governments are enjoined to do to make available to people a rich and full life. This part is very controversial, because there are different cultures that say, "Wait a minute, I don't agree that government can or should do this or that." Then you've got the list of what governments are *not* to do. There's much more agreement on things in this category, such as unjust imprisonment and torture. So you start to build negatively, but working underneath there is some basic understanding of the human person, and you wind up with a lot of commonality.

MICHAEL CROMARTIE: When we were planning this seminar the "George Bush's favorite philosopher" controversy had just come out. If you were an advisor right now to candidate Bush, what would you say to him about how he *ought* to talk about his faith in the public arena? What public language is available to express faith in a way that's both sincere and not offensive?

JEAN ELSHTAIN: He's an evangelical Christian, and there's a language in which evangelical Christians speak about the experience that was decisive for them. If you're talking specifically about your own faith commitment, there may not be another way to describe that. But if you're talking about the rationale behind certain kinds of policy initiatives, then I think there *are* other ways of describing it. Don't you think Bush has done that? In talking about charitable-choice provisions and so on, he's not saying, "My personal relationship with Jesus Christ tells me that this is a good policy." He talks about why *civically* this makes a lot of sense, which is the way that Gore talks, too. That strikes me as entirely reasonable. I'm not super-keen on having people make a public confession of faith. Part of that, I suppose, goes back to the fact that Lutherans are a very buttoned-up kind of people!

LEO RIBUFFO: This picks up on something Bill said but gives it a somewhat different edge. I would suggest, Jean, that you sever the normative argument from the historical/semihistorical argument. Let me give you a list of names, contemporaries. Mary Baker Eddy, Brigham Young, Henry Ward Beecher, Archbishop John Hughes, Charles Taze Russell, who founded the Jehovah's Witnesses, and members of the twenty-thousand Spiritualist or Theosophist groups in the United States. Now it's all very well, if you're building a usable past, to say that these all reflect a common religiosity in nineteenth-century America. But the people involved didn't think so, and I think it's indisputable that when Americans took religion more seriously there was more religious conflict. It seems to me that someone will make that point to you with less sympathy with your normative position than I have. And it strikes me that cultural conservatives have to *bite that bullet*. If you want more religiosity—religion taken more seriously, and thus more conflicts—you shouldn't be surprised that the theological liberals and the secularists are going to fight pretty hard, too.

JEAN ELSHTAIN: I think we have become astonishingly conflict adverse. It's not as if those conflicts threaten to rip the country apart. There are all kinds of interesting debates that reflect different sorts of commitments. In the past, accommodations got made; the conflicts didn't lead to total war.

DAVID VAN BIEMA: Jean, it was sort of discouraging to learn that I was a Rawlsian and to learn that you didn't like Rawlsians all in one lecture! My comment is this: Over the brief period I've been reporting on religion I've come to a respect for what evangelicals mean when they talk about their faith. But it does have a feeling of the whole enchilada about it, that it's a whole package and we either take it or leave it. It's not arguable.

You spoke about the importance of having power distributed along the periphery. But these groups on the periphery that help to keep the power in the center from becoming absolute often themselves speak in very absolute language. That's one of the reasons why I feel uncomfortable with them. As long as they're on the periphery, it's okay for them to speak in absolute language; but if I take them seriously, then I have to take seriously the notion that at some point they might be in the center and their power might be applied. I want to speak up for all the secularists and the Rawlsians, if that's indeed what I am, and say that this prospect is a bit scary.

JEAN ELSHTAIN: The Rawlsian position holds that civic argument must be free from the taint of religious conviction—and that position becomes a kind of absolute. The absolutists I run into are the Rawlsians. I just don't think it's possible for people to sever religious commitments from civic positions in this way. And I don't think such a requirement should be the price of civic admission.

That said, let me respond to the concerns you expressed. If someone says that his or her position is scripturally enjoined and that therefore there's no counterargument, while that person may *claim* unassailability, it's just not going to hold. Somebody else—not necessarily our Rawlsian protagonist but somebody with strong religious convictions who can also do the scriptural proof texting—is going to say, "I don't interpret that passage that way at all." So you're not creating a completely unassailable position. Argument over interpretation of Scripture is going to continue no matter how many people might want to fix and freeze it. How that translates into civic and political commitments is an enormous issue. And effecting that translation means you inevitably are going to enter the world of political jousting and debate and that dirty word "compromise."

I was in Prague right after the changes, and I was talking to Martin Palous, a friend of mine who is now deputy foreign minister in the Czech Republic. He's a political philosopher, and he said something like this: "One of the things we have to understand now that we have a democracy is that compromise is a principle. In the old regime, to compromise was to *be compromised*. Now compromise is a principled way that people have to learn, given that you just can't always get everything you want. You can't expect that whole translation of your views into a civic outcome." I think that's something that anyone who enters the civic arena realizes straightaway.

Often the role of a prophet is a tragic role, because while you're the one who stands on the mountaintop and raises the alarm, you're like Moses: you can't make it to the promised land. The promised land isn't of this earth, in a sense; you can't realize it politically. We shouldn't be so afraid of people who are playing the prophet's part. There will always be those who say to them, "Well, now, wait a minute. You might be absolutely right, but you have to get your plan through Congress or through the state legislature. You have to find a way to do this. Sometimes that's going to mean holding your nose and doing the best you can."

As soon as the periphery seeks to engage, it's transformed. It can't remain isolated and impermeable. My worry is the argument from those who say that independent sites of social power ought not to exist unless people reason a certain way, think a certain way, argue a certain way, because otherwise they are civically irrelevant or even dangerous.

WILLIAM MCGURN: Some people think that these controversies that divide our society should be settled through the judicial process. But I'm not sure that the solution is to have such questions adjudicated by the least representative part of the government so that the answers rest on a legal case—all or nothing. That seems very absolutist. I think legislators would love to have the courts settle these issues. When the Supreme Court issued *Roe* v. *Wade* they probably thought they had settled the matter. The question is not what people say, what they demand, but what people will settle for. And I don't mean that in bad way. My ideal version of America and what I'm prepared to settle for, and even be content with, are two different things.

DAVID VAN BIEMA: I think there is, with evangelicals, a vocabulary that is still very much of a piece and self-referential and not particularly open. When evangelicals bring that vocabulary into these sorts of arguments, they shouldn't be surprised that people who are not privy to that circle of words become a little exercised over it.

JEAN ELSHTAIN: People are going to react, and that's fine. The kind of principled *modus vivendi* that Bill and I are talking about is in fact anathema to the Rawlsians, who would argue that you need to have a sort of *overwhelming* normative theory of democracy, so that everyone is reasoning in the same way and talking in the same way, that a *modus vivendi* isn't enough. I think a principled *modus vivendi* is a hell of a good deal when you look at the other possibilities for politics out there.

STEPHEN CARTER: I want to do something that will surprise at least Jean and maybe some others: I want to speak up on behalf of John Rawls. Years ago Don Fehrenbacher in his book about the Dred Scott decision was asked why so many people were *complaining* about slavery but were not *doing* anything about slavery for fifty, sixty, seventy years. It was because while the slaveholders had an *interest* in keeping slaves, there was no *interest* in freeing them, although there was *sentiment* for freeing them. This is one of the things that the Abolitionists used and one of the things that religious advocacy does: it persuades people that they have an actual interest in ordering things to fit what was previously just a sentiment, so that now they want to change what has no direct effect on them.

So Rawls comes along—and in my view Rawls's most important antecedent in the twentieth century is John Dewey—and says that we've got to tame these passions. We have to construct a way to have civil discourse where we're not ruled by passion, where we're ruled by reason. Now what Dewey said earlier is that we need to find a way to teach people from a very early age to *reason*, even if this takes them away from the views of their parents. We have to teach them what it means to be an American. And a lot of Rawlsians, even more than Rawls himself, would say, "You know, this is exactly right. We need to teach people very clearly that to participate in public life, what's most important is not so much the values you hold but the way you engage with other people. Can't we come up with a way to avoid impasse, to avoid passion, to avoid people's sense of being frightened or oppressed by the words of others? Can't we design a public square in which we will be able to have conversations that have commonalities, where we're all speaking in effect the same language?"

The models fail, but why is the project not admirable? Why is it not admirable to say, "We do have a lot of passions—religion, ethnicity, and so on—and we're going to tame all of that by coming up with a common language for the public square, so that we don't always have this warring of interests, with everything up for grabs every couple of years"?

JEAN ELSHTAIN: Because it would shut down Martin Luther King and anyone else who's talking specifically in a language of advocacy that could not be what it is without the commitments drawn from religious faith. The problem is not the advocacy of reason; it is, instead, a far too narrow definition of what constitutes reason. Rawls isn't as bad as some of the Rawlsians, as I've been categorizing them, but there's a very, very narrow view of what counts as deliberation. There is the presupposition that people with strong religious convictions cannot be considered people of reason because they haven't deliberated about this—as if their convictions are an unthought thing, so that whatever they say has the epistemological status of a grunt.

This is a narrow view of reason and of deliberation, and one frightened of conflict. What is politics about if not the way in which we adjudicate these conflicts? The view that we should have politics with as few conflicts as possible doesn't make sense to me. The notion that you have to strip people of the markers of their identities, so that they're sexless, nameless, religionless, and then they can make the best decisions about the principles of justice and how to govern a society—that just seems wrong. You have to start where people are, with their passions, their interests, their convictions, and then politics is a way that those get molded, get civically filtered. We have ways of doing that. Half the time I don't understand what the problem is here, because there are ways in which we do that.

JOHN LEO: I'm interested in the way this stuff gets into the popular medium. I only became aware in the last year—possibly under the influence of Jean's writing—of how widespread among ordinary people this hostility to religion is. Even Mayor Giuliani, of all people, was lecturing the Catholics not to push too hard on abortion because not everyone shares their principles. Well, you discuss the issue as best you can and then you vote; that's what America is all about. I have a folder bulging with clips of common, ordinary people reflecting the attitude that there's something illicit about religion, and this is new. It has been around forever as an intellectual idea, but now it's in the culture. The cultural left has opened a broader assault on religion. You can see it in images on TV or comedy skits or *Dumb and Dumber*–type movies that are filled with a mockery of religion. The ability of gays to derecognize evangelicals at three or four colleges—that's something new, too. So something is going on here outside the intellectual arena. It has become respectable and ordinary for people to say that religion has to shut up. Am I just belatedly coming to recognize this or is it indeed a new thing?

JEAN ELSHTAIN: Let me reply first from within the academy. What happens there, what kinds of student groups are considered acceptable and can make their presence felt as RSOs, Registered Student Organizations, varies widely from campus to campus. The kind of thing you're talking about in the Tufts case or the Grinnell case, where student Christian groups were denied access or were kicked off campus because they didn't have the politically correct position on some issue or another—I think that's a minority phenomenon. More common is what so many campus spiritual advisers have commented on: they're seeing in many of the students a renewed interest in religion, a concern that they're ignorant of their own traditions and want to find out about them. The students are leading the way on this, which makes some of the university powers that be very uncomfortable.

There's a notion in some quarters that religious convictions are incompatible with the pedagogical mission, that somehow religious belief just doesn't comport with learning how to be a critical thinker, whereas other forms of advocacy or of identity claims are thought to be entirely compatible with the pedagogical mission. Where all that comes from I'm not entirely sure. I think that certain strands in popular culture, in portraying religious people as dummies, have had an effect. But I also think there's a lot of interesting stuff in the popular culture that doesn't deserve to be blasted and is engaging people of religious convictions. Some movies where you wouldn't expect it speak to suppressed theological and religious concerns. It's as if these ideas are yearning to breathe free and can't quite do it, but they're there and they're worth teasing out.

MICHAEL CROMARTIE: Vincent Carroll is writing a book on this subject.

VINCENT CARROLL: The book is going to be a defense of Christianity from various popular indictments. It's something only a journalist would do; no historian would be so reckless. It's a defense of the historic role of Christianity in terms of the things that the vast majority of Americans would agree are positive, whatever their political convictions, and whatever their attitude toward Christianity. So it's vast in scope.

One of the things it deals with is conflict, and it strikes me that there seems to be a widespread view that religious views tend to lead to conflict more often than nonreligious views, that they are less grounded in reason than nonreligious views and less subject to debate. I don't believe that's obvious at all. I don't think it is obvious that the wars of religion in the fifteen and sixteen hundreds were necessarily more savage than the secular ideological wars of the twentieth century, and yet it is almost conventional wisdom to think they were. Garry Wills wrote a column not long ago that started out with this notion, taking for granted that religious conflict is more vicious, more visceral, more brutal. I don't believe it's true, and I think the historical record is quite clear about this. We have this vision of the Crusades as somehow being worse than Tamerlane's brutalities. They weren't.

Anyway, in my job I get hundreds of letters to the editor every week, and I can tell you that arguments *not* generated by faith-based beliefs are no less passionate and indeed may be *more* passionate than faith-based arguments. The most hostile sort of reaction to anything that I've written over the years has come from gay militants. Not reasoned discussion but denunciation. In Colorado right now, ever since Columbine, the issue that is most passionately argued, *viscerally* argued if you will, is gun rights.

So I absolutely reject the idea that religious-based advocacy is any more passionate or less subject to reason than nonreligious-based advocacy. There is something attractive about idling discussions down and being able to engage at some level, no matter how far apart the two parties are, rather than just shouting at each other. Nevertheless, in the purely secular arena a lot of discussion is simply shouting, and no different from the most extreme religious sectarian shouting that has occurred throughout history.

JEAN ELSHTAIN: That has certainly been my experience, too, of just how ardently views are held and how passionately they are expressed. That radical separatist feminist position I mentioned earlier was often couched in the most extreme language, and it was almost impossible to have a reason-based discussion about it within the framework of feminism—not as an antifeminist but *within* that framework.

KENNETH WOODWARD: Is there a cultural failure to all of this that wasn't there before? Look, I think there is a moral equivalent of war, namely, reasoned argument over issues of fundamental importance to society and to all of us as human beings. But from where I sit it seems that the only kind of religion that creates a problem for secularists is a religion that makes judgments, insists on distinctions that secularists preclude or ignore, and is seen as threatening to society by the sheer weight of numbers. That's why, historically, Catholics have been perceived as a political and social threat in American society. But as American Catholics dissipate in various political and social directions, they are now seen as less threatening, with the possible exception of the abortion issue. My contention is that what leads us to discuss this question now is the emergence of evangelical Protestants as a movement of social and political consequence. If we removed these people from the scene, I don't think we'd be having this discussion.

On the contrary, what passes for "real religion" for many Americans who are otherwise disconnected from any religious formation or tradition is what goes by the name of "spirituality," and this dimension of American religion has so far been missing from our discussion. If you look at the best-seller list, you find the most innocuous kinds of religion, airy, meditative, *Celestine Prophecy* stuff that isn't going to make any judgments. I think that as a religion writer I have been a little too dismissive of this trend. It is all over the place, and those of you who are parents of young children are going to run into it a lot. "Why aren't we more spiritual, Mommy? Why do we have to be just religious?" So it's only the religious people who make judgments, and who look as if they might be able to make those judgments prevail over others, who are feared and fought against. Religion these days is very acceptable, even in political campaigns and at dinner parties, as long as it speaks the language of personal discovery, recovery, or spiritual quest.

JEAN ELSHTAIN: The heart of politics is making judgments, distinguishing what should be done from what shouldn't be done. Now we get this dominant view, in the name of spirituality, that *judging* is anathema. If making relevant distinctions and assessments is considered by definition something that only intolerant people do, then politically we'll just get dumber and dumber. Learning how to make reasoned judgments is at the heart of the civic community.

JAY TOLSON: I think that some of the really rending issues like abortion or homosexuality have not been scrutinized very deeply within certain faith traditions. It's as though theologically these issues are absolutely decided. I find myself wondering, am I at fault within my own faith that I haven't come to a decision? For instance, I don't find overwhelming scriptural evidence to prove certain positions on homosexuality. I think one of the fears about the entry of a powerful evangelical point of view into public discourse is that it will silence reasonable discussion, that there is a kind of absence of serious engagement of faith with reason. We're facing the prospect of kids who are not allowed to study even the possibility of Darwinism. If we have a public that more and more finds evolution an inadmissible subject of discussion, that's a little frightening,

JEAN ELSHTAIN: There are precious few places where such discussions can go forward as it is, and it might be that the upshot of some of the evangelical Christian claims in this area, their argument that Darwin shouldn't be taken as scripture, will be to force a discussion to occur rather than close one down. Certainly it has forced a discussion from some of the defenders of evolutionary theory like Stephen Gould, who will say, "Wait a minute. Orthodox Darwinism—there are real problems with that, too! Now, I'm an evolutionist, but I'm not that kind." So they start to nuance the view from science, which is good.

One of the things we need to be concerned about is the automatic authority that the hype of science confers. The Human Genome Project has people shouting hosannas and flipping cartwheels and thinking that in three years we're going to cure cancer. There's a utopian cast to a lot of what is coming to us in the name of science. First of all, the scientists and science writers shouldn't be making such grandiose claims. Second, these are issues that have to be discussed in other arenas, where people are not shot down with the notion that if you don't have the full scientific apparatus to bring to bear, you're out of the discussion. When the American Catholic bishops issued their 1983 pastoral on nuclear strategy, the reaction from some quarters was, "What the hell do the bishops know? They're not experts in throw weights of missiles, so they shouldn't be in this discussion." That's a way of saying that ordinary citizens can't talk about these things because they're not experts.

So challenging the automatic authority of science is a good thing. Having a public debate about science and its claims is like having a debate about religion and its claims. Both are important debates.

LYNN NEARY: I want to talk about reporting on a particular story, the Southern Baptists' decision to proselytize specifically to Jews. I had a certain moment of clarity as a reporter and an individual when I spoke to a Southern Baptist leader who explained the decision something like this: "We don't have a choice. This is our mission. We are evangelicals, and evangelization is what we're about. If we don't bring people to Jesus Christ we feel that we're doing harm, because the way to salvation is through Jesus Christ." So my question is, what happens when that primary goal—that we all should be Christian, and a very specific kind of Christian—hits politics or hits the public forum?

I was an educational reporter at one time, and I think the fear of this gets played out a lot in the schools. People worry about what's going to happen to their kids, and that's why you get cases like Santa Fe in the Supreme Court. [Santa Fe School District v. Doe, June 2000, held that student-led prayer at football games violates the Establishment Clause.] The people who brought that, as I understand it, were Catholics. So we're talking about people who would certainly think of themselves as Christian but who resented having a certain form of Christianity imposed upon their children. I think there are lots of communities around this country where people of a majority religious belief see no problem at all with having elements of that belief infiltrate many areas of public life. That to me is a fundamental part of what's going on, the fear that somebody else's idea of what religion should be is being imposed upon me or my children.

JEAN ELSHTAIN: I don't see what could be objectionable per se about people who regard themselves as evangelicals *evangelizing*. People can resist evangelization. They don't have to agree. The real problem would arise if people with evangelical commitments decided that they were going to evangelize using certain public institutions, that they were going to take over the public school and turn it into an evangelizing institution. That's completely improbable. And certainly if evangelicals set up Christian schools, no one *has* to go to those. I think that objecting to nonviolent, noncoercive evangelization is objecting to free expression.

PEGGY WEHMEYER: The Baptists-and-Jews story is fascinating. I did a report for *20/20* on it, and we got incredible feedback. The piece focused on a Southern Baptist who converted a twelve-year-old Jewish boy before his bar mitzvah. His parents went berserk, and so did the Jewish community. The issue raised is this: yes, they believe there's only one way to God, and that is through Jesus, and yes, that would be offensive to other people; but do they have the right to share that belief in the public square?

What happened in this case was that the Jewish boy was invited by his classmates to a Baptist youth rally. His mother allowed him to go to a Baptist church, and after going two or three times he decided to convert. Now, the mother had let him go to what she knew was a Baptist church. And the Baptists did what they always do *in their church*, telling people that if you come to Jesus, all your sins will be erased. The Jewish boy thought, "That sounds like a good deal to me!" He wanted his sins erased. And then he converted and canceled his bar mitzvah. Well, the community said, "How dare those Baptists! They're dangerous people!"

JULIE BUNDT: In response to Lynn I would say that I think two things are going on. One is that the evangelicals must share their faith and the truth of the gospel and Jesus Christ, but they usually do this one to one. That's pretty different from what they want to achieve in the public square. It's not that they want to get into the public forum and use it as a platform to share the gospel; they want to get into the public forum because that is where you have a voice on public-policy issues like abortion.

FRANKLIN FOER: What is the appropriate response to an evangelical who is trying to evangelize a Jew?

LEO RIBUFFO: Why not just treat it as you would someone calling you up and offering you a credit card? "No, thank you."

E. J. DIONNE: What Peggy said about the reaction to her story is fascinating to me as someone who grew up a Catholic kid in a Jewish neighborhood. My Jewish friend David would sometimes come to church with me. He liked the church. But if I had tried to persuade him to become a Catholic, the first thing my parents would have done is call his parents, out of respect for their rights over their own child. Our next-door neighbor who was from an Orthodox Jewish family married a Catholic, and my mother sat down with his mother and shared her worry that her son had married outside the faith, though of course my mother thought there was nothing wrong with being Catholic. A lot of people say that this is not about rights; they obviously have a right to do this. It's about the respect that a parent owes another parent of another faith.

MICHEL MARTIN: Part of the reason why a lot of these arguments take place in high school is that being okay is really important there. It's less important to an adult. I think a lot of evangelical Christians say, "I don't feel okay. We can talk about Kwanzaa in the schools and we can talk about Passover in the schools, so why can't we talk about the birthday of Jesus in the schools on Christmas? How come I'm not okay?" One of the things I hear Jean saying is that people need to stand up for their own okay-ness and stop expecting other people to withdraw. I do find that the mainstream denominations are not willing to step into the ring; they just want the other people to step out.

JEAN ELSHTAIN: The decline in membership in the mainline denominations suggests, in fact, that people are looking for something more robust, something more powerful and more demanding of them. I think the mainline folks ought to look to themselves more than they have.

MICHEL MARTIN: Journalism is often about conflict; that's the easiest way to do stories. Side A versus side B. Maybe part of our task as journalists is to think about how to write a story without reducing it to a side A/side B fight.

DIANE WINSTON: That was what I wanted to bring up, too. One of the dilemmas I feel as a journalist is how to tell stories in ways that will be interesting enough to get in the newspaper but will still be true to what's going on. People *are* religious, and they do feel strongly about their convictions, but they're very wary of bringing them up in the public arena because they feel such things would lead to conflict, and they don't want that kind of conflict. Part of what we can do as journalists is to encourage a process of reconceptualization that shows people that you can disagree civilly, and that there's more to it than "I'm right, you're wrong." Even evangelicals who believe they need to convert people say that they believe other people's beliefs should be tolerated.

ALISSA RUBIN: It seems to me is that people don't know how to argue very well. They don't know how to argue in a way that's constructive, where you can concede a point but not concede everything. It always seems that either you're going to win or you're going to lose, and those are your only choices. That makes the stakes incredibly high. I'm not sure how you create an environment in which people feel that it's safe to argue, that they won't simply be crushed.

MICHEL MARTIN: I often think of this when I watch the House floor and the level of argument has deteriorated to the point where people just scream. They only get to scream for about three minutes, so that makes it more intense. Often they're like a couple on the verge of divorce, and it's really painful.

WILLIAM MCGURN: You should watch the Taiwan legislature!

JEAN ELSHTAIN: My late friend Christopher Lasch lamented the loss of a culture of democratic argument. Our options, for a variety of complex reasons, seem to be either to shout somebody down or just to walk away. There is a therapeutic mentality in which a strong argument is thought to undermine people's fragile standing. "Oh, my feelings are really hurt and I'm going to leave the room right now because my self-esteem is in danger of plummeting to ground zero." The ability to engage in democratic argument comes from practice. It used to be a more standard part of civic education for people to learn how to do this. Debate wasn't just for a few students in debate club; it was something that everyone had to learn how to do. There's no reason in principle why we can't relearn those lessons. Too often people think that if you attack my position you're attacking me. That isn't so. People need to realize that you can stand outside yourself to have an argument.

E. J. DIONNE: I want to go back to where we were a while ago in this discussion and Jean's point about Rawls. I was glad that Stephen brought up John Dewey. I have a Dewey-eyed view of democracy, you know; I love the idea of democracy as a way of life. But I think constitutional democracy imposes certain disciplines on people who participate in it. I agree with Jean that you shouldn't have to translate everything into secular language, but it does seem to me that you can't base an argument in the public square solely on an appeal to scripture and faith. It has to be rooted in reasons that are accessible to other people. Yes, Martin Luther King's speeches seemed to use Southern Baptist language, but they were actually public arguments accessible to everyone.

STEPHEN CARTER: I've got about seventeen points here, but I'll narrow them down to just a couple. First of all, I want to disagree with my good friend E. J. Dionne and, to my surprise, with Jean as well. I think this vision of giving acceptable reasons is a nonstarter. I'm sure that evangelical activists who speak from nothing but scripture would say, "This is publicly accessible. Everybody can understand this! It's as plain as the nose on your face!" I think anybody should be able to say in public what they think. They may lose, they may fail to persuade anybody, but that has nothing to do with it. I strongly disagree about Martin Luther King. I've studied his work for a year now, and I don't think you can easily make the case that King's body of work is anything but a deeply religious testament. It's at least as full of explicitly scriptural arguments as the work of leaders of the Christian Coalition.

On the matter of threats to identity: a lot of black, church-going, inner-city parents feel very threatened by the rise of Islam. They're afraid their children are going to become Muslims and lose Jesus. But threats to identity in that constitutive sense will not always seem religious to outside observers. When parents protested the Kansas Board of Education decision to leave evolution out of the statewide science test that students had to pass, people looked at them and said, "These people are nuts!" But the parents who were protesting were saying, "It's a deep threat to our identity for our children to be required to say, as part of the price of graduating from school, that evolution is the explanation for how human beings emerge. That's different from the way we see it, and our view is crucial, in our judgment, to our understanding of who we are." And so the problem doesn't have a solution. I honestly think it has no solution. I don't think that a common language is the solution, or that Supreme Court decisions are.

We are going to have to live with deep, painful, offensive, troubling, scary conflicts because we are free. Because we're a free country we're going to continue to fight about this stuff as we have done all through our history. But we'll sometimes find ways to soften its impact, and we will find ways to live together because we've always done that.

E. J. DIONNE: I read Martin Luther King's *Strength to Love* when I was in high school, and I didn't realize he was a Southern Baptist. I certainly didn't have to share his faith tradition in order to understand his argument. I'm not arguing that constitutionally you can't derive your public argument solely from faith, and I'm not saying that your argument can't be steeped in your religious tradition. What I'm saying is that in a pluralist democracy, your public arguments need to be different from the kind of arguments you might make in deciding your church's view of gay rights or abortion. You are asking a government that does not recognize your particular religion—or any other—as guiding its view to make a decision.

JEAN ELSHTAIN: The first King I knew about was *Stride Toward Freedom*, which I read in high school, and I took him to be talking to me as an American citizen. You may know that what he says is coming out of his faith commitment, but he's talking about the Constitution and all sorts of things in a language that appeals to you as a citizen. I think it's analogous to the Catholic common-good argument. The question is, really, what kind of people are we?

STEPHEN CARTER: I'm not disputing that. I'm just saying that Pat Robertson, whatever differences I may have with his agenda, talks very, very similarly.

JEAN ELSHTAIN: He's not good at it! What he says doesn't have the power. It doesn't speak to normative questions in the way that King did.

STEPHEN CARTER: In the Western tradition we take the view that a legitimate government has the exclusive right to use force, that is, to use violence to achieve its ends. And although we have deeply worked out philosophies of law, law to the dissenter always looks like force, because law is the police with guns drawn, making you do what you *don't* want to do and preventing you from doing the things you *do* want to do. I think that people of faith ought to be very reluctant to place their hands on the levers that say, "For this, we as a society may kill." I tell my students on the first day of law school that every time we have an argument about what the law ought to be we're arguing about what we as a society would want to kill for, because we send armed police to go and enforce the law. So if you don't want to have a society that has to do violence in this cause, don't say it's a good cause in which the government ought to take sides.

The humility that is characteristic of so many fine religious traditions ought to give people pause before they say, "Rah rah, our side has won. We can now change all the laws we disagree with."

JEAN ELSHTAIN: Civil-rights laws are coercive, and they have sometimes been enforced at the point of a gun, but it's not everyday practice for the U.S. government to go out and kill its citizens. Law is coercive, but it's not violent. It's a mediated form of coercion. So when you say religious people ought to be very cautious about having that kind of power, that in effect says to me that the judiciary, the police force, the legislature all ought to consist of people who don't have Christian commitments, because Christians somehow ought to be humble enough not to trust themselves with this power.

Here I would offer as the counterargument, which I can't flesh out fully here, Augustine's fascinating discussion of why he opposed the notion of Christian empire. He says that if you're lucky you'll have a Christian emperor who behaves like a Christian, not a Christian empire. But does that mean that Christians should shun positions of judgment? Augustine said no. If your calling is to be a judge, that may well be a kind of tragic vocation in some ways, but it is necessary. It's important to have people—this is Calvin's argument, this is Luther's argument, this is the Reformers' argument for the most part, except for the Anabaptists—it's important to have people whose consciences are developed and who will therefore handle the reins of power in a way that is more just than unjust. That's Niebuhr's argument, too.

STEPHEN CARTER: There's a distinction between the notion of a calling or an obligation, which is what I think you're talking about and certainly what Augustine is talking about, and the notion that I've got to get my hands on political power so I can do this and that and the other thing.

JEAN ELSHTAIN: I would just say that the idea that if you get a couple of people in the judiciary and a couple of people somewhere else, then we'll be able to create the Christian nation—in a huge, complex, plural democracy it isn't going to work like that.

MICHAEL CROMARTIE: Stephen, are you making an Anabaptist point that the church, as the late John Howard Yoder used to say, should "not do ethics for Caesar"?

STEPHEN CARTER: No, I'm not making an Anabaptist point, and I'm not suggesting not doing it. I'm just saying, look prayerfully and with caution.

JEAN ELSHTAIN: I certainly do not disagree with that. That's exactly what the people I was citing would say. Absolutely.

LEO RIBUFFO: I'd like to go back to the difference between Pat Robertson and Martin Luther King, which I think relates to the broader question of why folks are so frightened of evangelicals and fundamentalists. King spoke religious language; he did not speak *supernatural* language. He was essentially a theologically liberal social gospeler—some Rauschenbusch, some Gandhi, some Thoreau. Robertson speaks about praying the hurricane away, about reading the newspaper to look for the Antichrist. Fundamentalists and evangelicals say they are Christians and the rest of us are not, and from their point of view they're correct. The greatest fundamentalist theologian of the 1920s, a man named J. Gresham Machen, said that liberal Protestantism was not just a new religion; it was a new *kind* of religion. So to say that they're all just religious thinkers leaves out the fact that when Robertson addresses the public sphere he brings in a lot of supernatural stuff that I don't see in King at all.

STEPHEN CARTER: I think that most people are wary of Robertson for good reason. They're not particularly aware of what his theology is; it's simply the causes this man is fighting for. If he were exactly the same kind of person working for a different set of causes, I think he would receive a very different reception.

MICHAEL CROMARTIE: It's not at all clear that Robertson is liked by most evangelicals either. The good news for anyone worried about Robertson is that the Christian Coalition really doesn't exist anymore. It's down to one staff person in Washington and a small office in Virginia Beach. It's not clear that Robertson has a constituency other than himself. And yet Tim Russert keeps calling on him to speak for the people he supposedly represents.

ELLIOTT ABRAMS: I want to go back to Lynn Neary's point about fear of evangelicals and what they might be up to. It struck me as a very odd statement. Think for example what a bunch of Southern Baptist evangelicals might do if they controlled the school board. Well, they were in control of *every* school board in the South for a hundred years, and yet they did not kill any Jews, nor did they kill any Catholics, nor did they drive these people of other faiths out of the South or destroy their religious identity. It seems to me that we're building a past here in which the dangers existed but did not eventuate, in religious terms (race is different), in this kind of horror that you now say you fear.

I am not an evangelical, but it seems to me that if I were, I would wonder what world this discussion generally has been describing. I'd say something like this: "You're describing a world in which we evangelicals are trying to change America, whereas in fact America has already been drastically changed by our opponents, and all we're trying *desperately* to do is to ask them to show a bit of humility and slow down! For example, the power to change overnight all American law with respect to homosexual sexuality, including marriage law—slow down! Can't we talk about this a bit before we do it? Must Justice Stevens make these rulings simply because he can put five votes together?" Lynn's statement implied that the evangelicals were to be feared because they were culturally the aggressors, whereas it seems to me, as I look at American culture today, that not only are they on the defensive, but they are big losers! Their world is collapsing around them. All they're doing is saying, Slow down.

JEAN ELSHTAIN: I was giving a talk someplace and was interviewed by the local public radio station. Even though it wasn't the subject of my talk, the fellow started asking me questions about the dire threat from evangelicals. I said, "It seems to me that what you're complaining about is that they're being politically effective. If they're electing people you don't like, there's a democratic solution to that: unelect them." The notion that there's something intolerable about these people *actually getting elected* to school boards and city councils seems to me radically antidemocratic. And the idea that we're helpless before them— well, for Pete's sake, get off your duff and go find candidates to unseat them. I just don't understand why somehow this constitutes a dire threat. People come into office and go out of office. They're reelected or they're not reelected. That's the deal.

PEGGY WEHMEYER: I think that we in the press have to be careful with our language. When I read that the Christian Coalition "took over" a school board, I wonder, when did the other side take over? When these protesting parents see condoms being distributed and evolution being taught in the schools, they say, "Oh no! They're offending our deeply held beliefs! We'd better run for the school board." And then the press says, "Look out! They're taking over!" It isn't a takeover any more than it was when the other side took over in the sixties, or whenever it was that they started running the school boards. What we really should do as journalists is to drop that "takeover" language and enlighten our readers and viewers as to what these people really fear, why they're doing what they're doing.

DAVID BOLDT: I wanted to respond to this consensus that seems to be emerging that the problem is fear of evangelicals, and that anti-Catholicism is a thing of the past. We don't really seem to see that quite so much in Pennsylvania. The principal issue there that involves religion happens to be school vouchers, and anti-Catholicism is still a very virulent force. It is also one that is difficult to deal with in commentary or in the news, partly because it's practiced by the people who are doing the writing. We shouldn't go out as Catholics thinking anti-Catholicism is completely gone.

JEAN ELSHTAIN: I agree. I think there's actually a lot of it. My friend Mary Ann Glendon has talked and written about this. It comes up in the academy in the form of attacks on the pro-life people, where a lot of the arguments are just flat out anti-Catholic. The idea seems to be that the pro-life Catholics are, again, antireason; they're doing what their church demands of them and they haven't thought the position through. It has also been my experience in the academy that even though you can't tell most kinds of antigroup jokes, anti-Catholic jokes are still okay. I heard them all the time when I was in political science departments.

DAVID BOLDT: The difference today is that it's a *secular* anti-Catholicism, not primarily a *religious* anti-Catholicism. Bob Jones is an anomaly in terms of anti-Catholicism, and I think that is what has changed.

WILLIAM MCGURN: One of the things that comes to mind in regard to school boards is the difference between a court decision and a process of change. The court produces a law that just sits out there and is imposed everywhere. But *processes* can be reversed, so if you go too far you can step back. We tend to think there's an end point, whether the controversy is abortion or something else, and that eventually we will reach it. Maybe we ended slavery with a civil war, but I don't think that in most cases there is a real end point. It takes a long time for consensus to build, and it's not always an attractive process. There will be very contentious matters, and a lot of bad feelings; still, it's the better way.

JEAN ELSHTAIN: I want to sign on to what Bill just said. It strikes me that a lot of the fear is a fear of democracy itself, the fact that it is about messy conflict and people working things out over time in a way that stops short of the use of power, something that we're all too familiar with in the history of political life. When too much is adjudicated by fiat and people feel they haven't had a say in what happens, for a period of time there is a kind of sullen withdrawal. Then when people do decide they've had enough, often the way that gets articulated—out of a sense of deep grievance—is far more scary than what would have happened if there had been more space created for people to messily butt heads over a period of time. That's where this winds up, with a robust and rowdy democracy.

The New Christian Right in Historical Context   7
A Conversation with Leo Ribuffo
and David Shribman

LEO RIBUFFO: Intermittently since 1980 pundits and liberal activists have been saying that the New Christian Right is either on the verge of taking over American life or on the verge of decline. Among the high spots and low spots was the 1992 Republican Convention, where Pat Buchanan declared "cultural war," a term that has, alas, entered our discourse. I'm going to try to make sense of some of this through the history of American religion and religion-related conflicts. We'll see some similarities and continuities.

A couple of methodological considerations at the outset. The American religious stew has always been immensely complicated. This was certainly true in colonial days, when religion tended to be a mix of Puritanism and animism and witchcraft, and you were less likely to be a church member before you were married than to be pregnant or to have gotten someone pregnant. Similarly, beware of sweeping categories. The term "Judeo-Christian tradition" goes back only to the 1930s. "Fundamentalist" was coined in the 1920s to describe one wing of theologically conservative Protestants; it is now used ubiquitously to label groups from Tulsa to Tehran. It's a little like referring to Jerry Falwell as, say, "a Protestant Hasid," or Pat Robertson as a "Protestant Sufi Muslim." We may expand our definitions to some degree, but let's at least try to preserve some nuance.

It seems to me that if you want to understand the New Christian Right, then you have to understand the American religious crisis of the late nineteenth century, the transformation of American politics in the 1930s and 1940s, and the cultural crisis of the 1960s and early 1970s. I want to go back to that overwhelmingly Protestant culture in the late nineteenth century, when it was facing various challenges. Darwinism suggested that man, instead of being a little lower than the angels, was just a little higher than the apes. "Higher criticism" of the

Bible told the faithful that the book of Isaiah was written by three people, none of whom was named Isaiah. These intellectual challenges had to be assimilated. Then there were social challenges such as the "new immigration"—almost thirty million Catholics and Jews who, in an overwhelmingly Protestant culture, seemed very, very strange.

The institutionally dominant Protestant response was what was known as "new theology," or "liberal theology," or "modernism," entailing five major positions: a new view of the Bible as not necessarily inerrant; a new view of Jesus as a good guy, not necessarily divine; a new view of God's kingdom as the good society here and now; a tendency toward ecumenicism within Protestantism; and an optimism that the world was getting better and better. A minority of those theological liberals were also politically liberal or radical, and they espoused what became known as the social gospel. They had an immense popular appeal with best-selling books like Charles Sheldon's novel *In His Steps*, where the citizens of Topeka are instructed in how to live their lives "as Jesus would." This is Al Gore's tradition! When he said that he wakes up every day asking himself "What would Jesus do?" he was harkening back to *In His Steps*.

And what did theological conservatives believe? In a nutshell, liberalism turned on its head. The Bible is inerrant, period. Jesus is the Son of God who died for your sins. God's kingdom will be established when Jesus returns. We are ecumenical only among fellow theological conservatives. The world will get worse and worse until Jesus returns. Increasingly that worsening process was interpreted through a framework called *premillennial dispensationalism*. You may not have heard of it, but more Americans can tell you its essential features than can tell you the essential features of Keynesian economics. All time is divided into ages or dispensations (usually seven); we are in the next-to-last age; things are getting worse and worse; Satan's agent, the Antichrist, will arise and eventually dominate the world; this will be followed by the second coming of Christ and the establishment of the Millennium, the thousand-year reign of Christ. The scholar Paul Boyer says today there are eight million *avid* followers of this form of Bible prophecy; if there are eighty Keynesians left, I'd be surprised.

There's a lot of complexity here. Not all theological conservatives were also political conservatives; William Jennings Bryan stands out as a theological conservative who was politically a progressive. The theological conservatives fought among themselves (notably Pentecostals, who believed that spiritual rebirth brought special gifts such as speaking in tongues, versus classic fundamentalists). Indeed, theological liberals and conservatives were not fully polarized before World War I. Similarly, before then there wasn't a clear segmentation on the political spectrum; it's hard to tell a so-called progressive like Theodore Roosevelt from a so-called conservative like William Howard Taft.

As the Hun Scare moved quickly into the Red Scare, World War I polarized American culture and religious life. There was militancy on all fronts, but for theological conservatives the war had a particular impact. First, it proved pessimism was right; and second, according to Bible prophecy Jews would return to Palestine before the return of Jesus—*right before*—and the Balfour Declaration promised a Jewish homeland in Palestine. So the theological conservatives, usually called in an oversimplified fashion "fundamentalists" after 1920, came out of the war on a roll. In 1919 they founded the World's Christian Fundamentals Association, whose major focus was fighting the teaching of evolution in the public schools. In retrospect, in this first fundamentalist controversy, as in the second of the 1970s and beyond, it's hard to discover which side fired the first shots.

Actually, the first fundamentalist controversy had two fronts. One was within the denominations, with their heresy trials and so forth, where the rhetoric was tough. The *Christian Century* called fundamentalism a "neurotic" and "extremist" movement. The fundamentalist Billy Sunday, though in many ways atypical, had his good lines, and suggested to liberal Christians that going to church doesn't make a person a Christian any more than going to a garage makes him an automobile.

Outside the denominations there was a wider fundamentalist controversy. The Scopes trial plus the debunking carried on by people like H. L. Mencken, Upton Sinclair, and Sinclair Lewis (with his *Elmer Gantry*) left a permanent mark, alas, on our view of theological conservatives down to the present. While these stereotypes linger, the more typical fundamentalists were quieter figures who differed among themselves in style, intelligence, and politics. Above all, beware of the claim that preachers could mobilize fundamentalists like robots. Rather, this was a rank-and-file movement responding to cultural threats to the things they held dear, the threats being perhaps evolution in the classroom, perhaps Theda Bara's bared flesh in those very sexy silent movies.

In politics, most fundamentalists joined their liberal colleagues in opposing Al Smith, a Catholic, for president in 1928, but for a substantial number his religion was less important than the price of wheat or the preservation of white supremacy. Somewhere between two and five million Americans joined the Ku Klux Klan, most as casually as if they were joining the Elks. But not all fundamentalists were bigots, and not all bigots were fundamentalists. Perhaps the worst was the *pro forma* Christian Henry Ford, who distributed a collection called *The International Jew*, an Americanization of the virulently anti-Semitic *Protocols of the Learned Elders of Zion*. This was put together by his aide William Cameron, a Christian Identity type of that day. Those interested in the Christian Far Far Far Right can find here the antecedents of some of the current militias.

Clearly the twenties was a time of great cultural conflict with political ramifications, but I'd say that the political spectrum still was not clearly segmented. As Hoover put it, "We are a nation of progressives. We differ as to the road to progress." It was the Great Crash of 1929, the Depression, and the response to the New Deal that accomplished the segmentation. Cultural questions of the 1920s were reorchestrated in a less prosperous economic context, and we can now see the spectrum that we are more or less familiar with: liberal advocates of the welfare state; Roosevelt pushing to turn "progressives" into liberals; conservatives (many of whom adopted the term regrettably, saying they were the true liberals), who opposed the welfare state; a radical left of communists and socialists. We will focus here on the emergence of a distinct Far Right, the Old Christian Right, the spiritual ancestors of the modern Christian Right. Many Far Right figures were famous or notorious at the time. The names still familiar are Father Charles Coughlin, the "radio priest," and Senator Huey Long, whom I would put in this category though he is somewhat problematical. Among the many less well known today are Gerald L. K. Smith, my favorite Gerald Winrod, William Dudley Pelley of the nativist paramilitary group the Silver Shirts, and Elizabeth Dilling, the Phyllis Schlafly of her day, though much, much more conservative.

A critical question for historians is how this Far Right movement differed from such mainstream conservatives as Herbert Hoover and Senator Robert Taft. I would say three things. First, it had greater dynamism, not just to preserve American society but to restore American virtue. Second, the Far Right was more prone to ungrounded conspiracy theories, particularly those of an anti-Semitic sort. Third, this Far Right sometimes urged economic redistribution, and in that it was somewhat liberal to radical. Fourth, much of its rank and file came out of a theologically conservative Protestant background and made those arguments part of its politics.

Liberals or radicals of those days didn't see a "far right"—they saw the coming American fascism! And they were willing to support restrictions on speech and assembly, indictments, the House Un-American Activities Committee, and the like to shut these people up. I call it a "Brown Scare." Now, broadly speaking, there is an analogy between the American Far Right of the thirties and Hitler or Mussolini, in the sense that there would be an analogy between Wilson and David Lloyd George, or between Clinton and Blair. But these are very different countries. The American Far Right, particularly its religious wing, tended to be less militarist, more rooted in religion, and less disposed to genetic theories of interpretation regarding Jews than its European counterparts.

Let me give you only one example of my favorite, Gerald Winrod, a classic 1920s fundamentalist, fighting Prohibition and Theda Bara movies, politicized by the Great Depression. Winrod interprets the New Deal in theological terms. He notices that the blue eagle used as the emblem of the National Recovery Administration has the same number of feathers as the Beast of Revelation had arms. This was proof positive to him—and I suppose to many of the sixty thousand people in Kansas who tried to send him to the Senate—that there was an international Satanic conspiracy stretching from the Crucifixion to Franklin Delano Roosevelt.

Let me emphasize that only a minority of theological conservatives joined Far Right groups in the thirties. Most voted for FDR because they were Southern Democrats, poor, or both. Fundamentalist leaders spent most of the decade praying for the revival that didn't come then, and also building an important infrastructure of Bible institutes, periodicals, and radio stations that would survive totally ignored by sociologists and journalists (though not by all historians) until the 1950s.

World War II and its aftermath produced both a religious revival and a movement of the whole political spectrum rightward. It would be useful if we came to understand that our left-right-center spectrum is not a standard imprinted on an iron bar in the National Bureau of Standards. Rather, it's more like the old-fashioned Turkish taffy at the New Jersey shore: the location of the center depends on the "pull" on the extremes. The revival came during World War II; it's sometimes called the Fifth Great Awakening. In 1940 only 49 percent of the population claimed to attend church regularly; by 1960 it was 69 percent. Despite spurts and ebbs, I would say that yes, it was a real awakening; yes, it was the fifth; and yes, it's still going on. It involved Eisenhower's God float in the 1953 inaugural, "under God" added to the Pledge of Allegiance, "In God We Trust" made the national motto. It involved the self-help guides of Norman Vincent Peale and his Catholic and Jewish counterparts, Fulton J. Sheen and Joshua Loth Liebman, and it involved Martin Luther King's renovation of the social gospel in support of racial equality.

But what surprised all of the leading social scientists was the rebound of fundamentalism instead of its demise. (After all, if Seymour Martin Lipset and Daniel Bell said it was going, it had to go!) It adapted and thrived. That adaptation is largely symbolized by its most famous figure, Billy Graham, who began as a classic fundamentalist, indeed, a protégé of William Bell Riley, the founder of the World's Christian Fundamentals Association. Graham went for a time to Bob Jones University and Wheaton College. Early on, he tottered on whether the Catholic Church was the whore of Babylon, and he still opposed Darwinism. But he became more sophisticated and somewhat more liberal, and began to call himself an "evangelical" rather than a fundamentalist. While he still believed that the return of Jesus was relatively imminent, he didn't announce dates.

A similar renovation was the adoption by Pentecostals of the more stylish name "Full Gospel" or ultimately "Charismatic." The key figure there was Oral Roberts.

Not all theological conservatives of the fifties were happy with this drift. Young Jerry Falwell, who founded the Thomas Road Baptist Church in 1956, said he was still a Separate Baptist and a fundamentalist.

By the time we get to the mid-1970s with this Fifth Great Awakening, there's a large constituency. How large depends on definition. Who knows? Forty, sixty, eighty million, ready to be politicized, moved rightward by the sixties—by the Vietnam War, the civil-rights movement, secularizing court decisions, changing sexual mores, a society that seemed to be moving left politically and culturally. Such changes would have seemed virtually inconceivable in the 1950s, when both the liberal left and the right clung to what Arthur Schlesinger called "the vital center," liberals forgetting that they ever had popular-front allies, conservatives forgetting that they ever had anti-Semitic and isolationist allies.

But in 1964 the new conservatism nominated Barry Goldwater, running for president against what some Republicans saw as Eisenhower's "dime-store New Deal." Goldwater emphasized economic and foreign-policy issues but promised to restore school prayer. He himself was a *pro forma* Episcopalian who we now know had arranged an illegal abortion for his daughter. His overwhelming defeat also brought in the most liberal Congress at least since the thirties. But it was the turmoil around the Vietnam War that opened up all sorts of questions about those in authority and authority itself.

And so we get "The Sixties," which I would say really extend from 1965 to 1973 or 1974. That's where we find the recent political origins of the New Christian Right. Leaders like Falwell and Robertson have cited various issues: court decisions ending prayer in schools and lifting restrictions on pornography, increased acceptance of gays, the legalization of most abortions with *Roe* v. *Wade*, the rise of militant feminism, the Internal Revenue Service's moving against Christian academies as segregationist. Whatever the specifics, I think we have to recognize in retrospect that the much-misunderstood sixties was not a radical era but a *polarized era*. Even in 1968, 43 percent of Americans still claimed to attend religious services weekly. That same year, George Wallace got over 13 percent of the presidential vote, and Nixon won as a moderate and champion of what he called "Square America." In 1972, Nixon got 80 percent of the theologically conservative vote and was the first Republican to carry the Catholic vote. The Right's part in this cannot be dismissed in Richard Hofstadter's terms as "a paranoid style." It's a response to real issues and real changes.

But a sense of cultural grievance doesn't automatically produce a national movement. To understand why the New Christian Right emerged as it did by

1980, we have to consider two things: the ironic role of Jimmy Carter, and the shrewd tactics of professional conservative Republican activists. Clearly there would have been some sort of religious mobilization in the late seventies through early eighties without Carter. After all, remember the shock and the outrage from religious conservatives over Betty Ford's endorsement of *Roe v. Wade* and her comment on *Sixty Minutes* that her teenage daughter might have a love affair, which generated more White House mail than even the Nixon pardon.

But Carter attracted attention to "born-again" Protestants and showed their political potential. There is still an enormous amount of confusion about Carter's religion. I would say that he had an evangelical style—he signed letters "Your brother in Christ"—but was a fairly sophisticated theologian, essentially a liberal. He didn't highlight that in 1976 for obvious reasons. His conversion experience in 1966 involved much less anguish than, for example, John Foster Dulles's return to Presbyterianism in the 1930s. Carter rejected dispensationalism, accepted evolution, and was much influenced by the neoorthodox theologian Reinhold Niebuhr.

All this information was readily available and could have been explained to the press by perhaps two thousand academics in the United States. But somehow it didn't get through, and the presidential race of 1976 between the most devout pair of candidates since McKinley and Bryan was covered very badly. Carter got an estimated 56 percent of the evangelical/fundamentalist vote and was the first Democrat to carry Southern Baptists since Truman. That is a major reason why he won. Unfortunately, that constituency over four years discovered that Carter was theologically and politically more liberal than anticipated, and that he was in that line of Baptists going back to Roger Williams and John Leland who believed in the firm separation of church and state.

All sorts of issues in the Carter years provided occasions for a Christian Right mobilization. My favorite is the 1980 White House Conference on Families, which Carter promised in 1976 to Catholics. It was initially called the White House Conference on the Family, but junior members in the administration said that was too exclusive. So it became the White House Conference on Families, to emphasize the "pluralistic" nature of families. Theological conservatives like Phyllis Schlafly and Connie Marshner mobilized on behalf of the "traditional" family, a women's movement as powerful as any on the left. Beverly LaHaye was involved. James Dobson was involved. The White House Conference on Families occurred no closer to the White House than Baltimore. Nonetheless, it provided a convenient reason for mobilization, and such shrewd political pros as Paul Weyrich and Richard Viguerie worked with Falwell, Robertson, and others to put together groups like the Moral Majority, the Christian Roundtable, and the Christian Voice—what soon became known as the New Christian Right.

This all attracted national attention at the famous 1980 "national affairs briefing" for twenty thousand evangelicals, where candidate Reagan said he "approve[d] of what you are doing." Exactly what he approved of seemed deliberately vague. Reagan was a devout, eclectic Christian, more reminiscent of Eisenhower than of Carter or Ford. He had a Catholic father and a Protestant mother. He was also influenced by Hollywood's flexible mores. He had a vague interest in Ba'hai, dispensationalism, the Shroud of Turin, and astrology. In other words, he was a *regular American*. Again, the fact that Reagan was not in the grip of the Christian Right could have been explained by several thousand scholars. He opposed abortion, favored school prayer, and endorsed "equal time" for the Bible and evolution as elementary fairness. But he said that God heard the prayers of the Jews, despite what the Southern Baptist leader Bailey Smith said, and he was proud of the nickname "Gipper," taken from a Protestant convert to Catholicism he had played in a movie.

Reagan's election, it seems to me, brought a second Brown Scare—books with titles like *God's Bullies* and *Holy Terror* about the evangelicals taking over; a major new liberal lobby, People for the American Way. The *Washington Post* ran a long article saying Reagan might launch a nuclear war to bring Armageddon closer.

Religious and political groups had a role in the mobilization that led to Reagan's win and the Democratic loss in the Senate, but I think it's quite clear in retrospect that the Christian Right became a very junior partner in this coalition. This was the most remarkable coalition since Roosevelt's, which went from segregationists to communists; Reagan's went from Jerry Falwell in Lynchburg to Frank Sinatra in Las Vegas. The Christian Right criticized the appointment of Sandra Day O'Connor to the Supreme Court and the establishment of diplomatic relations with the Vatican. But Reagan managed to keep the Right content for a while with symbolism and schmoozing. Walter Mondale tried in 1984 to present Reagan as a tool of the Christian Right and did even worse than Carter at the polls. By that point, 70 to 80 percent of the theological conservative vote was solidly Republican. By the late 1980s, amid the Swaggart and Bakker scandals, pundits were predicting the end of the Christian Right. It didn't happen.

It is in this context that Pat Robertson emerged, the son of a Democratic senator from Virginia, a secularist, as he explains, living in New York and New Haven in the 1950s, his moral decay evidenced by the Modigliani prints and Courvoisier he had in his apartment. Finally, returning to God, he became a Pentecostal, having a so-called second blessing. By the mid-1980s Robertson's Christian Broadcasting Network, established in 1959, had an estimated worth of $230 million. In 1988 Robertson spent as much as George Bush in the primary but wound up with only thirty-five delegates.

Although Bush had effectively wooed the Christian Right, he ultimately made fewer appointments among evangelicals than Reagan, did less schmoozing, and intermittently did things that annoyed the Christian Right in a big way—inviting gays to several White House signing ceremonies, for example, and supposedly acquiescing, though not very eagerly, in what Robertson called the "gay and lesbian agenda" of the National Endowment for the Arts. It was in this context that Robertson formed the Christian Coalition, which under Ralph Reed's guidance went up to probably two million members.

Ralph Reed, as everybody knows, is very smart. He has a Ph.D. in history, and he went back to abolition, temperance, William Jennings Bryan, and the civil-rights movement in attempting to build a usable past for the New Christian Right. He tried to broaden the appeal by using the vague term "people of faith," which some saw as the Right's "weasel word," akin to "people of color." I think the best guess is that post-Reed the Christian Coalition has about a million members. Some say six hundred thousand; Robertson still says two million. One million seems about right.

There are, of course, other figures around. Pat Buchanan certainly deserves mention. He may not be very popular, but he does seem to be the Christian Right's most popular Catholic, and he apparently got about a third of the evangelical vote in the 1992 primaries. He's also interesting intellectually in that he too finds a usable past in the 1930s, in Father Coughlin and the more bigoted of the noninterventionists, not to mention the Catholic Church pre–Vatican II.

Certainly no presidential couple since Roosevelt and Eleanor Roosevelt has been hated as much by religious conservatives as the Clintons. By all accounts the feeling was mutual. That's not at all surprising, and there are two serious points beyond anecdote here. One, the Clintons were without question culturally the most liberal presidential couple in history. Two, this is the latest version of an inter-Christian battle. The Clintons present themselves as serious Christians, and in a way they are. You may wonder, "How can that womanizer be a serious Christian searcher?" So was Lyndon! He probably was more of a womanizer and maybe more of a searcher. Hillary for her part is an old-fashioned Methodist social-gospeler who says she believes in the literal second coming of Christ; she also mixes in various self-help gospels like those of Tony Robins and Marianne Williams. In other words, she is, in lots of ways, a *regular American!*

Before I offer some speculations about the future, let me summarize briefly the main differences between the New Christian Right and the old one of the thirties and forties. First, Falwell, Robertson, and their compatriots accept the basic dispensationalist framework. If you want more of that, turn on your cable TV any hour of the day. They see ubiquitous signs of the Antichrist, but they no longer name names. A previous generation tried Napoleon III; it didn't work out. Mussolini —oops. So we're not getting Tony Blair as the Antichrist.

There was also more significant updating. Evangelical-fundamentalist culture has, like the rest of America, gotten culturally more liberal since the 1920s and 1930s. The sins are not dancing and alcohol; they are homosexuality and abortion. Unlike Gerald Winrod and many others in the 1930s, they no longer believe the Antichrist will be a Jew associated with the international Zionist conspiracy. Although fundamentalists and evangelicals believe in inerrant scripture, they have to interpret what they read in the Bible, too, and that is affected by other events. Among those events is the Holocaust, which brought about a rise in the *philo-Semitic* interpretation of the book of Revelation. Robertson still cooks up some anti-Semitic folklore, but he drops the Jewish part out of it. I think Buchanan qualifies as a real live anti-Semite, and I don't use that term casually at all.

There is also a move away from the kind of anti-Catholicism that was quite routine in the twenties and thirties. There is good evidence that in the 1950s anti-Catholic sentiment was on the rise in the United States, for reasons related to Catholic power. I think that's one of the reasons why Kennedy had particular problems. But you don't find anybody now, really, with the exception of Bob Jones III, who says that the pope represents the "scarlet whore" of the book of Revelation.

This New Christian Right is more economically conservative than the old, primarily because, I think, we do not have 25 percent unemployment and the poverty level is about 13 percent, not 33 percent. The thing that's least new, one that pundits have marveled at for a generation, is that Christian Right leaders have managed to find someone who knows how to operate a television camera. Actually, cultural Christian conservatives in the twenties used radio earlier than many other constituencies. I would say that for eighty years they have been far ahead of, say, organized labor in using new technologies as they come along.

What of the future? I would say that we will have a Christian Right with us in some form into the foreseeable future. And certainly the New Christian Right will continue to be a major player in the Republican Party. There's a broad evangelical culture on which to draw. In the mid-1980s, 62 percent of Americans had no doubt about Jesus' ultimate return; 80 percent expected to be judged by God personally; 40 percent still claimed to attend church, compared to 14 percent in Britain and 12 percent in France. Though the numbers wax and wane, that's a pretty solid core constituency. The issues also wax and wane. There was a time when I thought abortion as an issue might last as long as temperance and prohibition. Now I'm not sure.

But to describe these conflicts as a cultural war is both off base and irresponsible, an example of what the great sociologist David Riesman called the American penchant for "big talk." We all share it. I don't want to write an article called "The Cultural Tempest in a Teapot"! But I think we'd be better off if we referred to this as a cultural *shouting match*, which is an American way of life that we've had for a long, long time. We haven't had a cultural *war*, really, since the cavalry attacked the Mormons in the 1850s.

Here are a few more possibilities to keep in mind as you watch the visions and shifts usually missed by the secular eye. There's evidence of an evangelical, even fundamentalist drift in various New Agey directions, or theologically liberal directions, particularly among the young. This is not surprising; since the twenties, theological conservatives have not been immune to the lure of bright lights, big cities, and Sunday baseball. One of the interesting aspects will be how evangelical pop music—the so-called "heavy metal missionaries"—will actually work: will it keep young people in evangelical-fundamentalist cultures, or will it serve as a bridge to the more secular society? Who is co-opting whom? The power of the country to sop up dissidence of all sorts—here Daniel Bell and Seymour Martin Lipset were right—is very, very strong.

I don't think there will be much success in rallying culturally conservative Catholic voters to an alliance with Far Right Protestants. They are more liberal on issues such as race, and still suspicious.

Finally, as you deal with all this, don't lump together everybody who seems to be pious. Beware the still powerful Mencken and Sinclair Lewis stereotypes from the 1920s. Don't lump together the Christian Coalition, Christian Identity militia, and the Branch Davidians as religious nuts. The Branch Davidians—poor souls—if they had been supported by fundamentalists and had had a national constituency, instead of being called a cult, might still be alive. If Timothy McVeigh had remained religious he would now be running Catholic bingo games in upstate New York with his father. Think about what bigotry may mean. Bob Jones has a theological animus toward Catholicism: is that bigotry? If you look at his website, you have to dig pretty hard to find the anti-Catholic stuff. It's a lot like life—complicated.

DAVID SHRIBMAN: Over the years I have developed something of a healthy obsession with the Religious Right. Actually I prefer to use the phrase "religious conservatives." It seems a little more elegant and much less loaded with partisan rancor. I find the presence of religious conservatives at the very center of our politics one of the more fascinating aspects of that politics. Surely that presence has helped move the politics of religious conservatives to the center of our politics.

I have talked with hundreds of religious conservatives over the years and have found them to be almost uniformly pleasant, thoughtful, intelligent, committed, and patriotic. They do not look like revolutionaries, and for the most part they don't consider themselves revolutionaries. They're not insurrectionaries by nature or by inclination. They're not doing anything especially dangerous or subversive or even unusual. They're talking politics, organizing, and voting—doing the pretty unremarkable things that union members, small business owners, capitalists, art lovers, gun owners, refrigerator salesmen, and everybody else have been doing for decades. The difference is that religious conservatives have recently fomented, I believe, a quiet American revolution. That revolution is a combination of morality and politics. It helps explain the 1998 drive to impeach President Clinton, which began with outrage over the president's personal morality and was fueled by the demand of religious conservatives and others that their representatives in Congress punish the president.

But this is a revolution with a difference. Though religious conservatives have not taken control of the Republican Party and suffered a setback in the 1998 midterm elections, though they don't hold Hollywood in their thrall, and though a well-publicized effort to make inroads among blacks fizzled terribly, they have achieved something far more profound and potentially far more significant than any one of those things. Religious conservatives have changed the American conversation. They have changed who participates in that conversation and what assumptions are brought to bear on it. They have changed the tone of the conversation, and they've changed the content of the conversation. Eventually they may even change its conclusion. But it's the content that is the most important part.

Largely as a result of their efforts, President Clinton will go into history as the first president to be impeached in 130 years. Dozens of undecided Republican lawmakers decided to vote with impeachment forces, at least in part out of fear of being challenged by the Right and by religious-conservative candidates in Republican primaries. A powerful legislator only days from winning the House speakership, Robert Livingston of Louisiana, was forced out because of his own history of adultery, forced to announce his withdrawal from the position that in the twentieth century has been occupied by some of the most notorious womanizers in Washington history.

In the entire half-century course of postwar America, only three movements can lay claim to having changed the American conversation: the civil-rights movement, which made the social order in the South and the industrial cities of the North seem odious and downright *anti*social; the women's movement, which freed half the population from the burdens of tradition and stereotype and in the process changed the lives and expectations of the other half; and the religious-conservative movement, which like the others was spawned by a deep sense of ethics, caused tension among friends, prompted violent debate among commentators and ordinary people, turned the natural order on its head, and then sent even more waves coursing through American politics and American life.

In winning a subtle but real change in the key in which American politics is sung, religious conservatives also challenged the way historic social movements sweep across the country. The civil-rights movement and the women's movement originated generally from the left, the religious-conservative movement from the right. The first two began in the streets and the nation's homes before moving into its electoral politics; the Christian Right began in the political world and then muscled its way into national life. The first two movements shifted American values, while the Christian Right thrust the whole notion of values to the forefront of American life. Now these issues are not only *on* the table of politics, they *are* the table of politics. Now the word "values" passes the lips not only of conservatives but also of liberals, not only of Republicans but also of Democrats. Now the notion that religion is at the center of national life and not at its periphery is voiced not only by Republicans but also by Democrats. Democrats cannot afford to ignore the values politics that the religious conservatives have forced the Republican Party to talk about.

Religious conservatives stir unusually strong passions. Opponents try to portray them as being on the fringe, but they have fought their way to the center of American political life. No accounting of American politics today can fail to include them. Like union members before them, religious conservatives built their power by understanding the nature of power. I once had a long discussion about this with an unusually sharp observer of Republican politics, Patrick Kelley. He's the managing editor of the *Emporia Gazette*, a Kansas paper that to all of us is a storied and beloved institution, once edited by William Allen White. Here's what Pat Kelley said: "They didn't change American politics, they *took advantage* of American politics. After Vietnam and after Watergate, nobody wanted to work for the old parties, and there was a vacuum for them to fill. All they had to do was to attend meetings and vote themselves into office. They're doing their politics better than anybody else. That formula found big results in Kansas." Religious conservatism may have a Southern face, but right now it has a Midwestern soul. And nowhere is the strength of the Christian Right greater than in the Grain Belt. While the *Emporia Gazette* trumpeted a sound, traditional, and respectable brand of Republicanism, religious conservatives in Lyon County noticed when members of the GOP Old Guard retired or moved or died, and they swiftly filled the vacuum. Once the stealth phase ended, the real battle began. Politics increasingly became a struggle over abortion. Soon Kansas, where blood had been shed over the moral issue of slavery in the middle of the nineteenth century, became a modern political battleground.

There's no denying the role of the Religious Right in the Republican Party as one of the signal developments of American politics in the last quarter century. But how much influence is enough? How much is too much? How close should the worlds of religion and politics be? Can people of faith separate their religious beliefs from their political beliefs? Should they? Should they have to? Are religious conservatives a threat to the political system, or are they its salvation? These questions loom large in the political landscape.

Religious conservatives now argue that politics is not an event but a process. After the tumult of the past dozen years, they themselves are clearly, indisputably, part of that process.

Discussion

JEAN ELSHTAIN: Just for clarification, Leo: You talked about the influx of Catholics and Jews and how strange our grandmothers seemed to people who were already here, and then you said, unless I missed something, that the Protestant response to this was the new theology. Are you arguing a causal relationship?

LEO RIBUFFO: No, I was just giving the social context of why there was so much upset. It wasn't solely an intellectual thing.

JEAN ELSHTAIN: So the new theology is not a response to integrationists; these tendencies were already at work in Protestantism?

LEO RIBUFFO: It was the context that made things scarier to them.

JEAN ELSHTAIN: Now a question for David: I don't disagree at all at your putting in the trio—civil rights, feminism, and religious conservatism—as movements that profoundly shifted the conversation. But I wonder if in some ways the story of religious conservatives isn't even more remarkable.

The civil-rights movement and feminism, after at least a period of time, had what we usually call "elite opinion" on their side. But religious conservatives have been bucking elite opinion and have in fact been often anathematized. Isn't that a rather important difference?

DAVID SHRIBMAN: Yes, but the civil-rights movement and the women's movement were mounted by or on behalf of outsiders. I think that this is less so of the religious-conservative movement.

JEAN ELSHTAIN: That makes sense to me regarding the civil-rights movement but not feminism. What do you mean when you say that the women's movement was mounted by outsiders?

DAVID SHRIBMAN: I mean before 1919, when women were not able to vote.

JEAN ELSHTAIN: I thought you were talking about the more recent wave of feminism, which was clearly managed by very educated, upper-middle-class women, primarily from the Northeast, although it became a bicoastal conversation early on. I know a lot of women who said, "This is not a movement for women; this is a movement on behalf of this particular socioeconomic group and has nothing to do with us or our lives." So it strikes me that the analogy with civil rights doesn't quite work there with feminism.

STEPHEN CARTER: I think you're both right about the difference in the elite reaction, but it strikes me that you can explain that simply by looking at two things. First, the issues themselves are very different. Even if we look at the civil-rights movement and say that in various parts of their movement the texts are the same—I'm thinking for instance of the Christian gospel—still what's at stake is different for different constituencies.

DAVID SHRIBMAN: Economically?

STEPHEN CARTER: No, politically or culturally. A few years ago when Oliver North, the Iran/Contra hero, was running for Senate in Virginia, I got a telephone call from a reporter who was doing a story about North's candidacy. She had discovered that there were people *praying* for him to win. What did I think about that? I told her I didn't think anything about it, one way or the other. But she thought this was peculiar—not outrageous, not a church/state separation problem, but just very odd that people would pray for something like that.

If your religious faith in any tradition is very deep, one of the things that it seems to me *has* to be true is that you are a different person because of that faith. It changes the way you look at the world, changes the things you value. So it's not plausible that people of deep religious faith could, no matter how hard they tried consciously, separate their faith from their political views. Now, surveys have found that people who participate more in their church also tend, apparently, to vote more Republican. And so one wonders, when people express strong discomfort with involvement by Christian Right people or other people with strong faith, is this really about issues or is it just partisanship?

LEO RIBUFFO: I agree that it's not simply issues.

STEPHEN CARTER: A lot of discomfort is expressed, by the elites on campuses and by political commentators and journalists, with the idea that heavily organized religious people using religious language talk about political issues. Do you sense this is a general discomfort with religiosity?

DAVID SHRIBMAN: In trying to explain the concept "compassionate conservatism" Marvin Olasky points out something about the Establishment Clause. He says that the Founders, or the caucus that voted to approve the First Amendment, conceived of a freedom *of* religion and not a freedom *from* religion. But since the 1960s—and the school-prayer decision was probably the most visible symbol of this—the prevailing elite thought has been that government and society should be free *from* religion, rather than free to foster religion. I think that gets to what you're talking about. There is indeed an unease among elites about spirituality, and more than spirituality, religiosity.

JEAN ELSHTAIN: There's an interesting division, in regard to the First Amendment, between those who emphasize disestablishment and those who emphasize free exercise. Religious conservatives are sure to emphasize free exercise and to resent constraints on that. But, David, you said that the revolution is a combination of morality and politics, and I think that's different from religiosity. What people may be wary of is that combination of politics and morality, given the question, how do you define morality? We're not just talking about a religious faith, we're talking about what the moral code is, and that can be interpreted very differently.

DAVID SHRIBMAN: I think that journalists live in a peculiarly isolated world in which honest and open expressions of religious belief are discouraged—but I see a lot of shaking heads.

JAY TOLSON: I think one of the dangers of historicizing the subject as Leo brilliantly did is suggesting that the religious experience has always been the same. It hasn't. Religion has become less and less about observance and more and more about belief and the moral complex that goes with belief. To some extent, that is the effect of the "Protestantizing" of all faiths in our culture. It puts a huge emphasis on the creedal aspects, on what I believe.

JODY HASSETT: Leo mentioned the Branch Davidians, and it got me thinking, well, yes, most conservative Christians would not theologically identify with them, but certainly the specter of jackbooted thugs did contribute to the circle-up-the-wagons mentality. Today there are so many conservative-Christian subcultural things—a big increase in home schooling, Christian diets, banks, rock, and now the Cal Thomas cultural thing about how to engage politically—that I'm wondering, Leo, how this fits into your view of conservative Christians.

LEO RIBUFFO: I think that's two points. On the Branch Davidians: afterwards theological conservatives and fundamentalists saw them as victims of the jackbooted thugs. Before they were cultists. All I'm saying is if the Branch Davidians had had any wider support in society, they would be alive. The Waco siege was, I believe, the largest number of civilians killed by the federal government in this century. The president of the United States said that they were "a bunch of crazy people who murdered themselves." The FBI, trying to figure out what David Koresh was talking about in translating the seals of the book of Revelation, thought they were like the seals at Sea World. Had this been *any other group* we could think of, had this been one guy shot by Guiliani's police, the mainstream would not have forgotten it.

As to the separate Christian culture, it seems to me not so different from parish Catholic schools when I was growing up. I think there will be the same pressures and pulls to assimilate over the long term and counterpressures to be more separate, to try to preserve the purity.

JODY HASSETT: John Green and others have suggested that the main voting issues for conservative Christians in the next ten years will be same-sex marriage and other kinds of homosexual rights. What abortion was to the nineties, gay rights will be to this decade. It seems to be the one area where conservative Protestants and Catholics are indeed coming together and mobilizing politically.

DAVID SHRIBMAN: But I think that abortion is still going to trump just about any other issue like that, in part because of the defenselessness of the victims and in part because of the heavy authoritarian potential for the government in this kind of decision. Who was worse, the fascists in Spain or the fascists in Italy?

DAVID PLOTZ: I'm changing the subject slightly. I've been reading the *Left Behind* novels, and I wonder what is behind the fascination with dispensationalism now. Why is it so popular? Is there any political stake involved in that popularity?

JAMES GUTH: May I comment on that? I've been writing on some of these topics for a while, and I think there are two things to say about dispensationalism today. First, its current manifestations have moved dramatically away from the central core of the dispensational tradition theologically. Historically, dispensationalism was connected to some degree of *non*politicization, in part because of the view of the futility of human effort. More recently, the premillennial dispensationalists were at the core of the Christian Right, and adherence to those beliefs was associated with very strong Republicanism and conservatism on social issues, and ironically a greater propensity for political activism.

JOHN LEO: There's a tendency at conferences like this to get to the point where we view religious conservatives as garish loonies. I don't think they're loonies, and I don't think it's an exaggeration to call what's going on a cultural war. Leo brought up the 1980 controversy over "the family/families." That was a very crucial debate, in my opinion. It wasn't just about the singular word and the plural and making room for single mothers. It amounted to a radical attack on the traditional family. And I think twenty years later that those people who reacted in 1980 to that little burp of change were on to something. Their entire value system, in their opinion, is under assault—honor, patriotism, family, work, self-discipline, right across the board. Yet we blame the religious Christians for reacting to attacks on their value system. I think it's folly to pretend that issues like this will go away.

Religious conservatives tend not to be represented at conferences like this. They don't get hired in journalism. I think the massive lack of sympathy for their point of view colors journalism and to some extent the academic world. We need to talk more about the elite worldview and what it's doing to religious people. I think we've gone too far in kicking them around. The contempt that a lot of us have for perfectly sincere religious people has gone too far.

PEGGY WEHMEYER: I happen to be a very unusual person in that I'm in network television and I attended an evangelical church when I was hired. The Associated Press spread all over the country a quote from my boss saying, "We really struggled with the idea of hiring a Southern born-again Christian." Can you imagine thinking, "There are forty, sixty, eighty million of these people and one slipped into the newsroom—it's terrifying!" People seemed to think that I must be a biased, shallow, unsophisticated swamp woman from the South because I attended an evangelical church. As journalists we analyze and talk about and write about these huge groups of people without really knowing any of them. I think that religious conservatives are not represented in our coverage of their issues in the same way that, say, gays and lesbians are represented on gay and lesbian issues.

MICHAEL CROMARTIE: That's one reason why we're having these meetings: to help educate journalists about religion in American life.

E. J. DIONNE: I found that when you tell somebody in the newsroom that you go to church, you discover that there are a lot of closet religious people. Back to a point that Leo made: I'm not sure I agree entirely that the press did such an awful job of covering Jimmy Carter—even if he was, as Leo has said, seen too much early on as a Martian for participating in a faith shared by tens of millions of Americans. For example, we certainly heard about Carter as a fan of Reinhold Niebuhr; that came out during the campaign.

LEO RIBUFFO: I'm not saying that the coverage of Carter in general was worse than the coverage of Ford. The oddity of Carter as religious, that came across. With Ford, here was a guy who played football, who skied all his life; he had bad knees in his sixties, and once in a while he stumbled and fell down. Did anybody talk to a bone doctor about why this was no big deal? Ford was the guy who fell down, and Carter was the guy with the strange religious relatives. I thought the press took the easy line on both.

DAVID SHRIBMAN: My memory of it is that Carter was treated like an alien being from another planet.

MICHAEL CROMARTIE: John Leo, do you remember how Carter was covered? How did you cover him?

JOHN LEO: We thought he was an exotic loon. I was at *Time* at the time; we put him on the cover looking like Jack Kennedy, and that got him elected!

LEO RIBUFFO: I want to say something as a historian. We're kicking around a perennial American historical issue, and that is this: to what degree is this an extraordinarily diverse country and to what degree is there a consensus? Conflict to a manageable degree is normal in America. The conservatives among us who see or want to see some unbroken line of respect for religion down to the 1960s, after which it all went to hell, need to realize that such a view simply does not fit the historical record. There were fights over disestablishing the state church in Massachusetts in the 1830s. In the late 1880s the problem was Republican politician Robert Ingersoll, who was also a prominent agnostic speaker. I wish you all luck in fighting it out, but as a historian I swear to you that these issues are not going to go away. There was no golden age, and there probably won't be one soon.

ALISSA RUBIN: It's not that people don't respect evangelical beliefs, but that when evangelicals propound them in the political arena and suggest changes in laws that then affect people who don't hold their beliefs, it seems impossible for there not to be arguments. Because we're a nation of law, we're going to come back to the Supreme Court and to Congress, and these questions are going to be argued out there. We need to keep adding information to these debates but not necessarily resisting conflict. There are people with very different ideas about the right way to live.

STEPHEN CARTER: That sounds true, except that I just spent the past couple of years reading proslavery and antislavery sermons from the late eighteenth and early nineteenth centuries, and that's exactly what all proslavery preachers said: "These darn Northern preachers, trying to impose their religious visions on us. Can't they just let us live the way we want to and they can live the way they want to? Why do they have to go changing the laws?" Change in law doesn't really get us anywhere. The conflicts are still going to be here, and somebody has to win.

LEO RIBUFFO: The Civil War was a *real* war. I think the issue we've been discussing is a lot closer to Prohibition. In the late nineteenth century the Women's Christian Temperance Union was the largest women's organization in the world, and probably the most powerful. And temperance wrenched the country apart, probably more than abortion has done.

FRANKLIN FOER: Leo, when you were giving your history of the Old Christian Right, it seems to me that you didn't pause at the two points that are traditionally considered the turning points in the movement: the 1925 Scopes trial, after which evangelicals disappeared from public life, and then the 1970s prayer disputes, where they suddenly reappeared. I have evangelical friends who tell me that the impact of the Scopes trial is usually exaggerated.

LEO RIBUFFO: I don't think it makes sense to refer to "left," "right," and "center" before the 1930s, when that terminology first began to be used. But certainly there were cultural conservatives—religious among them—before the Scopes trial, and they didn't all go home and lock themselves away right after the trial. They were all still around and still active in the thirties and forties. And I did deal with the seventies, except I call them still the sixties. I would say it's that period from 1964 and 1965 to 1973 and 1974.

FRANKLIN FOER: My second point is that I think we could sum up the differences between the Old Christian Right and the New Christian Right by saying that the movement was kind of bourgeois-fied, that the members absorbed a lot of middle-class and bourgeois values.

LEO RIBUFFO: I wouldn't put it that way. I think that before they were bourgeois-fied they became more tolerant. The two go together. But I also think that World War II had an impact on religious conservatives as on all other Americans. We've been able to say, "Look what intolerance can lead to."

WILLIAM MCGURN: On a related point, I think that evangelical leaders like Chuck Colson are way ahead of their people in their view of Catholics. If you look at the novels by Beverly LaHaye's husband, you find the Pope as the An-tichrist and a member of the Trilateral Commission and so on. After Colson signed that statement with Richard Neuhaus on a sort of evangelical/Catholic rapprochement, two evangelicals criticized Colson for doing so on the basis that Catholics are not Christians.

LEO RIBUFFO: I would say that for well over a hundred years Catholic/Protestant rank-and-file relations have been fairly calm. The Christian Protestant Right even in the thirties came to the discovery that the Pope was better than Franklin Roo-sevelt. Politics has always been complex. In the late 1890s there was a group called the American Protective Association, which McKinley courted very shrewdly. When you joined it you pledged not to join a union with Catholics, go on strike with a Catholic, vote for a Catholic. McKinley courted it. Then he appointed a Catholic attorney general, promoted him to the Supreme Court, and for the first time a Catholic took part in the inaugural.

MELANA VICKERS: Much of the Christian Right remains in ethnically homoge-neous pockets of the South, whereas Catholics are ethnically very diverse, as are many mainstream Protestant groups. I wonder what the Christian Right view of ethnic minorities has been—not racial minorities but Italians, Eastern Europeans, Jews to an extent.

LEO RIBUFFO: "Ethnic group" is another term we don't get in common use until the 1950s. A number of groups that are now lumped together with other white groups used to be considered pure ethnic groups. Norwegian and Swedish Lutherans in Minnesota, for instance, were once considered quite distinctive. There was also a time when groups we now put together as "white Protestants" were divided theo-logically as well as ethnically. Theologically liberal and theologically conservative Lutherans would have had their own ethnic conflicts. On the whole, I would say that the members of the Christian Right who are Northern European—sometimes self-described as Nordics or the Nordic-Celtic civilization—were pretty firmly in the vanguard of anti-immigrant nativism and were probably disproportionately anti-Semitic, though that's hard to judge, down through the 1940s.

I think it is safe to say that today anti-Semitism is quite small on the Christian Right, as it is among Americans generally.

DAVID SHRIBMAN: Wisconsin with a .5 percent Jewish population has two Jewish senators, and one Jew has succeeded another Jew in the senate in Minnesota, which also has a less than 1 percent population of Jews.

ELLIOTT ABRAMS: We've been talking about evangelicals in a certain sense as if there were a flat, cohesive population group that was there a hundred years ago and is there now. But clearly, over time, it's not the same group. So what is it? Either we're talking now about the great-grandchildren of the people of the 1890s or we're talking about a self-renewing group, one that gains members every day because, say, somebody whose father was a Methodist secularist becomes a born-again evangelical. How much of this is a genetic inheritance from your family and how much of it is voluntarism?

LEO RIBUFFO: Part of the confusion is that nineteenth-century evangelical Protestantism in general includes just about all Protestants. It's replenished by immigration. I don't know the percentage that is directly descended from the same population in the 1890s.

ELLIOTT ABRAMS: Replenished by immigration from where?

LEO RIBUFFO: From the rest of the world.

ELLIOTT ABRAMS: You can't replace Southern Baptists by immigration from Korea.

LEO RIBUFFO: But you could replace a lot of Pentecostals with Koreans. Granted, I have yet to see a Korean major figure in the New Christian Right, but if you go to Aimee Semple McPherson's church in Los Angeles, you find it's almost all Hispanic and Korean.

ELLIOTT ABRAMS: Evangelicals as a religious group used to be, probably even twenty-five years ago, white. Now the constituency is becoming more and more nonwhite.

LEO RIBUFFO: The black religious tradition is too complicated for us to get into. There are some theological overlaps, but on the whole it's a separate movement. But yes, evangelical/fundamentalist Protestantism is becoming less white.

JAMES GUTH: Let me say a little about the question of where evangelicals have come from. If you look at the entire evangelical tradition you see lots of elements.

You see Korean Presbyterians—who are for the most part very evangelical—and other Asian Christians who are an increasing influence on the evangelical community. Also, a lot of the rapidly growing evangelical denominations have a high proportion of former Catholics and former mainline Protestants who have experienced some sort of religious conversion. If you look at data on religious migration from the General Social Survey, you find that over the years Americans are not nearly as stable in their religious homes as you might think. A subtle movement goes on continuously. It used to be fed by social mobility—the old pattern of once you learned to read you were no longer a Baptist, you were a Methodist—but that doesn't work very much anymore. A bigger cause today is theological perspective. You're a United Methodist, you discover that United Methodists don't stand up for historical biblical beliefs, and you go somewhere else.

KENNETH WOODWARD: Are the children of evangelicals likely to become evangelicals themselves?

JAMES GUTH: They have a much higher retention rate than other Christian groups, even Catholics. So there's both more retention and more conversion. That's why the evangelical community has retained its one-quarter share of the population over the past few decades.

LYNN NEARY: There's a thread coming in and out of this conversation about why it is that people feel threatened by or concerned about the Religious Right, about conservative Christians being politically active. I've been covering religion now full-time for six years, and what I'm wondering is, what happens when a theological belief translates directly into a political belief? In regard to these issues like homosexuality and abortion, there's a certain point where the discussion really ends. There can be no discussion beyond that point on certain beliefs because they are such deeply held matters of faith. A person believes what he believes because it says so in the Bible, or because that's what Catholic teaching says.

When you take that into a larger political context, where do you go with a discussion about abortion or homosexuality? It becomes problematical when the political belief is the same as the theological belief.

LEO RIBUFFO: There is this tension in what Americans think they want. On the one hand, they want people to stand up for principles; on the other hand, they don't want too much noise and trouble. "We're nice Americans, and we're supposed to compromise." I would say for myself that if people disagree with me on principles, I tell them my principles. That's as legitimate a social fight as any other.

The Rights and Wrongs of Religion in Politics   8
A Conversation with Stephen Carter
and Jeffrey Rosen

STEPHEN CARTER: I come to these issues of religion and politics as a scholar, but also as an evangelical Christian. I didn't start out as an evangelical; I became one in the course of writing about law and religion and politics. And so although I try to maintain a tone of scholarly neutrality, some of it has become personal in a way that I wouldn't have expected fifteen years ago.

I'm going to begin by telling a story by way of introduction to a theory I want to advance about religion in public life. Fannie Lou Hamer was a powerful and marvelous black woman who was the guiding spirit, inspiration, and founder of the Mississippi Freedom Democratic Party. That party was founded in the early 1960s as a counterweight to the state's then lily-white Democratic Party. In 1964, the Mississippi Freedom Democratic Party threatened a credentials fight at the Democratic National Convention against the lily-white slate. Lyndon Johnson, who was going to be nominated, wanted the convention to look like a coronation; he wanted no bumps on the road to his nomination for his first run for president in his own right. So when the credentials fight was threatened, he sent his vice-president-in-waiting, Hubert Humphrey, to negotiate with Mrs. Hamer, giving him explicit orders: find out what she wants and give it to her.

Humphrey met with Mrs. Hamer in a hotel room in Atlantic City and asked her what she wanted. "I want the beginning of a new Kingdom right here on earth," she replied. Humphrey hadn't thought of that yet; that wasn't one of the things that Johnson had empowered him to offer. So he took a different tack. "Well, you know, I've been fighting for civil rights for a long time, since before it was fashionable," he said, which was true; he had made a pivotal speech in support of civil rights at the 1948 Democratic convention. "It would be really important to have me in the White House as a strong voice for racial equality," Humphrey continued, "and if I can't reach a deal with you, I'm not going to become vice president."

Fannie Lou Hamer had survived beating and torture in a city jail for insisting on her constitutional rights, and she was not particularly impressed. She answered, "Senator Humphrey, I know lots of people in Mississippi who have lost their jobs for trying to register to vote. I had to leave the plantation where I worked in Sunflower County. Now if you lose your job as vice president because you do what is right, because you help the Mississippi Freedom Democratic Party, everything will be all right. God will take care of you. But if you take the nomination this way, why, you will never be able to do any good for civil rights, for poor people, for peace, or any of those things you talk about. Senator Humphrey, I'm gonna pray to Jesus for you."

So that was the end of the negotiation. Humphrey went back to Lyndon Johnson and reported that he had failed. But Johnson was a master of politics, and he knew that for every inspirational leader, there are plenty of pilot fish swimming in the leader's way, people who are in the organization as much to serve their own ambition as to serve some vision. So he went to Mrs. Hamer's various lieutenants and horse traded: You can get this project; your wife can get a position on this commission. As a result they voted, in effect, to turn Mrs. Hamer into a figurehead and then to accept the shameful compromise under which the party was allowed to have just *one seat* on the floor of the convention where the lily-white delegation was seated. And that was pretty much the end of the Mississippi Freedom Democratic Party.

I tell this story for two reasons. One is that it shows the limits, not so much of religious advocacy as such, but of action based on deep religious conviction when it runs up against the wall of practical politics. The other reason is that it shows what can happen to religiously radical movements when they become involved in the electoral side of politics. Now, I'm an avid defender of religious voices, whatever tradition they may be from, in our public life, on policy issues, and so on. I am a big believer in that. However, I want to draw a distinction between two different ways of conceptualizing the politics we talk about when we talk about religious voices in politics. One of those, the one that Fannie Lou Hamer ran up against, is electoral politics, the actual process of selecting those who will hold the coercive power of the state in their hands. The other kind of politics is the politics of philosophers, the politics of Madison, the politics of conversation, dialogue, self-governance, what we do as a people in trying to come to a public consensus or at least to a public decision. While it is a good and deeply American thing for these religious voices to be raised along with all the other voices in society in our *conversational* politics, it can be a dangerous thing when religious voices become involved in *electoral* politics—dangerous, I want to propose, not so much to democracy or to America, but to the religious institutions or people who seek that involvement.

About a half century ago, C. S. Lewis wrote a well-known essay entitled "A Meditation on the Third Commandment." Lewis never quotes or describes the third commandment, since he was writing for a literate audience in an era when, if you were well educated, you would know the Ten Commandments. The essay was written in opposition to a proposal by a group of Tories to break away from the Conservative Party and form a Christian party. Lewis was against attaching the word Christian to the name of a party. A couple of his arguments are quite salient to our subject here today.

One of the arguments we can summarize by saying, though he didn't put it quite this way, that a Christian party was, for Lewis, an oxymoron. On the one hand, he said, if it were truly *Christian*, it would preach the whole gospel and nobody would vote for it. On the other hand, if it were truly a *party*, it would mute some parts of the gospel and exaggerate others or make some stuff up in order to win elections, and therefore not be truly Christian. And so his biggest objection was that a Christian party was an oxymoron.

But Lewis had another objection. He felt that the temptations that come when you hold the levers of power in your hands are enormous, and for Christians—he could have broadened this to people of deep faith in general—could be extraordinarily dangerous. The temptation is not just a temptation of *using* the power but also of *confusing* what God wants with what you want and have the power to do. Stanley Hauerwas made the point that the Inquisition became possible when the medieval church gave up the power to die for its beliefs in exchange for the power to *kill* for its beliefs. You lose something precious when you hold in your hand the power to *force* other people to do something. And I suggest that what you lose is the power of prophetic ministry, the power of standing outside the structures of authority and pointing out what you think they're doing wrong. What's quite striking about the prophets of Israel is that they stood *outside* the corridors of power. They tried to tell the king what to do, no question, but they didn't try to say, "I'm going to be king."

Now why should that matter? Well, one of the reasons why deep religious conviction is valuable to democracy is that it leads to genuine diversity. A religion that doesn't change who we are and how we look at the world is hardly a religion. We're different persons because of what we believe than we would be otherwise. The more religious diversity you have, the more centers of deeply profound meaning you have, the more genuinely diverse your society is going to be. When I say "genuinely diverse" I mean diverse in the sets of ideas that are brought to the table. The very fact that people's fundamental principles differ sharply leads to having a variety of ideas in play.

The main reason why a lot of evangelical parents, including myself, become so concerned about what goes on in the public schools has less to do with the desire to proselytize than with the desire to protect. It has less to do with wanting to make other people's children more religious than with keeping one's own children from being seduced by secularism. In my travels I've talked to a lot of parents in small communities in the Bible Belt. When they talk, for example, of prayer in public schools, they don't advocate classroom prayer because they want everyone else to learn their religion. It's because they raise their own children to believe that everything that's important in life is through prayer, and for the state to say "This is important but it excludes prayer" is an affront to their religion. I still think they're wrong on the merits, and I'm still against organized classroom prayer, but I don't think their position is ridiculous or irresponsible.

Similarly, parents who fight against teaching evolution are not, I think, trying to proselytize. I myself analyzed some of those cases that way in some of my early writings, but I was mistaken. Instead, those parents are trying to have their children taught what they believe to be true. A large proportion of Americans believe, or at least say they believe, that the Genesis account of creation is a literally true historical account of how the world came about. Parents want their children taught what they think is true, and not taught what they think is false.

All that is by way of protecting what I would describe as their ability to create centers of meaning, centers of understanding, that are distinct from what they see coming from the dominant culture. It may be that the white evangelicals who backed, say, Jerry Falwell, have a different vision of what they want to protect than the black evangelicals who backed Martin Luther King. Yet while substantively the visions may be different, analytically there's a similarity in that both are trying to create a world in which they can comfortably raise their children. In both educational theory and political theory, some voices tell us that this a very bad thing for parents to do. This theory, which goes back as far as Horace Mann, holds that it's very important to use the public schools as a way of giving children diverse ideas and diverse experiences and of teaching them a critical style of thinking. These are things they will need in order to become responsible adults. They can then make sensible choices about religion rather than having religion imposed upon them.

To a lot of religious parents this is terrifying stuff. Again, for evangelicals—and this is true of Judaism as well—there is not a sense of religion as choice. God chooses *you*; you do not choose God. The notion that you can decide what to do is contrary to a religious message that many parents are trying to teach their children. Now that does not go to the issue of who's right and who's wrong; it only helps to explain why so many of these battles are so hard fought. People are trying to protect their religious visions. When they feel you are pressing on what's most important to them, they're naturally going to press back, and I think that a lot of the fervor we see today in some of these conservative organizations is a pressing back.

But there's a problem with these organizations, and to talk about that problem I need to go back to Fannie Lou Hamer. As recently as the 1950s, it was still very respectable for black Americans to be Republicans. While my parents were both Democrats, my grandparents on both sides were Republicans back for generations. The 1964 Civil Rights Act was actually supported by a higher proportion of Republicans than Democrats in Congress. So what happened? The Republican Party's opposition to a lot of initiatives that blacks thought were important in the years since 1964 is certainly part of it. But you also have to look at what happened to black clergy.

One of the striking things about the great sermons of Martin Luther King— not the "I Have a Dream" speech but a lot of the other great sermons—is a remarkable radical energy, a vision of a very different America, an America built on radically different premises than the America he saw and the America we have. It's a vision that never comes to fruition even though, or perhaps precisely because, the black clergy make the choice, and it is a choice, to become part of the electoral coalition of the Democratic Party. As the black leadership and clergy get more involved in the Democratic Party, what you see is a falling off of radical energy; radicals get pushed to the sidelines, and pragmatists take control. Now from the point of view of politics that is a good thing. You want pragmatists to control. Politics is the art of the possible; you want compromisers. That makes sense once you make that choice to be part of a political coalition. But it comes at a price. A lot of black preachers I've talked to in recent years have complained about the things they do not feel free to say in the pulpit because such things are against the interests of the Democratic Party or positions that Democrats take.

I believe that the same thing is going to happen or is already happening to the energy of a lot of white radical evangelicals, radical perhaps for different causes. Take for example the Christian Coalition. It continues to be a reliable building block of the Republican electoral coalition and a relatively powerful entity in the primary battles. But something interesting has happened.

In 1995 the Christian Coalition published with much fanfare its ten-point "Contract With the American Family," presented, as its then director Ralph Reed said, as "ten suggestions, not the Ten Commandments." There are two striking things about these "suggestions." The first is that there is nothing striking about them. That is to say, these ten suggestions could have emerged from any moderately conservative think tank inside the Beltway. There's nothing distinctly Christian about them, whatever that might mean. There is also nothing "Restorationist" about them when you think of the Restorationist theology of the early Pat Robertson and the early Christian Coalition folks.

The second thing that is striking about them is the arguments pressed on their behalf. There is, as I recall, one biblical verse cited briefly in the discussion of one of the ten. Otherwise the argument is stated entirely in ordinary political language. Now immediately a lot of liberal critics say, "Well, it's subterfuge. There's a radical position working back there that they're just not saying." Maybe that's true. Could be. But the fact that they feel the need to *resort* to subterfuge is an indication of how far the group has been successfully subverted by its involvement in politics. The "Contract With the American Family" is written by a group that is blamed for hurting the Republican Party and wants to move into the mainstream, wants, in Ralph Reed's famous phrase, "a place at the table."

Now, Ralph Reed took a lot of flak from his right wing for this document. And note that his defense is really quite innocuous. He said things like, "Well, a lot of religious people care about the capital gains tax." That's true, but the conservative evangelical who gets this thing in the mail might understandably think, "I don't need them to help me with the capital gains tax issue." In this document the Christian Coalition largely abandoned the so-called social issues that helped to give it birth. Whether subterfuge or not, whether it marks the solidifying or the fragmenting of the group, it does exemplify what C. S. Lewis was talking about: that once you get involved in politics on the side you want to win, suddenly you find you can compromise.

Dietrich Bonhoeffer wrote that "compromise is the enemy of the Word." He wrote that, of course, at a time when the German Protestant churches were under pressure, and most of them were happily moving to become in effect the Nazi Church. And so I don't want to lift that out of historical context. But Bonhoeffer was, I think, also making a richer theological point: that there is something about pure doctrine, as opposed to malleable doctrine, that ought to be attractive to a person of deep faith. What happens too often in politics is that the doctrine gets softened in the effort to win, or in the effort just to stay at the table.

That's a dangerous thing for religion, but it's a good thing for political organizations. If you view the Christian Coalition as primarily a political organization, then you can see this as a good thing. But to the extent that you view it as a religious organization, there's a problem. There's a problem when you alter what you previously said was not negotiable, or soft-pedal things previously important in order to attain a particular political goal. That was what C. S. Lewis was worried about.

Another point in Lewis's essay is about the other problem with a "Christian party": the allies it has to take on in order to win. You take on allies because you think they're with you on a particular issue; then they disagree with you sharply on another issue, and only then do you realize what a terrible mistake you've made because of the rush to win.

In practice this has a couple of implications. The first is that people who are concerned about radical religious energy in politics—who think it's a bad thing—should be glad for the Christian Coalition, should be glad that there are ways to take that energy, tame it, mainstream it, and fit it into the electoral coalition of the existing political framework. The people who should be upset that there is a Christian Coalition are people who think that the religious voice in politics in its genuine, authentic self is very important and ought to be liberated, ought to be untamed.

The second implication is that if anything like what happened to many black clergy happens also to white clergy on the evangelical side, then we're going to see a great loss of energy at the level of leadership. It's not clear what will happen at the level of followership. Maybe a lot of radical energy will be left floating around out there and not really represented by the politically connected leadership. This is a more dangerous situation because of the potential for demagoguery in trying to take advantage of that. But it's probably less dangerous than it seems, because the long history of America shows that once you've been organized you're in trouble; you're bound to be co-opted sooner or later.

The other point I want to make has to do with the idea that maybe religious conservatives, instead of trying to persuade the dominant culture to be more accommodating of their deeply held convictions, should back off into separate institutions. I find it quite intriguing to think about the retreat, if you will, of religious energy into parallel institutions, in part because I owe a debt, in my work, to Roger Williams. For all his bad qualities, Roger Williams had some really good ideas. He is probably the best American source to point to for the origin of our practice of separation of church and state. The "wall of separation" image comes from his idea of a "hedgerow" that separates the garden from the wilderness, the garden being the place where the people of faith would congregate to hear the voice of God and the wilderness being the world. The wall protected them from the wilderness. They needed that protection so that they could reason together without interference and live the lives God would want them to live without having the larger society impinging on them in any important way. Roger Williams's garden wall was to protect the garden from the wilderness, not the wilderness from the garden.

Now, that is only one of many important strands in Protestant thought about separation of church and state. But here's why I said that Roger Williams has had an important impact on my work. I believe in the importance of nurturing competing centers of meaning, so that neither the state nor the culture can say that it is the only right way of looking at the world. Therefore I believe very deeply in the importance of the wall for guarding the garden, for protecting a lot of places where people can freely build communities, creating meanings different from those you or I might want to impose if we happened to run everything.

When I mentioned this idea in a church in Pittsburgh somebody said, "Well, okay, but not home schooling, because if you have home schooling a lot of people will teach their kids that creationist stuff." Well, so what? If that's what I want to teach to my kids, it doesn't mean that other people have to teach it to their kids. I'm always quite wary of the idea that there is just one way to be American, one set of understandings we all must have, one way of approaching the world. I myself am much more comfortable with having a lot of very diverse approaches. People say, "But some parents will teach their kids really evil things." Well, we don't need to work out an intricate view of church and state to do something about that. If we believe that a lot of parents are going to teach their kids evil things, then we have much more to worry about in America than what we teach in schools or where we draw these various lines.

I like diversity. I believe very deeply in dialogue across our different traditions, and I sharply disagree with the notion that such dialogue is impossible. I think Martin Luther King is a great exemplar of this kind of border crossing. His speeches were all sermons. Although you may find one or two where the evangelical rhetoric is toned down, for the most part they are open and unabashed sermons for a particular, narrow religious tradition. But sometimes, when we least expect it, those seemingly narrow arguments from a tradition we may not share can cross that border—the border between denominations, between traditions, between religion and nonreligion—and touch the human heart, where we simply know right from wrong.

JEFFREY ROSEN: It is slightly harrowing to respond to one's former teacher, especially in a group that knows far more about this topic than I do. I will focus my response on the particular point of the legal boundaries of the public and private sphere and how this matter relates to the Roger Williams vision that Professor Carter endorses.

A question: why is Stephen Carter not happier than he is now? He has won, hasn't he? The remarkable arc of the legal treatment of religion over the past decade is a vindication of Stephen Carter's important work. He spent the first part of his career arguing eloquently against the *strict separationist principle*, which (1) advocated a public sphere denuded of any kind of religious expression and (2) opposed any kind of direct government aid to religion, even when it was part of a scheme that put public and private institutions on equal terms. That strict separationist vision has been rejected by the Supreme Court, and the *equal-treatment vision* is ascendant there. It is likely to be reaffirmed soon in the *Mitchell* case. [In *Mitchell* v. *Helms*, decided June 28, 2000, the Court held that distributing government funds to provide such equipment as computers both to public and to private, religiously affiliated schools does not violate the Establishment Clause.] So strict separationism has been vanquished, and the equal-treatment vision—what I think Professor Carter is arguing for—has been vindicated.

Moreover, the third vision, the one we might call *religious supremacism*, also opposed by Carter, has been rejected as well. The supremacists argue for an openly religious public sphere in which students can pray in schools and public displays of religion such as crèches are permissible. This supremacist vision has at least three adherents on the Supreme Court. We saw Justices Rehnquist, Thomas, and Scalia in recent cases wistfully looking back to a time when it seemed that a supremacist majority was in their grasp, and indeed this is the vision that candidate George W. Bush has embraced. But they've lost for now. So why aren't Professor Carter and those who share his views celebrating?

I think it's in part because this equal-treatment vision, while extremely appealing in theory, is very hard to carry out in practice. It's so subtle and so complicated, and requires such delicate adherence. This is why I want to think about the *Santa Fe* case. On the way to that I want to trace the rise and fall of separationism and the triumph of Carterism and see how this applies in the *Santa Fe* and *Mitchell* cases. I will conclude by asking Professor Carter whether or not the Roger Williams–like vision he so eloquently posed—that the purpose of separationism is to protect the church from the state, not the state from the church—applies to many of the new state/church partnerships whose constitutionality will increasingly be upheld under this new equal-treatment vision. I'm thinking of course of charitable choice. This is not an age when the church is retreating deeper into the wilderness. It is a time when the church is administering welfare benefits on an unprecedented scale.

The arc of the rise and fall of separationism in America follows the rise and fall of anti-Catholicism; the basic impulse to keep state funds from sectarian schools was rooted in a robust antipapacy. This whole debate that we're having about the appropriate boundaries between the public and private sphere couldn't have existed in an eighteenth-century world where welfare and education services were essentially privatized. When the church monopolized education and welfare, we didn't have to worry about keeping the church from the encroachments of the state. It wasn't until schools began to be state sponsored in the mid-nineteenth century that the great school battles developed. The Blaine amendment to the Constitution proposed in 1875 and narrowly rejected would have prohibited tax money from going to any sectarian schools. The resurgence of anti-Catholicism in the 1940s culminated in Hugo Black's famous "wall of separation" metaphor: we must keep the wall high and impregnable; we cannot tolerate the slightest breach. This is Hugo Black, on one hand the great civil libertarian and textualist, on the other hand the robust antipapist who just wanted to protect the good Protestants of America from the encroachments of Rome.

So separationism found its brief flowering, and it's important to stress how brief this era was. It was really just in the 1970s and 1980s. The *Lemon* test, of course, is the notorious instantiation of it; it requires that governmental action be entirely secular in both purpose and impact and that it avoid excessive entanglement of the state with religion. It culminated in decisions like those that prohibited religious groups from participating on equal terms on public property—the school cases that said that, for example, the Christian group couldn't meet on school property but the gay and lesbian group could. This was the principle that inspired the opponents of separationism to argue for its demise.

The intellectual leader in defending equal treatment has been Professor Carter, who has made the case most powerfully in the public square. One of the legal architects was Michael McConnell, who argued first for the equal-treatment principle in the 1981 *Widmar* case, in which the University of Missouri had made its facilities available to all student groups except those that had a religious purpose. At the time McConnell was, somewhat improbably, clerking for Justice William Brennan, and he persuaded Brennan to lead an eight-to-one majority rejecting this exclusion and embracing the idea that public facilities should be available to religious and nonreligious groups on equal terms. This extraordinarily powerful idea (which is really a First Amendment idea, a free-expression idea) has gained such ground in the past few years that it seems to be leading almost inexorably to the eventual upholding of vouchers.

How could the architects have anticipated that this simple nondiscrimination principle would prove so powerful in eradicating the excesses of strict separationism? We saw it function in the 1995 *Rosenberger* case, in which the Supreme Court struck down the University of Virginia regulation that made student-activities funds available for all student magazines except religiously oriented ones. We also saw it in the 1997 *Agostini* case, where the Court struck down the refusal to allow public school teachers in New York City to provide remedial instruction to disadvantaged students in religious schools. I expect we'll see it in the *Mitchell* case as well.

So now we have this equal-treatment vision: how does it apply to prayer? The *Santa Fe* case strikes me as a much harder one than this arrogant, overconfident Court suggested. The imperialism of this Court knows no bounds. Here's the *Santa Fe* case: In a modified policy issued by the school district, students vote by majority, first whether or not to have an invocation at football games, and then, if they vote yes, to select a person to deliver it. A further modification by the district court said that the invocation had to be nonproselytizing and nonsectarian. In my view, the narrowest way of striking this down would have been merely to say that the requirement that the school guarantee a nonsectarian prayer by itself constitutes an illegitimate entanglement. This is the worst of all worlds: the school is imposing the prayer on unwilling students and then dictating the content of the prayer. In *Lee* v. *Weisman*, the requirement that the rabbi's prayer be censored to ensure that it was nonsectarian represents an affront to the Roger Williams principle that it is bad for the church when its message is diluted by the state. That degree of entanglement by itself might be enough to invalidate the policy.

Now let's think about the majoritarian mechanism in *Santa Fe*. The Court says the fact that there's a majoritarian election means that it's not a true public forum, because minority voices are by definition stifled. The quintessential example of private religious speech that should be permissible is that there's an election of the speaker and then the speaker can say whatever he or she likes, can pray or not pray. Now, although a Kentucky court struck down a similar scheme, I think this is a good example of purely private speech even on state property; the mere fact that the school owns the megaphone shouldn't settle the question. Is the fact that there's a majoritarian election for an invocation by itself enough to make it not a question of private speech, and essentially to put the school in the business of choosing the message? Maybe or maybe not. I'm not sure I'm convinced by the Court's notion. Justice Stevens says it would be like having a vote about whether or not to have a political rally, and then a second vote about whether to have a Democrat or a Republican. This wouldn't be an open public forum; it wouldn't be the case that anyone could say whatever he or she might choose to say. Basically there's an up-or-down vote about whether to have a prayer. It seems to me to be very close.

This is why Stevens then has to go further and say, Do we really know, with regard to the *Lemon* test, that this was an illegitimate state purpose? The earlier draft of the Santa Fe policy had not allowed an invocation and/or *message*, but an invocation or benediction; it was purely prayer oriented. Now Rehnquist has a very good dissent. He says, If the concern is that this will be applied illegitimately, why not wait for an actual illegitimate application of it? Again, my own instinct is that the result was right because of the nonsectarian aspect, but the Rehnquist objection was strong here.

In *Santa Fe*, Rehnquist and Scalia and Thomas—the three religious supremacists— are slyly concealing their true colors. Remember that in *Lee* v. *Weisman* they just came out and said they thought that a nonsectarian, nonproselytizing prayer would be an appropriate recognition of the religious heritage of a religious people. Here they just want neutrality, and if there's a problem with the application, they said, they'll deal with that when it occurs. *Santa Fe* shows how just how elusive neutrality is. On the one hand you have these supremacists who were hiding their true colors. On the other hand you have the majority, led by Justice Stevens, who has this nice argument about entanglement. Then he just goes to pieces so to speak and starts citing *Lemon* and stressing that the real problem with this prayer is that some people might perceive it as offensive; this would send an illegitimate message that would make people feel excluded. Stevens cites some O'Connor opinions about not wanting to make people feel traumatized by being exposed to offensive and vulgar language. This is the most troubling part of the opinion, this whole vestige of the worst strains of separationism, which would make the permissibility of speech, let alone prayer, turn on the perception of the listeners and its "offensiveness." This shows how hard the old habits die.

Among those joining Stevens in the majority opinion are Ginsburg and Breyer, secular Jews who came of age in an era when Leo Pfeiffer, the great head of the American Jewish Congress, was advocating separationism of the most uncompromising kind. For that generation of Jews and for some mainline Protestants (Stevens lists his religion as Protestant; the others identify themselves as Methodists or Lutherans and so forth), the old separationist habits die hard. And I guess I would say that if even the Supreme Court justices can't make a strong case for neutrality and equal treatment, it's not surprising that this principle hasn't found resonance in the public square. So maybe this is why Professor Carter isn't so happy. Legally he has achieved this paradigm-shifting Supreme Court victory, but it's impossible in culture to convey a sense of how complete and how central this triumph is, because the battles will never stop.

I'm going to conclude with the question I began with, which is, Does this Roger Williams–like vision apply to many of the new church/state partnerships that will be permitted under the equal-treatment vision? I think it will be a good thing if charitable choice, which allows religious providers to compete with non-religious providers on equal terms in the administration of welfare benefits, is upheld by the Supreme Court; it's one of our richest and most interesting social experiments. If one is concerned, as Stephen Carter so eloquently is, about protecting the church from the depredations of the state, from the temptation to dilute and compromise its message, I pose the question whether some of these church/state partnerships may not cause even greater threats than simple electoral politics.

The charitable-choice law in some ways protects churches from a requirement that they remove the most visible aspects of their iconography in the administration of welfare benefits. No doubt the ACLU is gunning up for a really fun decade of litigation! There's a lot of money involved here. And as this money becomes a serious, substantial part of the budgets of certain churches—especially African American churches, which are applying for and receiving these contracts in much greater numbers than other churches—how could pressures not operate that might pull them aside from their central message and lead them to focus their energies on nonpastoral polities that would change their very essence? So as I congratulate

Professor Carter on his important victory, I also ask whether the inadvertent fruits of this victory might threaten some of the church autonomy that he so powerfully defends.

Discussion

STEPHEN CARTER: I'm very flattered that Jeffrey thinks I'm responsible for a change in the legal climate, but I think it's just a matter of common sense. On the question he asks at the end: I'm very troubled by these religious court decisions; I'm very troubled by vouchers. When I say troubled by them, I don't mean I'm *opposed* to them. But I do think that churches that fight for this money need to think carefully about what they're taking, about what will happen years down the road when the strings start being applied and they have used a lot of public money to build their schools, to build this and build that. I'm not saying that they shouldn't take it or that it's unconstitutional; I'm saying it's worth being very thoughtful about, very prayerful about.

DAVID VAN BIEMA: I'm interested in the Southern Baptists because they seem to be very involved with political questions and yet they seem extraordinarily vigorous. It seems to me that there's really a two-track thing going: you keep your rank and file in line because you're talking about inerrancy, and then you pursue political policies in Washington and elsewhere. Do you foresee, as a result of the political activity, some sort of weakening or dissipation of the energies of the Southern Baptist Convention?

STEPHEN CARTER: Certainly it's a group of people with a lot of radical energy within mainstream terms. But it is important to distinguish between institutions that do church work, like the Southern Baptist Convention, and institutions that get heavily involved in the political side of things, like the Moral Majority in the past or the Christian Coalition in the present.

DAVID VAN BIEMA: There is certainly some blurring when you see someone like Jerry Falwell being welcomed back into the fold. I think he has been described as still an independent Baptist, and that may indeed be the case, but I believe his church is now in the Convention.

STEPHEN CARTER: I think we'll have to see what happens in the long run. Falwell is kind of a moving target, a person who has remade himself a number of times. His most recent remaking of himself in dialogue with gays and lesbians, for example, is very interesting stuff. You've raised a good question, but I think we'll have to wait and see. What I present is a kind of speculation more than a settled historical view.

E. J. DIONNE: I come from a Catholic tradition that has always had no problem with involvement in day-to-day politics. But Stephen, if I heard you right, you are laying out a recipe for withdrawal from politics by religious people. Is that the logic of your position? If not, what are the proper terms of engagement for religious people in politics?

Second, a question on *Santa Fe*: I agree with Jeffrey; I can't see how the Court could come out any other way, but I also didn't like the feelings language. However, I was actually quite convinced by the majoritarian argument, and I want to know what I was missing by being so convinced. The example I thought of was a Southern Baptist quarterback having to play in a public school in a Catholic neighborhood where they pipe in a "Hail Mary" before every game. I think that would raise a serious religious-liberty problem.

My third point is on charitable choice. A lot of folks are suggesting that the solution for the churches is to set up 501(c)(3)s—I think there will soon be a church named St. 501(c)(3)! In a way that seems like a very good idea, because you could hive off certain activities and then the state wouldn't get involved in the core work of the church. But a lot of advocates of charitable choice see this as a kind of separationist Trojan horse, where the separationist side is trying to say, Well, we'll have charitable choice but we won't *really* have charitable choice. I would like to ask both Stephen and Jeffrey to comment on that.

STEPHEN CARTER: To your first question, how should religious people get involved in electoral politics, I'd reply: the way porcupines make love—very, very carefully. I'm most concerned at this point about the corruption of institutions, partly because institutions, even in nonhierarchical denominations, are the custodians over time of a body of doctrine.

On the 501(c)(3) thing: I think this is not a swell idea. I think the tail has been whacked off from it. If the idea is that you should be able to participate like everybody else, then once you organize to participate, you are really looking at money that is going to dictate how you organize as a church. You've already lost, it seems to me, when you start saying, "I'm going to remake myself in order to get eligible for this money."

On the *Santa Fe* case: I'm not entirely persuaded by any part of the Court's argument. I think the dissent was probably right in saying that the case was not ripe for decision. It can't be that on its *face* electing a student to speak is problematic, which is what everyone said. What has to be the case is that it's problematic because of what we *think* they're going to do. But outside of certain statutes that are said to chill free speech, ordinarily the Court doesn't decide cases that way. It doesn't base decisions on what *might* happen.

The emphasis on offense, I agree with Jeff, was gratuitous, but also extremely interesting. From the point of view of the religious parent, it raised interesting notions. If some people are going to object to a prayer that they see as religious because it offends them, then what do you say to evangelicals who say, "Christianity is not a religion. The others are all religions, but this one is God-given truth. I object to nonreligious things that offend me, too. So if evolution is taught, I should be able to object because that offends me. It strikes at the heart of my religious sensibility. Therefore nobody should be exposed to it, so that *my* kids won't be exposed to it." The only clean way to write this opinion would be to say there could be no prayer of any kind, student initiated or state initiated, at any public school function whatsoever. That would be a clear constitutional law. It would be a *lousy* constitutional law, but it would be a clear one, and people could accommodate themselves to it. But because of its failure to declare a clear rule, the Court is inviting school districts to go back and try again and keep on trying.

JEFFREY ROSEN: Yes, that seems exactly right. The question is, and Rehnquist poses this, Is this an argument against all majoritarian elections? So if you don't accept a clean Carter rule and say that an elected speaker should be able to speak about whatever she or he likes, then you just want to ensure that people are not campaigning on particular messages. What invalidates the rule here perhaps is the fact that first you decided whether to have an invocation or message—that itself was content based; essentially, there was an up-or-down vote on whether to have a prayer—and then you chose who delivered it. That's what made it not a public forum. A genuinely majoritarian election where you can elect a speaker to say whatever he or she liked would be permissible. But what makes it so tricky is that the fact that it was an invocation *or* message might arguably mean that you would just decide whether or not to have a speaker, and then the speaker could choose to say whatever he or she liked, which means that Stevens was surely right that it might have been more prudent to wait to see how the thing operated in practice.

JEAN ELSHTAIN: Jeffrey, I wonder if one reason that Stephen isn't quite as happy as you think he ought to be is that in fact the stake hasn't been driven into the heart of separationism with quite the decisiveness that you suggest. You yourself talked about Stevens's "gratuitous referencing of *Lemon*" in the *Santa Fe* case, so it strikes me that the *Lemon* test is still lurking in the interstices as an ever-present possibility. We don't know what the makeup of the Court will be in the future; this stuff could be resurrected at any point. Certainly it is alive and well in political argumentation and political philosophy, given the dominance of the sort of Rawlsian tendency in liberal political philosophy.

Stephen, this picks up a bit on what E. J. Dionne said: it struck me as I was listening to you that Catholics would refract the issue of civic engagement in a very different way. In part this is because the great social encyclicals make it clear that we have available to us a civic language that appeals to all persons of good will, the persons to whom the social encyclicals are addressed. You can make a partial translation—not a full and complete translation, but at least a partial and rather effective translation—of the deep religious commitments into a language that invokes natural-law principles and that makes available these common-good concerns in a way that doesn't water down the faith. It doesn't require that faith commitments be *totally present* at every point in time in order to make effectively a certain kind of argument. People have access to these arguments through reason, whether or not they have the faith commitment.

STEPHEN CARTER: I agree with that entirely. The Catholic social tradition is a great and noble one. I think *Rerum Novarum* is one of the great pieces of pastoral theology. But I am not trying to say that churches should not be involved in politics, only that when it gets to the point of deciding who should be *elected*, we have a different kind of homiletic. I quite agree that religious traditions can remain true and authentic while speaking very effectively in a prophetic voice from outside the corridors of power. There's a long history of that all over the world, and certainly in the United States. But when they get into the business of *selecting*, they don't speak through their own best voice, I think, and then there's a danger of backlash. I think it was in 1854 that clergy were petitioning for the abolition of the slave trade, and Congress warned that the clergy were going to take over: if you listen to this petition, Congress said, suddenly our nation will be run by clergy, and that will be a terrible thing.

JEAN ELSHTAIN: That position you just articulated is fully compatible with John Paul's insistence that clergy not stand for electoral office, even as you have this robust engagement in what I usually call civil society.

STEPHEN CARTER: I think there's much to be said for the view that clergy should not stand for public office, not because they will destroy America, but because they will lose their best selves. That's true whether it's Pat Robertson or Jesse Jackson.

JEFFREY ROSEN: In a wonderful essay about pluralism Stephen talks about the need for people with hyphenated identities to feel free to proclaim their identities in this newly diverse public sphere. So maybe the best strategy is just to talk the language of identity politics and nondiscrimination, which is a form of language that really has resonance today, and to stress that it's a form of discrimination—the only unforgivable sin in this age—to prohibit religiously identified Americans from proclaiming their identity along with everyone else. It's a powerful rhetoric, and it links to some other things we've been talking about, such as, why is it that you can come out as gay or lesbian but you feel embarrassed coming out as religiously devout? Why not just feel proud and go on the "Oprah" show to talk about it! Maybe by talking this nondiscrimination language we could get to a point where the devout feel as free to proclaim their identities as everyone else.

LEO RIBUFFO: We historians and you constitutional lawyers look at the Constitution differently. We can say, "Well, that's an eighteenth-century document from two or three worldviews ago," and that's that. But you guys have to put the behavior of a twenty-first-century country into the framework of an eighteenth-century document, and then you complain that the Court—which is essentially a nine-person committee—doesn't do this in an intellectually coherent way. To the several billion people in the world who are not American constitutional lawyers, this might seem a rather bizarre way to run a country.

STEPHEN CARTER: I'd like to say that I agree.

LEO RIBUFFO: Okay. Both of you don't want the *Lemon* test, I gather. Does either of you have neutral principles to serve as guidance on how religion-state relations *should* be decided, or are you sort of *ad hoc*-ing here and there?

STEPHEN CARTER: In a way I want to throw up my hands and say that all this legal doctrine is a lot of nonsense and you can never fix it. To some extent I believe that. But in my youth, the youth that Jeff referred to, I offered two principles. First, the state cannot discriminate among religions, and second, except for the most compelling interest, the state cannot interfere with the free exercise of religion. That's the whole of the religion clause of the First Amendment. And that would ban classroom prayers as interference with the free exercise of religion, which includes the exercise of parents' right to raise their children in a particular religion or no religion at all. It would also mean that when Major Goldman wanted to wear his yarmulke, the Supreme Court was wrong in saying that the Air Force could, without violating the First Amendment, enforce the regulation forbidding the wearing of "headgear." That was a bad Supreme Court decision because it interfered with the fundamental principle of religious liberty without a sufficiently telling reason.

Now, when one makes an argument like this about how to read the Constitution, certainly historical challenges can be raised, but I'm more interested in the practical challenges. A few years ago I was moderating a debate between two very distinguished constitutional scholars, Michael McConnell, whom Jeff mentioned earlier, and Katherine Sullivan, now dean of Stanford Law School. It was a debate about the limits of religious freedom, and someone in the audience raised a question about human sacrifice. I figured, "That's a no brainer! That's absurd!" But to my astonishment both of these very distinguished constitutional scholars, two of the most thoughtful voices on religious freedom in the country, said that such a practice might be allowable as long as it involved consenting adults and there were no coercion!

I do think we could reach a rich consensus on a lot of places where we *should* draw the line, recognizing that in the margin there will be some differences. For example, suppose that there were no constitutional right to abortion and that a certain state had laws against abortion in all circumstances, but that someone belonged to a religious tradition that permitted or even required abortion under certain circumstances. Would the state law interfere with religious freedom?

In Kansas City a few years ago, a young woman in law school was offered a job with the attorney general of the state of Georgia. She subsequently engaged in a same-sex marriage ceremony permitted by her religious tradition, in her house of worship, and the job offer was withdrawn. The attorney general was very careful to say that he was not withdrawing the offer because of her sexual orientation but because of the same-sex marriage ceremony, which he said is against the public policy of the state of Georgia. It strikes me that he had the matter backwards: if he had refused to hire her because of her sexual orientation, that would have been within his prerogative, but by binding his action to the same-sex marriage ceremony he was actually punishing her for what went on within the four walls of her house of worship. To me that's a violation of the fundamental principle of religious liberty.

In my view, when the religious-liberty issue arises, the question should always be "What is the compelling reason why the state should be able to prevent it?" rather than "What is the religious basis for it?"

JEFFREY ROSEN: Here's a simpler question that's a different instantiation of the same impulse: public religious speech bad, private religious speech good. All the hard questions are questions of state action, and we try to figure out on which side of the line a particular problem falls. So that's why we have our debate about *Santa Fe*, about whether the intervention of the election mechanism converts it into the school's speech rather than the student's; that's the central question in all the voucher cases, whether or not the intervention of private choice converts it from a state to a private decision. It's hard, and you can have very different intuitions on all these cases, but it's very different from this expressive-harms notion, the question of the received effect of the speech or even the dominant purpose of the speech. It avoids the sort of touchy-feely questions about stigmatic injuries and expressive harms and focuses on this hard question of what's public and what's private.

This is why, as Leo Ribuffo pointed out, we constitutional lawyers have a much harder task than historians. We have an entirely different society than the one the framers inhabited; the boundaries between the public and the private sphere are both radically contested and utterly different. That's why the dreariest of the Supreme Court's religion decisions are the sort of one-step originalism stuff. Something like Rehnquist's dissent in *Wallace* v. *Jaffree*—just grimly reciting the history of the first Congress and pretending that that could possibly solve all these interesting questions—is just too simplistic to be interesting. These translation questions are really hard, and there's no obvious answer from text or history. You just have to make better and worse arguments about which side of the public/private divide a particular question falls on.

JAMES GUTH: As I was listening to Stephen talk about the distinction between entering into the conversation as religious actors, which he sees as a legitimate role for religious people, and taking part in the electoral process, which he sees as in some sense off limits, I recalled an argument made by John Mark Hansen, who teaches political science at the University of Chicago. Hansen said that the only way you really become a part of the conversation in the United States is to demonstrate electoral impact. Is that a kind of understanding you're willing to accept, Stephen, that the participation of religious groups in the public realm is going to be constrained very severely if they choose not to engage in electoral politics?

STEPHEN CARTER: Yes, I accept that description, but I hope it doesn't make my views quite as paradoxical as they seem. What I think that religious people—especially when they're organized in groups—have to do is to hold a very fine and delicate balance. Because it *is* the case, to restate the point more crudely, that the more votes you can deliver, the more impact you have. No question. The problem for me from the Christian point of view is, Why do I want to get into the conversation, to be persuasive or to be coercive? Those are not the same activity. Sometimes arguments that are couched in terms of values can have resonance and can cut across lines.

JOHN LEO: In line with your distinction between advocacy and electoral politics, what would you say about the Catholic clergy and bishops who've been drawn beyond the general principle on abortion to pushing candidates?

STEPHEN CARTER: I really think it's a mistake to put the imprimatur of God's name next to a political candidate, not because God doesn't care, but because the possibility of error is so great. In the African American church it is very common to find a lot of clergy endorsement and quasi endorsement, voter guides, and the like. I think it's a terrible mistake. The kinds of arguments that are made within a religious tradition *should* affect people. Our religion makes us different people than we would be without it. But I nevertheless think there's a difference between feeling the weight of your tradition pushing you in a different direction and being told in effect that to be a godly person you *have* to move in this direction.

KENNETH WOODWARD: It seems to me that when you talk about *church* you really are talking about the small evangelical congregation. For me as a Catholic, that doesn't do enough. If you imagine *church* differently, perhaps you can imagine more involvement. The tradition I'm talking about looks at two things. One is that people are going to be formed by their society no matter what. You can't be a perfectionist and say, we're going to live like Amish; even the Amish are affected by the kinds of formation that take place when you are living in a society, even at its margins. To some extent you have to play in the larger field. Secondly, it seems to me that there's a danger of perfectionism in what you're talking about. If you want any portion of justice achieved, you're going to have to get your hands dirty. You're going to have to see ideals compromised if as a Christian citizen you want to see at least half a loaf accomplished, on behalf of minorities or whatever the cause may be. You can't not be involved in that sense.

STEPHEN CARTER: I don't think that getting one's hands dirty is inherently a bad thing. The problem arises when people get involved in politics and decide, "Gee, this is the place for me!" That's where the temptation comes in. It's not so much that one should never be involved in politics at all; it's that there are dangers to institutionalizing one's involvement. And the model isn't so much a small evangelical church. I think that over the years there's been a much greater political involvement of both the Catholic Church and mainline Protestant denominations. Sometimes their efforts are great, and sometimes they have a lot of difficulties.

KENNETH WOODWARD: How about Catholic Charities or its Protestant equivalent, where they are using a lot of government dollars?

STEPHEN CARTER: What I'm talking about is not the risk of getting one's hands dirty but the risk of becoming so reliant on that money that when the strings come, when a later administration with a different view imposes conditions that should cause concern, one says, "We really need that money, so we'll adjust to those conditions." In 1982, when the Supreme Court decided it was not a violation of religious freedom for the IRS to withhold the preferred tax status of Bob Jones University because of its segregationist policies, Bob Jones gave up the money rather than change its policies. While I think those policies are wrong from a Christian point of view, one has to give them credit for integrity. Giving up money is very hard to do.

FRANKLIN FOER: Professor Carter, you gave Fannie Lou Hamer and the civil-rights movement as an example of the bad things that can happen when religiously motivated people try to achieve their vision through political involvement. But it seems to me that that movement was victorious, that Fannie Lou Hamer's prophetic vision was in large part achieved.

STEPHEN CARTER: I think what was achieved was the bureaucratization of civil rights. The vision and achievements came to be limited to things that are measurable in the fight against racial injustice. Not a bad solution if you can't do anything else, but Fannie Lou Hamer's broader vision of economic justice, of redistribution of land, and a lot of other things—it's gone. It's off the table. And it's something that preachers who want to be part of the Democratic coalition can't talk about. So there was indeed a civil-rights victory, and I'm not diminishing it or the work of the people who bled for it. The transformation in the law and in some parts of society was enormous. But the richer *radical* vision, I would say, was not achieved. I'm not sure whether it *should* have been achieved; I'm only describing what actually happened.

MICHAEL BARONE: We talked earlier about what could happen with charitable choice, particularly the kind of thing that Bush is talking about. I think that different religious faith traditions are going to cope with this in different ways. The Catholic Church has a set of institutions, a vocabulary, and a two-thousand-year history of interacting and getting along with the state and inserting its moral principles and vocabulary. They're old pros at this, and much of that will continue to go on as it has. I think a lot will depend on how this stuff is administered. If you have some Ruth Bader Ginsburg–type separationists in the regional offices of HUD and HHS in Dallas, say, you're going to get very different results than if you have people who are sympathetic to the program at that local level. There is tension built into that program. It suggests that the results are not going to be totally satisfying on any grounds. There may be some real messes created here or there. Some organizations may follow the suggestion implicit in what Stephen Carter said, which is, "Hey, just stay private. Raise your own money so you can do what you want to do."

A question of the last thirty years that fascinates me, one I have not seen addressed, is the relationship between the black churches and the plagues of crime and poverty in the underclass black communities. Have the black churches done a lot to help? Why have they not done more?

MICHEL MARTIN: My sense, from a reporting perspective, is that many of these churches have felt their primary mission to be mediating a relationship between the community and the outside world, that is, the white power structure—speaking truth to power, as it were. They see themselves as the mediators between the powerless and the powerful. What is going on right now is a real shift in emphasis, achieved after a great deal of pain and in some cases saying, "You know, we are killing ourselves now. Promiscuous sex, drug use, and various sorts of irresponsible lifestyles are as great a danger to our communities and constituencies as the Ku Klux Klan ever was." That's why I think we're seeing a paradigm shift.

STEPHEN CARTER: I think Michel is exactly right, but there's another point here also. If you look at black preaching, you find there was a lot said about these issues of, say, sexuality and marriage as recently as the 1950s and 1960s. That fell away in the 1970s and 1980s and early 1990s. Now it's starting to come back a little.

Why is it that black preachers talked about these things very sanely in those earlier decades, then stopped, and then started talking about them again in the 1990s? It's an interesting question.

Index

About the Contributors

Elliot Abrams is a special assistant to President George W. Bush and was an assistant secretary of state during the Reagan administration. He is the editor of several books, including *The Influence of Faith: Religious Groups and U.S. Foreign Policy* (2001).

Jay Ambrose is a columnist with Scripps Howard News Service.

Fred Barnes is the executive editor of the *Weekly Standard* and cohost of the *Beltway Boys* on the Fox News Channel.

Michael Barone is a senior writer for *U.S. News & World Report*. He is the author of biennial *The Almanac of American Politics* and *The New Americans: How the Melting Pot Can Work Again* (2001).

Peter Beinart is the editor of the *New Republic*.

David Boldt is a columnist for the *Philadelphia Inquirer*.

Karlyn Bowman is a resident fellow at the American Enterprise Institute. She writes a weekly column called, "POLLitics," for *Roll Call*, and is the editor of "Opinion Pulse" in the *American Enterprise Institute Magazine*.

David Brooks is a columnist for the *New York Times*, senior editor at the *Weekly Standard*, a contributing editor at *Newsweek* and *Atlantic Monthly*, and a commentator on *The Newshour with Jim Lehrer*. His books include *On Paradise Drive: How We Live Now (And Always Have) in the Future Tense* (2004).

Julie Bundt is assistant professor of political science at the University of Northern Iowa.

Vincent Carroll is the editor of the editorial page at the *Denver Rocky Mountain News*.

Stephen Carter is the William Nelson Cromwell Professor of Law at Yale Law School. He is the author of many book *God's Name in Vain* (2000); *Civility* (1998); and *The Dissent of the Governed* (1998).

Ming Hsu Chen is the coauthor of *Sacred Places, Civic Purposes: Should Government Help Faith-Based Charity?* (2001).

Richard Cizik is vice president for governmental affairs for the National Association of Evangelicals.

Michael Cromartie is vice president at the Ethics and Public Policy Center. He is the editor of several books, most recently *A Public Faith: Evangelicals and Civic Engagement* (2003).

Claudia Deane is a reporter for the *Washington Post*.

Karen DeWitt is a news journalist with ABC News *Nightline*.

John J. DiIulio Jr. is Frederic Fox Leadership Professor of Politics, Religion, and Civil Society at the University of Pennsylvania. He is also senior fellow at the Manhattan Institute, senior counsel to Public/Private Ventures, and founding director of the Center for Public Management at the Brookings Institution. His books include *What's God Got To Do With the American Experiment?* (2000).

E. J. Dionne is a columnist for the *Washington Post* and senior fellow at the Brookings Institution. His most recent books are *Stand Up Fight Back: Republican Toughs, Democratic Wimps, and the Politics of Revenge* (2004) and *One Electorate Under God: A Dialogue on Religion and American Politics* (coeditor, 2004).

Gregg Easterbrook is a senior editor of the *New Republic*, and a contributing editor to *The Atlantic Monthly*. He is the author of several books, including *The Progress Paradox: How Life Gets Better While People Feel Worse* (2003).

Larry Eichel is a columnist for the *Philadelphia Inquirer*.

Jean Bethke Elshtain is Laura Spelman Rockefeller Professor of Social and Political Ethics at the University of Chicago. She is the author of *Just War against Terror: The Burden of American Power in a Violent World* (2003); *Jane Addams and the Dream of American Democracy* (2002); and *Who Are We? Critical Reflections and Hopeful Possibilities. Politics and Ethical Discourse* (2000).

Franklin Foer is a senior editor at the *New Republic* and author of *How Soccer Explains the World: An Unlikely Theory of Globalization* (2004).

Hillel Fradkin is senior fellow and director of the Center on Islam, Democracy and the Future of the Muslim World at the Hudson Institute.

Nancy Gibbs is the editor-at-large for *Time* magazine. She is the coauthor of *Through The Night with God (Quiet Moments with God)* (1999).

John Green is distinguished professor of political science at the University of Akron. He is the Director of the Ray C. Bliss Institute of Applied Politics. Green is the coeditor of *The State of the Parties: The Changing Role of Contemporary Party Politics* (1999) and the coauthor of *The Bully Pulpit: The Politics of Protestant Clergy* (1997).

James Guth is William R. Kenan Jr. Professor of Political Science at Furman University. He is the editor of *The Bully Pulpit: The Politics of Protestant Clergy* (1998).

Barbara Bradley Hagerty is the religion correspondent for National Public Radio.

Jody Hassett is a correspondent for ABC's *World News Tonight*.

Nathan O. Hatch is provost and Andrew V. Tackes Professor of History at the University of Notre Dame. He is the author of *The Democratization of Christianity* (1991).

Deborah Howell is chief of the Washington bureau for the Newhouse Newspaper Group and editor of the Newhouse News Service.

Bob Jones is the national editor for *World Magazine*.

Charles Krauthammer is a syndicated columnist and a 1987 Pulitzer Prize winner.

John Leo is a contributing editor for *U.S. News & World Report* and author of *Incorrect Thoughts: Notes on Our Wayward Culture* (2000).

Mary Leonard is a staff writer for the *Boston Globe*.

Kathy Lewis is a columnist for the *Dallas Morning News*.

Joseph Loconte is senior fellow at the Heritage Foundation. He is the editor of *The End of Illusions: Religious Leaders Confront Hitler's Gathering Storm* (2004).

Michel McQueen Martin is a correspondent for ABC's *Nightline*.

Terry Mattingly teaches at Palm Beach Atlantic University and is senior fellow for journalism at the Council for Christian Colleges and Universities.

William McGurn is chief editorial writer and a member of the editorial board of the *Wall Street Journal*. He is the coauthor of *Is the Market Moral?: A Dialogue on Religion, Economics, and Justice* (2004).

Richard Morin is a staff writer for the *Washington Post*.

Caryle Murphy is a *Washington Post* staff writer and author of *Passion for Islam: Shaping the Modern Middle East: The Egyptian Experience* (2002).

Lynn Neary is a correspondent for National Public Radio.

Mark O'Keefe covers values and philanthropy at Newhouse News Service.

John Omicinski is the national defense correspondent and columnist for Gannett News Service.

Richard Ostling is a religion writer for the Associated Press. He is the coauthor of *Mormon America: The Power and the Promise* (2000).

Gerard Perseghin is an assistant editor at the *Catholic Standard*.

David Plotz is Washington bureau chief of *Slate.com*.

Ramesh Ponnuru is a senior editor for *National Review*.

Thomas Pratt is the president of Prison Fellowship.

Leo Ribuffo is Society of the Cincinnati George Washington Distinguished Professor and professor of history at George Washington University. He is the author of *Right Center Left: Essays in American History* (1992).

Jeffrey Rosen is the legal affairs editor for the *New Republic* and an associate professor at the George Washington University School of Law. He is the author of *The Unwanted Gaze: The Destruction of Privacy in America* (2000).

Hanna Rosin is an editorial page staff writer for the *Washington Post*.

Alissa Rubin is a reporter for the *Los Angeles Times*.

Timothy Shah is the director of the South Asian Studies Program and a research fellow at the Ethics and Public Policy Center.

Robert Shogan is a former staff writer for the *Los Angeles Times*. He is the author of *The Battle of Blair Mountain: The Story of America's Largest Labor Uprising* (2004).

David Shribman is the Pulitzer Prize–winning Washington bureau chief, assistant managing editor, and columnist for the *Boston Globe*. He also writes a regular column for *Fortune Magazine*.

Jay Tolson is a senior writer at *U.S. News & World Report*.

David Van Biema reports for *Time* magazine.

Melana Zyla Vickers is a columnist for TechCentralStation.com and a senior fellow at the Independent Women's Forum.

Grant Wacker is professor of church history at the Duke University Divinity School. He is the coauthor of *Religion in American Life: A Short History* (2003).

Steve Wagner is the president of QEV Analytics.

Peggy Wehmeyer is the religion correspondent for ABC News.

George Weigel is a senior fellow at the Ethics and Public Policy Center and author of several books, including *Letters to a Young Catholic* (2004).

Jack Wertheimer is provost and chief academic officer of the Jewish Theological Seminary. He is also Joseph and Martha Mendelson Professor of American Jewish History and director of the Joseph and Miriam Ratner Center for the Study of Conservative Judaism. He is the author of *Jews in the Center: Conservative Synagogues and Their Members* (2002).

Diane Winston holds the Knight Chair in media and religion at the University of Southern California Annenberg School for Communication. She is the coeditor of *Faith in the Market: Religion and the Rise of Urban Commercial Culture* (2002).

Larry Witham is a writer for the *Washington Times.*

Adam Wolfson is the editor of the *Public Interest.*

Kenneth L. Woodward is a contributing editor for *Newsweek.* He is the author of *The Book of Miracles: The Meaning of the Miracles Stories in Christianity, Judaism, Buddhism, Hinduism, and Islam* (2000).